Islam: what every Christian should know

Islam:
What every Christian should know

Bassam M. Chedid

EP PUBLISHING WITH A MISSION

EP BOOKS
Faverdale North, Darlington, DL3 0PH, England
e-mail: sales@evangelicalpress.org

EP BOOKS INC.
P. O. Box 825, Webster, New York 14580, USA
e-mail: usa.sales@evangelicalpress.org

web: http://www.epbooks.org

First published 2004
Reprinted 2009

British Library Cataloguing in Publication Data available

ISBN 978 0 85234 698 3

Printed in Great Britain by the MPG Books Group,
Bodmin and King's Lynn

To those who carry their cross and follow Christ,
enduring daily persecution:
may we never be silent about your suffering

Acknowledgements

Many thanks to:

Rebecca Hobbs, Rev. Dale Van Ness and Yoybe Baird for reading and processing the manuscript and offering valuable suggestions.

My wonderful wife Norma, for her encouragement and patience during the writing of this book, and for our three children: Chad, AnaLina and Dora — they are our joy!

My father and mother, God's servants in the Middle East for more than fifty-five years.

Contents

Introduction

Why another book on Islam?

This book is written in response to a genuine need, especially among Christians, who are constantly receiving mixed signals from the media about the nature of Islam. Additionally, publications on Islam have now become a familiar sight in the bookstores. Some are written by Muslim authors attempting to show Islam in a positive light, while others are written from a purely secular position. However, there are still very few books by evangelical authors, and I hope more will be published in the days to come.

We are all aware of the challenges the church is facing today, including religious pluralism and relativism. It is evident that these trends are not only widespread, but increasingly deemed enticing to many in our own society and in the global community. When Christians stand for the truth of God's Word, they are often labelled as uncharitable and radical. What is forgotten is that God himself, by his own Scripture, does not allow for a blind endorsement of claims that are incompatible with his own revelation in the Bible. The Scripture is clear at this point. While God has chosen to make himself known in more than one way (cf. Rom. 1-2), he has made only one provision for salvation, and that is Jesus Christ, who said, 'I am the way and the truth and the life. No one comes to the Father except through me' (John 14:6). Likewise, the book of Acts is very exclusive about the way of salvation. It says, 'Salvation is found in no one else, for there is no other name under heaven given to men by which we must be saved' (Acts 4:12).

For this reason, the present treatment of Islam is written from an evangelical Christian perspective. Concealing the absolute uniqueness of Christ and the biblical claims in the process of writing this book would be the height of dishonesty, hypocrisy and disservice to our Muslim friends. The foremost reason that we proclaim the gospel faithfully is because the Lord Jesus Christ has commanded it (cf. Matt. 28:18-20). Thus personal opinion about Islam, if not based on biblical principles, is, in the final analysis, irrelevant. As Christians we have no right to judge other religions except by the authority and under the revealing light of the Word of God. Moody said it well: 'The best way to show that a stick is crooked is not to argue about it or to spend time denouncing it, but to lay a straight stick alongside it.'

To whom is this book written?

In writing this book, I had in mind lay people, pastors and Bible students who sincerely yearn to know more about the true nature of Islam and desire to communicate the gospel to their Muslim friends and neighbours.

During my travel and speaking engagements in churches, mission conferences and Christian gatherings, I have found an increasing interest in learning about Islam. I have been asked numerous good questions, many of which are included in this book. Moreover, other questions and discussions are accumulated from my own files, personal writings and correspondence.

None the less, the book is not written exclusively for Christians. I invite our Muslim friends to examine the evidence presented with an open mind and to make an informed decision about the claims of both the Bible and the Quran, and I sincerely welcome any feedback.

What is the purpose of this book?

My sincere prayer is that this guidebook will be found informative and practical. Though I have tried to discuss the questions in an intelligible and direct way, I am also fully aware of the shortcomings imposed by the limitations of space when it comes to giving comprehensive and definite answers to these questions. But this book will have been worthwhile if what I have written about Islam helps you in any, or all, of the following ways:

- 'to contend for the faith that was once for all entrusted to the saints' (Jude 3);
- to 'be prepared to give an answer to everyone who asks you to give the reason for the hope that you have...' (1 Peter 3:15);
- to see Muslims not as antagonists, but rather as an opportunity for sharing Christ's redeeming grace. Most Muslims are still unreached and have not really had the chance to believe, because they have heard and seen little of the true gospel.

How is this book organized?

Chapter 1 deals with questions connected with early Islam and its encounters with Judaism and Christianity. They are arranged chronologically. However, certain historical themes, such as the discussion about the Quran and the *Hadith*, have been moved to chapter 3 under the heading, 'Questions about faith and practice'. To a large extent, these two themes are integral components of the whole Islamic belief system. This will allow for further examination of their impact on that belief system and their various implications.

Chapter 2 asks questions about the historical encounters between Islam and the West. It highlights the critical implications of these encounters and suggests some biblical guidelines.

Chapter 3 discusses the core beliefs and practices of Islam as a theological system. Though these beliefs are presented in an objective encyclopaedic fashion, they are examined in the light of the Bible. The fundamental conflict between Islam and biblical Christianity revolves around their concept of the nature of God and man. Thus this chapter attempts to appraise the Muslim belief system with our eyes on the Bible.

Chapter 4 surveys some of the peculiar cultural themes in Islam which I believe play a potent role in the exceptional resistance on the part of its adherents towards the Christian faith. Unlike Christianity, Islam, under the aegis of the Quran, plays the dominant role in shaping all facets of socio-cultural and political life. These themes and their implications are expounded.

Chapters 5 and 6 furnish some pertinent questions and answers about evangelism of Muslims. Evangelism must be carried out with understanding, unconditional love, humility and a passion to communicate the gospel, echoing the words of Paul: 'Brothers, my heart's desire and prayer to God for' my people 'is that they may be saved. For I testify about them that they are zealous for God, but their zeal is not based on knowledge' (cf. Rom. 10:1-2).

1.
Questions about early Islam

Who is an Arab?

The etymological origin of the word 'Arab' (عرب) has been debated among philologists and historians who depend for their investigation mainly upon isolated ancient inscriptions and statements. While Genesis chapter 10 records the earliest account of the inhabitants of the Arabian Peninsula, the word 'Arab' makes its first appearance in an Assyrian inscription dating from 852 B.C. Historically, 'Arabs' were nomadic people living in the far north of Arabia. They may be identified with the Arabs of the later books of the Old Testament. The ancient inscriptions found in Yemen, south of Arabia, reveal that the term 'Arab' means Bedouin (بدو), as distinct from the sedentary population. The Bedouin have maintained more faithfully than others the traditional Arab way of life and language and have continued to do so right up to modern times. It is within this group that we find the roots of the power of tradition in Arab society and preservation of culture.

This cultural preservation, which became the basis for traditional authority, provided a blueprint for Muhammad as he skilfully developed within a very short time a new Islamic society. In contrast to biblical Christianity, which 'renders unto Caesar the things that are Caesar's, and unto God the things that are God's', Muhammad, from the beginning, was preparing his followers to establish a state of their own. Thus social and cultural considerations were of the utmost importance to him.

Central Arabia continued to play an important role as a transit area between two neighbouring civilizations: Yemen (Abyssinian) in the south, and Syria (Byzantine) in the north. However, in contrast to the civilizations both to the south and to the north, central Arabia developed its own distinctive culture, which later became a formative launching pad for the rise of the Islamic religion and its traditional culture as we observe it even today.

What religious life was there in Arabia before Islam?

The religious life of pre-Islamic Arabia was characterized by paganism, known as *wathaniah* (وَثَنِيَّة). The religious practices corresponded to those of the Semites. The tribes were idol-worshippers and often associated their worship with objects in the sky. Abed Shams is a well-known Arabic name meaning 'slave of the sun'. The Quran contains *surahs* (سورة), or chapters, pertaining to the sun, the night, the moon, the day and the *jinn*, or demon. 'Abd-najm' means 'slave of the star' and 'Abd al-thuraiyah' 'slave of the constellation'. Other names include Gad, the Canaanite deity, which refers to the god of fortune (Isa. 65:11), and Baal, which was associated with the fertility god, particularly among the northern Semites. Today, the name *Baal* (بعل) is still in use among Arabs to refer to fertile land that does not require artificial irrigation. Among other gods is the god Sa'd (سعد), meaning 'fortune'. Today, the name Sa'd and its derivations are widely used among Arabs. The god *Ruda* (رضى), 'Goodwill', was largely worshipped by the members of the Arabian Tamim tribe; the name Abd-Ruda (Slave of Goodwill) was used before and after Islam.[1]

The name and concept of 'Allah' (الله) as a supreme deity is not an Islamic distinctive. The testimony of the Quran (قرآن) itself leaves no doubt that the worship of Allah was an integral part of the worship system of the pre-Islamic pantheon (29:65; 31:31; 26:61-63).

Where did the confusion in Islam about the Trinity come from?

Muhammad's charge against pre-Islamic religious groups contributed to his false understanding of the Christian teaching concerning the Trinity and Christ's being called the Son of God. We read in the Quran: 'They surely disbelieve who say: Lo Allah is the third of three; when there is no God save the one God' (5:73). Another verse says, 'And they say: Allah hath taken unto Himself a Son... Nay, but whatsoever is in the heaven and the earth is His. All are subservient unto Him' (2:116).

In fact Muhammad's charge was not directed against orthodox Christianity, but against some heretical groups existing in Arabia prior to Islam. Muhammad had to deal with the Jews, or *Yahoud* (يهود), and the Christians, known collectively as *Nasarah* (نصارى), including the sects of the Nestorians, the Jacobites, the Copts, the Melkites and others.

Among the most important pre-Islamic deities were the Manat (المنات), the al-Lat (اللات) and the al-Uzza (العزّة). These three are also mentioned in the Quran and referred to as 'the daughters of Allah'. The Manat was an ancient Semite goddess. The etymological derivation is perhaps connected with the Aramaic *m'nata* (portion or lot). The Arabic word *manaya* (منايا) came to mean 'fate' and was associated with the concept of death. Manat was a prominent goddess among the many deities, and a popular sanctuary was erected for her near Mecca.

Al-Lat was another venerated Arabian goddess. Most philologists derive the name from the form *ilahat* (الهات), which means 'deities'. Her sanctuary was located at the valley of Wadiji near the town of Taif in Arabia.

Al-Uzza was the third goddess in the pre-Islamic Arab pantheon. She was principally an important idol associated with the tribe of Khata-fan, but later her worship also spread to the main tribes, including Quraysh (the tribe of Muhammad). The historical significance of al-Uzza and the exact meaning of the name is uncertain among the Arabs. However, it has been suggested by some that Uzza should be identified with the Queen of Heaven (cf. Jer. 7:18).

Recognizing the deep attachment of the Arabian tribes to their deities caused Muhammad to compromise. Afraid of causing opposition to his message and division among the tribes, he went so far as to recognize the pre-Islamic pagan trinity (al-Lat, al-Uzza and al-Manat) as mediators with Allah. This reinforced the prevalent idea that the members of this trinity were, in fact, the 'daughters of Allah'. However, Muhammad later retracted this position.

Thus in the Quran we read, 'What think ye, then, of al-Lat and al-Uzza, Manat, the third idol besides?' (3:9). In connection with this verse, Thomas Hughes, in his *Dictionary of Islam*, relates the following interesting discussion between Muhammad, the idol-worshippers, Satan and Gabriel. Al-Tabari, a famed Arab historian and scholar born in A.D. 839, relates that '... on a certain day, the chief men of Mecca, discussed the affairs of the city, when the prophet [Muhammad] appeared, and seating himself by them in a friendly manner, began to recite the 53rd chapter of the Quran; and when he had reached the verse: "What think ye then of al-Lat, and al-Uzza and Manat, the third idol besides?" the devil suggested words of reconciliation and compromise with idolatry, namely, "These are exalted females and verily their intercession is to be hoped for." These words, however, which were received by the idolaters with great delight, were afterwards disavowed by the prophet, for Gabriel revealed to him the true reading, namely, "What think ye then of al-Lat, and al-Uzza and Manat, the third idol besides? Shall ye have male progeny and make God female? This, then, was an unjust partition! Verily, these are mere names which ye and your fathers have given them." '2

One can argue persuasively that Muhammad was perplexed about the difference between the tritheism of pre-Islam and the true concept of the Trinity. Muhammad's attack was directed first of all against the polytheism of pre-Islam. Later, however, his charges against these pre-Islamic religious groups were a major factor leading to his false understanding of Christian teaching concerning the Trinity and what was meant by Christ's being called the Son of God, as demonstrated in the verses from the Quran quoted earlier. It is unfortunate that such a complete and utter misunderstanding of the authentic Christian teaching continues to plague the minds and consciences of Muslims around the world as they are taught from early childhood.

Who are the 'People of the Book'?

The Quran refers to both Jews and Christians as 'the People of the Book', *Ahl-al-kitab* (أهل الكتاب). The testimony of the Quran itself points to the significant role that Judaism and Christianity played in the formation of Islam. From the Quran's own record we read, 'And We caused Jesus, son of Mary, to follow in their footsteps, confirming that which was [revealed] before him, and we bestowed on him the Gospel in the Torah, and a guidance and admonition unto those who ward off evil' (*Surah* 5:47, Pickthall translation).

There is an inconsistency in that the Quran clearly testifies to the validity and authority of both the Torah (i.e. the Pentateuch) and the *Injil* (the Gospels), while at the same time it charges both Jews and Christians with corrupting their own

Scriptures, and thus invalidating them (2:75,101;
3:70,78,187; 4:46). Here we need only comment that Muslim
scholars have not provided any proof to justify this claim.

Who were the pre-Islamic Jews?

A number of historians trace the presence of Jews in south
and north Arabia back to biblical times. Archaeological dis-
coveries in Yemen point to the presence of a Jewish community from the early third century. Jewish communities also
spread in North Arabia in Hijaz, the coastal territory, and in
the city of Yathrib (the modern city of Medina). In his attempt
to reconcile the Jews to his cause, Muhammad gave them an
eminent place. After all, from the beginning he tried to model
Islam on Judaism.

Medina harboured three major Jewish tribes. First, the
tribe of Banu-Natheer owned land and engaged in money-
lending and trading. Secondly, the tribe of Banu-Kinkah possessed no land, but engaged in commerce and worked as
goldsmiths. This was the first Jewish community to suffer persecution by the prophet of Islam. Thirdly, the tribe of Banu-
Kuraida disputed with Muhammad and was reluctant to support his new faith; consequently they were persecuted (for
further details see the section, 'How did Muhammad treat the
Jews and Christians... during his life?', pp. 54-5)

How did Judaism Influence Islam?

Perhaps one of Muhammad's most pronounced leadership
abilities was his skilful appeal to traditional authority. He recognized the power of tradition (التقليد) over the Arabs, who are
by nature tradition-directed. Thus, his skilful incorporation of
elements handed down by previous generations caused his

contemporaries to view him as a reformer, *musleh* (مصلح),
rather than a revolutionary or innovator, *mubdeh* (مبدع).

Both pre-Islamic Judaism and Christianity played an important role in the formation of the new religion, not only with regard to its scripture, but also to its thought and culture. However, Muslims claim that the Quran originated in heaven and could not have been influenced by any earthly culture. None the less, even a cursory reading of the Quran shows the adoption of numerous rabbinic themes by the founder of Islam and leads one to the obvious conclusion that the influence of Judaism upon Islam is integral to the religion's very core. In his classic book, *The Original Sources of the Quran* (published in 1905), W. Clair Tisdall dealt with a subject never before discussed by anyone — namely, the origin of the Quran. While Muslims claim the divine origin of their holy book, Tisdall argues that its sources are found in pre-Islamic Arabian traditions, including Judaism and Christianity.

It is important to keep in mind that Muhammad's skilful borrowing from previous traditions later became the heart

and soul of the new faith. Many precepts that are included in the religious and cultural system of Islam are derived from Hebraic and Semitic traditions. Among the cultural rites derived from Judaism are usury, dietary laws, business transactions, the status of women and the relationship of children with their parents.

The following table compares some of the Jewish and Islamic beliefs and duties.

Jewish	Islamic
Beliefs	*Beliefs*
God	Allah
Unity (Deut. 6:4); Holiness (Lev. 10:3) Self-revelation in word and deed	Unity (2:163); Incomprehensibility (42:11)
Torah, Psalms, Prophets (Neh. 13:1; Luke 24:44)	Torah, Psalms, Prophets (5:44; 2:87; 21:105)
Angels (Gen. 3:24; 28:12; Exod. 14:19; Judg. 13:6; 2 Sam 24:16-17)	Angels (2:30; 6:61; 35:21-22; 43:19)
Prophets (Num. 12:6; 2 Kings 2:3-5)	Prophets / apostles (4:150; 21:1-112)
Day of Judgement (1 Chr. 16:33; Job 21:30; Ps. 9:7; 50:3; 96:13; Mal. 4:5)	Last day (3:185; 6:51,128; 54:1-5)
Election (Deut. 10:14-15; Ps. 106:5	Determinism / fatalism (2:7; 16:93; 6:2)
Duties	*Duties*
Shema (Deut. 6:4)	*Shahadah* (First Pillar of Islam)
Prayer (Exod. 27:20-21; 30:7-10; Lev. 10:9; 24:2-9)	Prayer (Second Pillar)
	Alms — *Zakat* (Third Pillar)
Fasting (Neh. 9:1; Ps. 35:13; Jer. 36:9; Joel 1:14; Zech. 8:19)	Fasting — *Sawm* (Fourth Pillar)

To what extent does the Quran correspond to the Old Testament narratives?

The overwhelming majority of the Quranic accounts, including creation, prophets and elements of faith, have their antecedents in the Bible and rabbinic traditions. However, a cursory reading of the Quran reveals significant reconstruction of

some of these accounts. For example, the traditional narratives describing Allah's covenant with Abraham and the sacrifice of his son are incompatible with the biblical account. While the Quran is silent about the identity of the son intended for sacrifice to God, Muslims insist that Ishmael was the recipient of Allah's promises. He is considered to be the father of the Arab race and the first to build the *Kaaba* (كعبة) along with his father Abraham (2:124-127). The title given to Ishmael is Abu-al-fida (أبوالفدى), which means, 'Father of the ransom'. While the Quran does not say that it was Ishmael who was to be sacrificed, Muslims hold that he — and not Isaac, as the Bible affirms — was intended as a sacrifice to God. Furthermore, Ishmael is regarded as a prophet in Islam and a recipient of revelation (2:136).

The Bible, however, gives special significance to Isaac in the context of God's historical redemptive plan. Isaac was the beneficiary of God's covenant with his father, Abraham. The promise was given that through Abraham's child of the promise — Isaac (Gal. 4:22-23) — and his descendants the Messiah would come, and all the nations of the earth would be blessed. But the Quran's account leaves no place for God's redemptive promises, which first appear in Genesis 3:15 and progressively move towards the perfect sacrifice on the cross. There is a theological reason for this. While the biblical account asserts that Adam's sin of disobedience resulted in the total corruption of human nature and carried with it far-reaching consequences, it is not so in Islam. The Quran states that Adam was created weak; his moral disposition remained the same as it was prior to the Fall (4:28). Thus, according to Islamic argumentation, since sin did not affect human nature, there is no need for a divine act of reconciliation (i.e., the cross).

Who were the pre-Islamic Christians?

Reference was made earlier to the emphasis some scholars place on the relationship between Islam, Judaism and Christianity, particularly in the formation of Muhammad's religious ideas. While it may have been the apostle Paul who first preached the unblemished gospel in Arabia (Gal. 1:17), the following centuries witnessed the introduction of various brands of Christianity, ranging from mainline orthodoxy to a number of heretical sects.

The three most significant groups that exerted religious and social influence on Islam were the Nestorians (نسطوريون) in the east, the Byzantines in the north and the Abyssinians in the south (in what is now Ethiopia). Historians tell us that

after the capture of Rome in A.D. 476 by the Germanic tribes, the great Roman Empire lost its Western dominance. The eastern half, however, continued to represent Christianity, even though it was plagued with internal divisions, theological disputes and veneration of saints and relics. Eastern Christendom was a house divided against itself by theological disputes.

A group in Mecca and Medina called 'the *Hanifs*' coexisted with the Jews, Christians and pagans. The *Hanifs* are highly respected by the Arabian tribes for their devotion to God.

Two Arabian states were formed on the border between Arabia and the Byzantine Empire. *Beni Ghassan* (بني غسان), a Monophysite Christian tribe, settled south of Syria and was directly connected with central Arabia, the birthplace of Islam. The *Lakhmid* (لخميد) tribe was largely Nestorian and occupied the eastern section of Arabia.

Although Arabia was never dominated by the Greek and Roman empires, it was not totally isolated from those civilizations. Arabia played an important role as a trade route connecting the Byzantine Empire in the north with the Abyssinian in the south. Muhammad was exposed during his childhood to the Jewish and Christian beliefs already in existence in Arabia and later through his trading activities with the Christians in the north. The Jewish community included the sect of the Ebionites (ايبونيّة).

What were the main heresies which led to Muhammad's misunderstanding of the Christian faith?

Muhammad never had direct access to the Bible, and certainly not in his own language. By its own admission the Quran acknowledges that some heretical Jews and Christians who conversed with Muhammad about the Bible distorted its teachings as they expounded their faiths to him: 'Some of those who are Jews change words from their context and say: "We hear and disobey; hear thou as one who heareth not" and "Listen to us!" distorting with their tongues and slandering religion' (Quran 4:46; see also 4:47-48).

However, the theological controversies of the early church up to the emergence of Muhammad had far-reaching consequences on the formation of Islam. These controversies were perhaps some of the most important factors contributing to Muhammad's misinterpretation of the Christian faith, which led ultimately to the development of Islam. The prominent seventh-century Christian theologian John of Damascus labelled Islam 'a Christian heresy'.

The following major heresies are believed to be the ones that most influenced Muhammad's false view of the Christian faith, ultimately leading him to fill the vacuum with a religion based on modifications of already existing religious systems.

Trinitarian heresies

Arianism

This rather extreme heresy in the early church was constructed by Arius, a fourth-century theologian, parish priest of the church in Alexandria. He maintained that the Son was not coequal or coeternal with the Father. He alleged that Christ was the first and highest of all beings, created out of nothing by God the Father. This view denied the true deity of Christ and held instead that he occupied a position somewhere between that of God and man. However, the Arians in fact misinterpreted certain Scripture statements relating to Christ's state of humiliation and wrongly assumed that temporary subordination to the Father meant original and permanent inequality. Origen, the most outstanding of the early church fathers, profoundly defended the divinity of Christ against Arianism.

The Arians asserted that Christ was not of the same substance *(homo-ousia)* as the Father, but of similar substance *(homoi-ousia)*. We may be tempted today to wonder how the whole Christian world could have been convulsed over the rejection of a single letter of the original Greek alphabet, but, in reality, the difference is between a Saviour who is truly God and one who is only a creature; between a Christianity which is able to save the souls of men and one which cannot. Under the influence of the great early Christian apologist Athanasius, the Council of Nicaea asserted the full and eternal deity of Christ, who was declared to be 'God of God, Light of

Arius' theological views were condemned at the Council of Nicaea,
which was convened by the Emperor Constantine (A.D. 325).

Light, Very God of Very God, being of one substance with
the Father'.

Because of the claims which Christ made, the authority
which he assumed, the miracles he worked, and the glory he
displayed, particularly in his resurrection, the great majority of
the early Christians recognized him as truly God. However, a
number of clergy and laity maintained erroneous views about
Christ in several parts of the Middle East and in close prox-
imity to Arabia, where Muhammad was born.

A similar Arian influence is also found in Islam. The Quran
contends that Christ was created by Allah: 'The similitude of
Jesus before God is that of Adam; He created Him from dust,
then said to Him be, and he was' (Quran 3:59). Moreover,
both modern-day Jehovah's Witnesses and Islam resemble
the Arians in their rejection of the orthodox teaching of the
Trinity and the deity of Christ.

Christological heresies

Apollinarianism

Apollinarius, the Bishop of Syria, was the first to grapple with the question of how the divine and human natures could unite in Christ. He developed his Christological views by asserting the divinity of Christ, while emphasizing the imperfections of his humanity. This assertion, which found its roots in the Platonic / Greek ideas that elevate the soul, or the divine, above the body, was condemned at the Council of Constantinople in A.D. 381.

In contrast with Apollinarianism, the Antiochan school of thought in the fourth century A.D. emphasized the real humanity of Christ. This emphasis came into conflict with the Alexandrian Christology, which focused on the divine nature of Christ. Exposed to such ideas, Muhammad shows a conflicting understanding of Christ's nature as we read the Quran. Unfortunately, Muhammad later totally rejected Christ's divine nature and concentrated exclusively on his human nature (cf. Quran 3:59).

Nestorianism

Nestorianism was another error that had a widespread influence in the early church, ranking next to Arianism in consequence, and even resulting in a considerable portion of the church splitting off from the main body. The error of Nestorius was that he carried the dual nature of Christ too far. This gave Christ a double personality, two natures and two persons instead of two natures and one person. Christ was thus regarded as being only a man in very close union with God. A similar view is found in the Quran: 'The Messiah Jesus, was a messenger of Allah, and His Word, and a Spirit from Him' (4:171). Of course, Christ is a unique person: in him true deity and true humanity are joined to form one

The Nestorians were mission-minded. They spread as far as China. However, when Islam controlled the region, they lost their influence. The image (early twentieth century), shows Nestorian Dervishes in Baghdad, Iraq.

person. He is as truly God as is God the Father and as truly man as we are.

Adding to the complexity of the theological disputes in the early church was the fact that technical theological words were often used. Nestorius' frequent use of abstract theological terms and his excessive emphasis on the humanity of Christ created confusion within the Christian church, and later among Muslims like Al-Tabari (d. 855). Al-Tabari was a Nestorian and a famous physician, who at the age of seventy converted to Islam. His main teaching was that the dual nature of Christ cannot be sustained within the confines of a monotheistic faith because confusion will arise as to whether Jesus was God or a second god. In some ways, he portrayed Christ as Muslims identified him, as a man and prophet sent from God.

According to the Muslim historian Hassan Ibrahim Hassan, Muhammad was exposed first-hand to Christian teaching from a Syrian Nestorian monk, Buhaira (بحيرى), during his many commercial travels to Syria. Being influenced by early Christian heresies such as Nestorianism, Muhammad replaced the Christ-centred message of the gospel with an intensely legalistic system based on the teachings of both the Quran (قرآن) and the Sunnah (سنة).

Monophysitism

This Greek term, meaning 'one nature', refers to the unorthodox doctrine that Christ, after his incarnation, had only one
nature. The adherents of this doctrine claim that Christ's divine nature was dominant and his human nature was subor-
dinated to it. Such teaching influenced a number of churches
in the subsequent centuries, such as the Coptic, Syrian and
Armenian churches in the Middle East. Monophysitism was
condemned by the Council of Chalcedon in the year 451.

As we noted earlier, among the most important pre-Islamic
deities were the 'Manat', 'al-Lat' and 'al-Uzza' (see pp.
19-21). These three are also mentioned in the Quran and referred to as 'the daughters of Allah'. A number of historians
believe that it was a pre-Islamic tritheism of this kind that created confusion in Muhammad's mind. He did not see the distinctive Christian doctrine, which maintains the unity of one
true living God existing in three persons — Father, Son and
Holy Spirit — in one substance. The Quran reflects this mis-
reading of the doctrine in the following verse: 'So Believe in
Allah and his messengers, and say not "Three, it is better for
you!" Allah is only one God...' (4:171).

What are some of the implications of these heresies?

This was the state of affairs in Eastern Christianity just before
the advent of Islam. Muhammad was able to incorporate into
his new religion some important beliefs and practices already
in existence among pagan religions, as well as among both
Hebraic and Christian traditions. Muhammad's misconception
of the orthodox Christian teaching about the Trinity and the
nature of Christ, however, paved the way for the outbreak of
Islam by giving him a reason to craft a new, facile religion appealing to the masses — a faith predominately based on
human initiative. Unfortunately, these misconceptions have

continued to permeate Muslim thinking from the very inception of Islam right up to our own day.

The Quran seems to describe Christ in conflicting terms, some of which correspond to the unorthodox Christian teachings which were the subject of controversies in the early church; others confirm the biblical teaching. In certain places the Quran denies that Jesus is the Son of God (2:116), describing him as a mere man (3:59). Nevertheless, in other places Jesus is described in lofty, highly favoured terms, elevating him above all other prophets. Unlike other prophets, Jesus' prophetic ministry was validated in the Quran by a number of distinctives. First, miracles were ascribed to him (5:112-13; 3:46). Secondly, he was united with the Holy Spirit (2:86). Thirdly, he was called the Messiah (مسيّا), (3:45). Fourthly, he was born of a virgin (3:47). Another important designation of Jesus is that of the 'Word' (cf. John 1:1). In *surah* 3:45 we read, 'O Mary! God giveth thee Glad tidings of a Word from Him: his name Will be Christ Jesus.' George Sale translated this verse more literally from the original Arabic: 'O Mary! God sendeth thee good tidings, that thou shalt bear the Word, proceeding from Himself; his name shall be Christ Jesus.'[3] The 'Word, proceeding from Himself,' seems to correlate with John's affirmation of Christ's eternal existence, and to be a more accurate translation of the Arabic text.

Who was Muhammad?

Muhammad, the founder of Islam, was a native of Arabia and a Semite by race. He is thought to have been born on 20 April 571, in the city of Mecca (historical accounts differ as to the exact date). The year 571 is called the Year of the Elephant (عام الفيل), which was later linked to a *surah* in the Quran describing the unsuccessful attempt by the Christian Ethiopian general Abraha to capture Mecca, using military elephants (see picture overleaf), upon learning of the desecration of

Christian sites. Muslims believe that the defeat of Abraha in the same year as Muhammad's birth was a prophetic sign from Allah designating Muhammad as the future conqueror of non-Muslim religions.

Muhammad belonged to the Hashimite clan of the tribe of Quraysh, who controlled the Kaaba shrines, which were associated with a number of polytheistic and pagan religions. His father's name was Abed Allah, indicating that the term 'Allah' was used in pre-Islamic paganism. Some argue that the term 'Allah' is purely Arabic and has nothing to do with the biblical name Elohim.

In any case, Muhammad was orphaned at an early age and was raised by his grandfather, Abed Almutalib. When Abed Almutalib died, Muhammad came under the guardianship of his uncle, Abu Talib, the head of the Hashimite clan. He was breastfed by a Bedouin woman named Halima. (In Arabic culture boys, being more favoured than girls, are usually suckled longer.) It was here among the Bedouins where Muhammad learned the classical Arabic language, which proved to be an important factor in his later religious life. Muslims claim that Muhammad was illiterate and would have been unable to compose a book in excellent Arabic, like the Quran; therefore, they say, the Quran must be an authentic revelation from Allah. However, a number of scholars, such as Tisdall, Saal and Pfander, efficiently dispute such a claim.

Muhammad was to a large extent familiar with other religious practices, including those of Christianity and Judaism. As we saw earlier, according to the Muslim historian Hassan Ibrahim Hassan, he was exposed first-hand to Christian teaching from a Syrian Nestorian monk. Moreover, according to *Harper's Dictionary of Religion*, in his quest for religious answers, Muhammad looked first to the religious traditions around him. Muhammad was not alone in his search for religious truth. Muslim tradition tells of at least three other men who broke with polytheism and adopted some form of monotheism just before or during Muhammad's time. They are called *Hanifs* (men who were truly seeking to worship God, analogous to the Bible's designation of 'God-fearers'). They were:

1. Waraka ibn Nawfal, Khadija's cousin (see below), who converted to Christianity;
2. Ubaydallah ibn Jahsh, who converted to Islam after Muhammad's mission, but later became a Christian;
3. Uthman ibn al-Huwayrith, who went to the Byzantine court, became a Christian and received high office.

Muhammad's material success in this part of his life is attributed to his commercial association with the rich widow, Khadija, and his later marriage to her. It is not clear whether she, or any in her family, provided Muhammad with any religious instruction, but, as mentioned above, she was related to the Christian scholar Waraka ibn Nawfal, who memorized large portions of the Bible. She did give Muhammad social standing and considerable personal support during his early religious experiences. She was the mother of all his children except Ibrahim. His three sons by her, al-Qasim, al-Ta and al-Tabir, died in infancy, as did Ibrahim. Muhammad's new social status enabled him to assume a central role in the rebuilding of the Kaaba, although later narrators have embellished the particulars of the story.

Muhammad exercised an annual ascetic withdrawal in the Hira Cave near Mecca. Not much detail is known about his routine but it lasted for approximately a month each year. Muhammad claimed that he received the first revelation from the angel Gabriel on Mt Hira, a nearby mountain. Frightened by this encounter, Muhammad doubted this revelation, believing it was from Satan, and contemplated killing himself to avoid being thought insane (which his critics called him anyway). When he experienced revelatory visions, he underwent bodily changes evident to those around him. He was accused of being the subject of seizures, or epilepsy, and some went so far as to suggest these experiences were satanic in origin. However, Muhammad came back to his wife Khadija and her

Hira Cave, near Mecca

cousin Waraka ibn Nawfal, who encouraged him and persuaded him that this was a valid revelation from Allah, similar
to revelation in both Old and New Testaments.

He persuaded a few to accept his new religion, including
his wife Khadija. However, his initial success was faced with
opposition from the Meccan tribes, although they refrained
from harming him for fear of embarking on a civil war, particularly one involving Muhammad's Hashimite clan, who
supported him more out of tribal loyalty than from conviction
about his religious mission. After failing to recruit the Meccans
to his religion, Muhammad moved to Medina and succeeded
in uniting its various factions against the Meccans, establishing
the first Muslim community *(Ummah)*, which he ruled strictly
under the injunction of the Quran. In A. D. 630 Muhammad
succeeded in conquering Mecca and made it the centre of his
religion. Between 630 and 632, he subjugated Arabia, thus
turning it from a pre-Islamic, multi-ethnic and culturally di-
verse society into an exclusive Islamic state.

Muhammad became ill and died in June 632. He was bur-
ied at Medina, where his tomb has become a major attraction
for Muslims. Muhammad died without providing a successor.
Later a series of successors, called caliphs, carried on the task
of ruling and expanding the Muslim community which was
established by Muhammad in Medina. Today the term *Ummah* (which originally designated that community) refers to
Islam worldwide.

Why do Muslims visit Mecca?

The Quran demands that every able Muslim should make the
pilgrimage to Mecca, known as the *hajj* (حج), at least once in a
lifetime. In *surah* 3:97 we read, 'Wherein are plain memorials;
the place where Abraham stood up to pray; and whosoever
entereth it is safe. And Pilgrimage to the house is a duty unto
Allah for mankind, for him who can find a way thither.' This

About two million followers of Islam from all over the world travel to
Saudi Arabia for the annual pilgrimage to Mecca known as the *hajj*.
Saudi Arabia allocates each country a quota of 1,000 to make the *hajj*
for every million Muslims.

duty is considered part of the Five Pillars of Islam (see chapter
3, and the question, 'What are the religious duties required of
Muslims?', p. 97) Contrary to the teaching of the New Testament, these 'pillars', including the *hajj*, are thought to provide
all the works necessary in order to secure salvation.

The *hajj* basically consists of the following beliefs and
rituals.

1. The origins of the hajj

From the verse in the Quran mentioned earlier, Muslims traditionally trace this ritual back to Abraham. They maintain that Abraham brought his son Ishmael in order to sacrifice him to Allah, and rebuild al-Kaaba (Quran 3:127). Muhammad reclaimed this shrine from pagans and converted it to a Muslim site which has become the most sacred place on earth for Muslims.

This Turkish painting shows Muhammad sitting outside the Kaaba, which became the most sacred site in Islam. Most, but not all, Islamic paintings show Muhammad with a veil covering his face.

2. The importance of Mecca

The pilgrimage to Mecca is performed once a year, during the last Islamic lunar calendar. It is considered to be the highest form of personal religious achievement. Some Muslims regard it as a form of personal rebirth whereby one can devote oneself unequivocally to Allah and the religion of Islam.

What does the Bible say?

In John 4:20, the Samaritan woman told Jesus, 'Our fathers worshipped on this mountain, but you Jews claim that the place where we must worship is in Jerusalem.' After all, the mountain to which she referred, Gerizim, had a significant role in the tradition of the Samaritans. Here Abraham prepared the sacrifice of Isaac, and according to their scriptures, Gerizim was the mountain on which the altar was erected. None the less, Jesus' answer was unmistakable: 'Believe me, woman, a time is coming when you will worship the Father neither on this mountain nor in Jerusalem ... a time is coming and has now come when the true worshippers will worship the Father in spirit and truth, for they are the kind of worshippers the Father seeks. God is spirit, and his worshippers must worship in Spirit and in truth' (John 4: 21,24).

3. Rituals of purification

The *hajj* commences with the performance of the ritual of outward physical purification and this is followed by wearing white garments.

What does the Bible say?

Although it is not wise to judge the motive of individual Muslims engaging in acts of worship, we need to see what Jesus has to say. Jesus gave a stern warning to the Pharisees, who were meticulous about the minute details of outward acts of worship and purification: 'Woe to you, teachers of the law and Pharisees, you hypocrites! You clean the outside of the cup and dish, but inside they are full of greed and self-indulgence. Blind Pharisee! First clean the inside of the cup and dish, and then the outside also will be clean' (Matt 23:25-26).

4. The state of cleanliness

After achieving the state of cleanliness, the pilgrims are ready to enter Mecca and begin what is called the *'umra'* (a secondary *hajj)*. This initiatory ritual involves *'tawaf'*, i.e., walking seven times around the Kaaba (see p. 38).

What does the Bible say?

The idea of true cleanliness and perfection of the heart corresponds with the idea of cleansing the conscience from true guilt which is associated with inward piety. In Hebrews 10:22 we read, 'Let us draw near to God with a sincere heart in full assurance of faith, having our hearts sprinkled to cleanse us from a guilty conscience.' Furthermore, the writer of Hebrews maintains that guilt cannot be expunged by the performance of good works or obedience to the law: '... the gifts and sacrifices being offered were not able to clear the conscience of the worshipper. They are only a matter of food and drink and various ceremonial washings — external regulations applying until the time of the new order' (Heb. 9:9-10).

5. Hagar's search for water

Closely connected with the *umra* (عمرة) is the ritual of running between the two hills, Marwah and Safa, near Mecca. This is intended to recall the desperate search for water made by Abraham's wife Hagar. Muslims believe that Hagar searched for water at this location, where she left her son Ishmael while she hurried back and forth between the two mountains in her frantic quest for water. When she returned to her child, the angel Gabriel appeared and led her to a spring of water called the well of 'Zamzam'. In similar fashion, Muslim pilgrims run between the two mountains. Then they visit the Zamzam well, where many purchase some of the precious water to take home.

What does the Bible say?

The book of Genesis says that Hagar was with Ishmael in Beersheba, south of Palestine, and both lived in Paran — modern-day Sinai in Egypt (Gen. 21:14,21).

6. Standing before Allah

The main pilgrimage begins with the critical ritual of *wuquf* (وقوف), which means 'standing', and is performed with the greatest solemnity. The obligatory standing before Allah in a position of prayer takes place in the barren plain of Arafat, about fifteen miles from Mecca. Any improper performance of this part of the ritual invalidates the entire pilgrimage.

What does the Bible say?

People tend to try to do something in order to earn the sanction of their conscience, and we often condemn ourselves when we sense that we fall short. The book of Hebrews, as we have already seen, gives concrete teaching that we can never satisfy the demands of conscience through our own attempts to expiate our sins (see Heb. 9:9; 10:22).

7. The stoning of Satan

On the road back to Mecca, pilgrims find pebbles for tossing at three pillars located in the nearby area while chanting, '*Allah Akbar*' (الله أكبر), which means, 'God is great'. This is said to symbolize the stoning of Satan.

The Arabic name for Satan is *Shaytan* (شيطان) or *Iblis*. According to the Quran (7:12; 15:27; 55:15), he was originally some kind of a *jinn*, and was created with fire as an essential constituent of his being. After defying Allah by refusing to bow to Adam, he was expelled from heaven and his rebellion against Allah made him *Shaytan* and caused him to become the sworn enemy of man. One is fully justified in commenting that there is an apparent contradiction in the Quran, which must be reconciled: how is it that the Quran repeatedly and emphatically calls on Muslims to bow down and worship none but Allah, while at the same time it teaches that it would have been right for Satan to bow down and worship Adam? Was not

Satan justified in refusing to bow down to Adam? Why then did Allah castigate and expel him for doing what was right?

What does the Bible say?

In describing the biblical teaching about Satan, we must never forget one very important fact which may in itself suffice to make clear that, contrary to Islamic teaching, Satan cannot be defeated by any human effort. According to Islam, the best defence against Satan is seeking Allah by the recitation of the Quran (7:200; 41:36). In contrast, in Genesis 3 we learn that Satan brought about the fall of the human race. There is an inherent correlation between Satan, sin and the fall of man. If we take the holiness of God seriously, then we can understand that the sin of Satan, Adam and Eve cannot be expunged by any human effort. According to the Word of God, the defeat of Satan comes only by the coming of the promised Messiah (Gen. 3:15). The Bible says that only Christ can destroy the works of Satan: 'The reason the Son of God appeared was to destroy the devil's work' (1 John 3:8); 'Since the children have flesh and blood, he [Christ] too shared in their humanity so that by his death he might destroy him who holds the power of death — that is, the devil...' (Heb. 2:14).

8. Animal sacrifices

The ritual sacrificing of animals follows. This ceremony commemorates Abraham's sacrifice of a ram to Allah instead of Ishmael. The title given to Ishmael is 'Abu-al-fida' ('Father of the Ransom'). It reflects the traditional Islamic belief that it was Ishmael who was to be sacrificed, not Isaac, contrary to the biblical narrative. None the less, all pilgrims are required to offer an animal sacrifice. The acts of sacrifice and the subsequent feast both last for three days and coincide with similar celebrations by Muslims worldwide. This feast is called the

'Greater Feast', while the feast which is observed at the end of the fasting of Ramadan is called 'the Lesser Feast'.

What does the Bible say?

Here again we see demonstrated the fact that we all have a tendency to want to do something in order to satisfy the demands of conscience. However, as we have already seen (see pp. 41, 42), the epistle to the Hebrews teaches that we can never be cleansed from a guilty conscience by any efforts of our own, such as the offering of animal

At the hajj Muslims perform the central ritual of animal sacrifices in memory of Allah's sparing Abraham's son. (Islamic tradition points to Ishmael as the intended sacrifice, not Isaac, as the Bible affirms.) The feast is called Eid al-Adha, or Eid al-Kurban.

sacrifices (Heb. 9:9). It can be accomplished only through the efficacy of Christ's sacrifice, which provides the ground for justification.

In the introduction to his commentary on the epistle to the Hebrews, F. F. Bruce points out that 'The Aaronic priests offered up sacrifices repeatedly, and our author pays particular attention to the annual sin-offering presented on the nation's behalf by the high priest on the day of atonement. But the animal sacrifice could not meet the real need of men and women. A sin-stained conscience is a barrier to communion with God, and the cleansing of the conscience could not be effected by such sacrifice as the levitical cultus provided. But Christ exercises His priestly ministry on the basis of a real and efficacious sacrifice — "the sacrifice of himself" (Heb. 9:26). The nature of this sacrifice our author finds expressed in the language of Ps. 40:6-8, where someone who knows the uselessness of animal sacrifices dedicated his life to God for the obedient accomplishment of His will.'[4]

9. The final rituals of the hajj

Following the sacrifice, the pilgrims often shave their heads to signify the completion of the *hajj* and return to al-Kaaba for another *tawaf* (completing seven circuits around the shrine, see pp. 41, 46) and a second stoning of the devil.

As the pilgrims return home they leave with the satisfaction of having, as they suppose, gained merit with Allah. Furthermore, they acquire a new religious and social status which is denoted by the title *'Hajji'* for a male and *'Hajjiah'* for a female. They are treated as ideal Muslims, who are worthy of respect and honour.

What is the Kaaba?

The Kaaba is the centre of the Muslim world and the most sacred shrine to which pilgrimage is made. It is a relatively small, windowless cube-like structure located in the centre of the Grand Mosque in Mecca. It is about twelve metres (or forty feet) long, ten metres (thirty-two feet) wide and fifteen metres (fifty feet) high.

Muslims believe that the Kaaba is built directly under the throne of Allah. It is difficult to see how this belief can be defensible when it is known that the earth is globe-shaped, and that its centre can therefore be at any point. Moreover, the

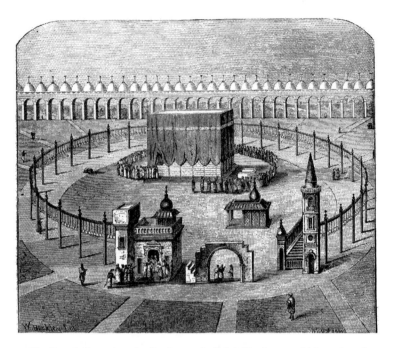

Muslims believe that the Kaaba was built by Abraham and Ishmael and, upon their death, it became a pantheon of pagan idols.

earth is constantly in motion as it tilts around its own axis and orbits the sun.

It is in the direction towards the Kaaba, known as the *kiblah* (قبلة), that Muslims around the world bow in prayer to Allah. The Kaaba, and indeed all the city of Mecca, is sacred territory reserved only for Muslims; all other people are forbidden to enter, *haram* (حرام). As we have seen earlier, the pilgrimage to Mecca (the *hajj*) is one of the basic tenets of Islam.

The ritual of circling round the Kaaba is called *tawaf* (طواف). Seven circuits are made around the Kaaba. Each circuit is called a *'shawt'*; seven *'shawts'* make one *'tawaf'*. This ceremonial walk must be performed by all pilgrims according to specific rules, which include the kissing of the Black Stone.

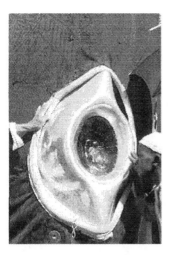

The Kaaba was built to enclose the Black Stone *(al-Hajar al-Aswad)*, the most venerated object in Islam. The Black Stone is semi-circular and measures about ten inches (250 mm.) horizontally and twelve inches (300 mm.) vertically. Its origin is not certain. Many believe it is a meteorite, similar to others found in Arabia. The Black Stone is set in gold and fixed on the eastern corner of the Kaaba. Muslim legends say that Adam erected the Kaaba and, according to the Quran, Abraham rebuilt it later, after the flood (2:127-128).

What is meant by 'Dar al-Islam' and Dar al-Harb?

According to Islamic traditions, the globe is divided into two domains: *Dar al-Islam* (دار الإسلام), the Abode / House of Islam and *Dar al-Harb* (دار الحرب), the Abode / House of War. *Dar al-Islam* is an Arabic term and refers more precisely to those territories controlled by the Islamic religion where the Islamic law, or *Shariah*, prevails. Non-Muslims may live there, but they are, none the less, considered to belong to the Domain of War, sometimes called *Dar al-Kufr* (دار الكفر), the Domain of Unbelief / Infidels.

Historically, orthodox Muslims have understood the Domain of War as being the foreign world which has not yet come under the majority rule of Islam. However, the more militant and fundamentalist Muslims reject any non-Muslim ethos. They appeal to the Quran as authority for the universal inculcation of Islamic values, even if this means taking military actions against *Dar al-Harb*.

What do Muslims believe about Abraham?

In an article by Jim Reed of *CBS News*, dated 27 September 2002, we read the following comment: ' "All the children of Abraham deserve peace." Thus spake U.S. President George W. Bush in a pronouncement on the White House lawn earlier this year. His biblical reference highlighted one core element of the agonizing and tragic dilemma that has stymied Middle East peacemakers: Arabs and Jews both claim Abraham as their ancestor. According to Holy Scripture, whether the Christian Bible, the Torah or the Koran, the same blood courses through their veins.'

Both Arabs and Jews claim Abraham as their forefather. On the basis of the Torah, the Jews maintain, 'Abraham is ours; he is our father,' the father of Isaac and ancestor of Jacob and his sons. They emphasize what they see as their divinely given entitlement, including both land and national identity, through their descent from Abraham. For the Jewish people Abraham is the most revered patriarch, and they are reluctant to share him with others. Raphael Patai says, 'One of the most tenacious popular beliefs transmitted from generation to generation of Jews is that of Abrahamic descent... This popular Jewish belief has become a psychological fact holding the Jews together... The image of "Abraham our Father" has been focal in Jewish consciousness throughout history, beginning with biblical times.'⁵ Moreover, Jews claim that God promised Abraham and his descendants a land 'from the river of Egypt to the great river, the Euphrates' (Gen 15:18).

Jews are not the only people who claim to be the true descendants of Abraham. Muslims also maintain that Abraham was the first *hanif* (حنيف), or monotheist Muslim. Moreover, he was the father of Ismail (Ishmael), the progenitor of the Arab race, including the prophet Muhammad. Muslims also cite other traditions in support of their claim to be descendants from the patriarch. The Quran incorporates several events in the life of Abraham similar to those found in the Bible. Nevertheless, a number of narratives are added in the Quran, such as Abraham's travelling to Mecca with his son Ishmael and building the Kaaba (2:125-127), quarrels with idol-worshippers (21:51-57) and arguments with his father (Azar) against idolatry (6:74). It is important to keep in mind that Muhammad's skilful borrowing from previous traditions, in the process of the formation of Islam, later became the heart and soul of the new faith. It is striking, however, that although Muhammad appealed to previous revelation (the Torah, Psalms and *Injil* — i.e. the Gospels) in support of his teaching, these traditions were ignored or rejected whenever he understood them to be incompatible with the accounts found in the Quran.

As stated above, Abraham is given the title of *hanif*, to designate his monotheism. The Quran reads: 'And they say: Be Jews or Christians, then you will be rightly guided. Say: Nay, but [we follow] the religion of Abraham, the upright, and he was not of the idolaters' (2:135).

Another title given to Abraham is taken from the Bible. He is called *Khalilu Allah* (خليل الله), or the 'friend of God' (cf. 2 Chr. 20:7; James 2:23).

In any case, any claim to ownership of Abraham must be qualified, according to what the Lord Jesus Christ said (John 8:31-41; cf. Matt. 3:9). There is a strong propensity among Jews and Muslims to interpret their connection with Abraham in religious, political and racial terms. Abraham's sacrifice is recorded in the Bible and also in the Quran as a religious act of worship. While both Jews and Muslims attach a symbolic meaning to it, the New Testament gives it an eschatological element. Paul says, 'Consider Abraham: "He believed God, and it was credited to him as righteousness." Understand, then, that those who believe are children of Abraham. The Scripture foresaw that God would justify the Gentiles by faith, and announced the gospel in advance to Abraham: "All nations will be blessed through you." So those who have faith are blessed along with Abraham, the man of faith' (Gal. 3:6-9). God commanded Abraham to sacrifice his son Isaac. However, Isaac was spared when God provided a substitute, a ram offered in his place on Mount Moriah (Gen. 22:13). This is a powerful anticipation of the Lord Jesus Christ's being sacrificed in our place on Mount Calvary. Forgiveness of sins is no longer achieved by animal sacrifices, but by the ultimate sacrifice of Christ (Heb. 10 1-18). The theme of sin and guilt offerings continues in the Old Testament (Lev. 4:1-35; 5;14 – 6:7), but only temporarily and symbolically as the preparatory stage for approaching God until the advent of the perfect sacrifice.

What is the *jihad*, and how did Muhammad spread Islam?

Muhammad was a man who was consumed by a deep sense of *dawah* (دعوى) which means in an Islamic context 'to propagate the faith by calling people to embrace Islam'. His unquenchable zeal for spreading Islam has left a lasting influence upon his followers.

Among the many uses of the term *'dawah'* in the Quran, perhaps the one with the most potent and far-reaching implications is in connection with the external mission of promulgating Islam — that is, the concept of *jihad* (8:74,75; 9:44). From the beginning, *dawah* has been associated with military conquest, the justification for which is laid down in the prescriptions of the Quran (2:69; 2:190; 2:217; 2:256; 3:103; 8:39; 8:61-62; 25:52; 61:9). Thus, the importance of the propagation of Islam has been ingrained in the consciousness of Muslims from the very beginning. Resulting from its connection with the divine imperative in the Quran, it was inspired by the actions of the prophet and stirred by his call for 'struggle in the path of Allah', *jihad fe sabeel Allah* (جهاد في سبيل الله). The idea of martyrdom *(shahadah)* and the use of the sword as well as the word was therefore not a matter of choice, but part and parcel of the way of life for devout Muslims. The *Hadith* tells us that Muhammad's own soul yearned for martyrdom for the cause of Islam. Abu Hurrairah, a companion of the prophet and respected traditionalist said, 'I heard the prophet say: "I would not remain behind an army that fights in the way of Allah... I love that I should be killed in the way of Allah then brought to life, then killed again, then brought to life, then killed again."'[6]

Another explicit reference to the idea of armed struggle points to the way in which Muhammad's thoughts and commands continued to be the normative standard at least during the early period of Islam. Ibn Umar reports Muhammad as saying, 'I have been commanded that I should fight these people [non-Muslims] till they bear witness that there is no god but Allah and keep up the prayer and pay Zakat. When they do this, their blood and their property shall be safe with me except as Islam requires, and their reckoning is with Allah.'[7]

It would be difficult for a Muslim scholar to reconcile the idea of *jihad* with the command in the Quran which says, 'There is no compulsion in religion' (2:256). Today, the idea of *jihad* as pertaining to the physical struggle against the enemies of Islam is regarded as an acceptable norm among the increasing number of fundamentalists who are actively calling for the return 'back to the fundamentals', ar. *usuliyah* (اصوليّة). (For more on this see the question: 'What is modern-day Islamic fundamentalism and how does it influence Muslims?', pp. 72-4).

Who were the caliphs?

The word *caliph* (خليفة) is the title for the main leader of the Muslim community. It is derived from a word which literally means 'to leave behind a successor or vicegerent'. This title is given to the successor of Muhammad who is vested with the absolute authority of the laws of the Quran and *Sunnah*. The first four caliphs are called 'the companions of the prophet'. After Muhammad's death, Abu Bakr (632–634), the first to accept Islam, was elected as the first caliph. Umar (634–644) succeeded him after two years, and spread Islam in most of the Middle East, including Arabia, Iraq, Persia, Syria and Egypt. Umar was replaced by Uthman (644–656), who governed for some twelve years during the peak of the Islamic expansion into Armenia, Cyprus and North Africa. With the death during the battles of the prophet and several of the key reciters of the Quran, Uthman greatly feared the loss of the original text of the Quran — or, as some believe, of what was left of the oral tradition. Uthman therefore commissioned a group under the leadership of Zayed Ben Thabit to produce an official written text.

A series of uprisings began during Uthman's rule, and a new period of schisms and civil wars started with his murder. Ali (656–661), who was the cousin and son-in-law of the prophet Muhammad, succeeded him. He became the fourth and last of what is called *al-Khulafa al-Rashidoon* (the rightly guided caliphs). Ali inherited the political and religious repercussions of Uthman's murder. After a series of civil rebellions, Ali was killed with a poisoned sword by a member of the dissenting Kharijite sect, which had seceded from Ali's ranks.

What areas did Muslims conquer?

Following the example of Muhammad and the injunctions of the Quran, Muslim armies continued to conquer and subjugate subjects in the Middle East, Africa and Asia. The East Roman Empire, called the Byzantine, was plagued with constant political, social and religious strife. It came under relentless attack by the invading Muslim armies in A.D. 636, and the Christian church in that part of the world has never recovered. Within a century, Islamic armies had subjugated Saudi Arabia, the entire Middle East, Central Asia and large parts of India. The Muslim forces continued their advance into North Africa and Spain. In A.D. 711, under the leadership of Tariq Ben Ziad, 7,000 Berbers and 300 Arabs crossed the Straits of Gibraltar into Spain. Soon afterwards, Mousa Ben Nusayer, Arab governor of North Africa, crossed with 10,000 Arabs and 8,000 Berbers. While the forces of the Spanish king were distracted by a rebellion in the north, the Muslim army swiftly conquered Spain and Portugal.

After their success in Spain, they invaded France, hoping to capture all of southern Europe and Constantinople, which they had failed to conquer during their invasion earlier from the east. The caliphs of Damascus hoped to control the whole Mediterranean Sea and turn it into a huge Arabian lake. Muslim armies advanced in France and were 125 miles from Paris when they were defeated at the Battle of Tours in A.D. 732 by European forces led by Charles Martel. One of the most critical battles in history, the victory at Tours would determine the future faith of Europe.

However, Muslim armies from the east later tried again to control all of Europe. The Turks, under Muhammad II, conquered Constantinople in 1453 and made it an Ottoman capital. Under Suleiman I (often known as Suleiman the Magnificent), much of the Balkan Peninsula — Hungary, Greece, Yugoslavia and Bulgaria — came under Ottoman control. By 1685 they had reached Vienna, where, once again, the Western forces defeated the advancing Ottoman Muslim armies.

How did Muhammad treat Jews and Christians, or
dhimmis (أهل الذِمَّة), during his lifetime ?

We noted earlier that the presence of Jews and Christians in
south and north Arabia goes back to biblical times. Jewish
communities also spread in North Arabia in Hijaz, the coastal
territory, and in the city of Yathrib (modern-day Medina). As
we saw when considering the question, 'Who were the pre-
Islamic Jews?' (p. 22), three Jewish tribes were present in
Medina: Banu-Natheer, Banu-Kinkah — who were the first
Jewish community to suffer persecution by the prophet of Islam — and Banu-Kuraida, who were persecuted because they
quarrelled with Muhammad and were unwilling to support his
new faith. According to the orientalist and historian Mont-
gomery Watt, this persecution took a variety of forms including killing, destruction of property and expulsion.

One of the cruel acts of persecution against the Jews by
Muhammad (recorded even by Islamic sources, such as the
History of Islam by Hassan Ibrahim Hassan) is known as the
Massacre of Banu-Kuraida. When the Jews of the tribe of
Kuraida sided with the Qurashite tribe in opposing Islam, they
provoked Muhammad's wrath. Islamic sources tell us that the
forces of Muhammad were able to encircle the tribe of Banu-
Kuraida and besiege them for over twenty-five days until they
surrendered. Consequently, the men of Banu-Kuraida were
brought out in groups and they were beheaded. Historian
Hassan Ibrahim Hassan estimates that about 700 men were
killed. Other sources believe that the number is much higher.

In his book, *The Dhimmi*, Bat Ye'or ascertained that the
oppressive Arab Muslim armies provoked revolts in the Byzantine Christian provinces. The Arab colonialists harshly re-
pressed these revolts and peasant insurrections. The insur-
gents were put to the sword, large sections of the local
populations (Persians, Armenians, Copts, etc.) were reduced
to slavery, and many were deported. Moreover, the *dhimmis'*
lands were transferred to the Islamic community. Those who

were allowed to keep some land were subjected to heavy land taxes, known as the *kharaj* (خراج), which to some extent guaranteed protection to the *dhimmis*. In addition to the *kharaj*, Christians and Jews were subjected to a poll tax called the *jizya* (جزية) in accordance with the Quran, which says, 'Fight against such of those who have been given the Scripture as believe not in Allah nor the Last Day, and forbid not that which Allah hath forbidden by his messenger, and follow not the religion of truth, until they pay the tribute readily' (9:29). This poll tax was to be paid in a humiliating public ceremony in the course of which the *dhimmi* was struck while in the act of paying the tax. Upon the payment of the *jizya*, he received a document that was to be worn around his neck and that was regarded as a mark of dishonour, identifying him as a *dhimmi* and enabling him to move from place to place without persecution.[8]

Al-Hakim (996–1021), the sixth Fatimid caliph at Cairo, in Egypt, is known for his severe and cruel persecution of Christians and Jews. He implemented harsh restrictions on groups and ordered the destruction of the Church of the Nativity, which fuelled the desire on the part of Western Christendom to liberate the Holy Land from the hands of Muslims.

Christians in a few Middle-Eastern countries, such as Lebanon and, more recently, Syria, have enjoyed a considerable measure of freedom. However, this has not been the case in most Islamic nations. Christians around the world still endure persecution. Adherents to the Christian faith face severe punishment, rape, murder, loss of their homes and possessions and separation from family. The U.S. Commission on International Religious Freedom lists Burma, China, Iran, Sudan, Saudi Arabia and Turkmenistan among the worst violators of religious freedom.

Who were the Umayyads?

The Umayyads were an Arab dynasty that traced its origin to the Quraysh tribe of the prophet Muhammad. Muawia (A.D. 605–680), who became the governor of Syria, was the principal founder of this dynasty. He opposed the fourth caliph, Ali, demanding revenge for the killing of his relative, the third caliph, Uthman, since he believed that Ali was behind the crime. Muawia became a caliph upon the death of Ali and established his capital in Damascus in A.D. 661. His son, Yazid, succeeded him in A.D. 683 and engaged in several battles with the *Shiah* (شيعة). The *Shiah* sect of Islam, also called the party of Ali (the son-in-law and cousin of the prophet Muhammad), recognizes Ali as the only leader of the Islamic community. The *Shiah* rejects the first three caliphs (خلفاء) and accords great reverence and authority to the descendants of Ali, considering them the only legitimate leaders in Islam. Ali's son, al-Hussayn, with a dozen of his relatives, was slain in the battle at Karbala, near Kufa in Iraq. The painful events are commemorated today among the *Shiah* in Iran, southern Iraq and Lebanon by ten days of mourning called *Ashura*, in which members of the *Shiah* parade and exhibit their grief by piercing their flesh with sharp objects.

The Umayyad reign, however, under al-Walid (670–715), saw the expansion of Islam in North Africa and Spain, halted by Charles Martel at the Battle of Tours (see above, p. 53). The Umayyad period was also marked by advanced architecture, such as the Dome of the Rock in Jerusalem, the great Umayyad Mosque in Damascus, and many other places still in existence today.

Who were some noted Christians during this time?

The Umayyad caliphs recognized the acumen of many of the Christians who mastered the Arabic and Greek languages,

Inside the Dome of the Rock

and employed them to advance the Umayyad culture. One of the great Christian statesmen and able apologists during this period was John of Damascus (675–749), who was appointed by the caliph Abdul-Malik as the Chief Minister of Finance. However, John never wavered in his faith in Christ and wrote at some length in defence of the Christian faith. Muhammad, he believed, had derived his ideas from Christian heretics. Then, pretending to be God-fearing, he spread rumours that the Quran was brought down to him by the angel Gabriel. Unlike Christ, John says, Muhammad had been neither foretold nor testified to in Scripture. Muslims call Christians polytheistic, but John says that Muslims should not accuse Christians of associating other deities with God. They themselves, he asserts, mention Christ as both Word, *kalimat* (كلمة), and Spirit, *Raouh* (روح). He wrote an apologetic work, *De Fide Orthodoxa*, in which he argued extensively that Islam is a Christian heresy, and he proposed an apologetic model for countering Islamic theological objections. John was the first to defend the truth of the gospel and to help fellow Christians in their faith in Jesus Christ while enduring the rule of Islam.

Who were the Abbasids?

The Abbasids, another Arab regime, ruled in Baghdad from A.D. 749–1258. They traced their descent from Abbas, an uncle of the prophet Muhammad. The Abbasids opposed the rule of the Umayyad dynasty in Damascus, demanding that the caliphate should reside in the hands of the prophet's own family. After a series of conflicts, the Umayyad were defeated in A.D. 750, shifting the centre of the Muslim caliphate from Damascus to Baghdad. The age of Haroon Al-Rashid was the zenith of the Abbasid dynasty. Al-Rashid ruled an empire stretching from North Africa to Central Asia. His capital, Baghdad, became a centre for learning and commerce. His close relationship with Charlemagne the Great (742–814) and the writing of the book *Thousand and One Nights*, made Haroon well known in the West during this period.

Unable to rule the vast empire, the Abbasids became increasingly fragmented. The rival Fatimid caliphate in North Africa took over Tunisia and Egypt. The Abbasids lost their dynasty to the invading Mongols, who captured Baghdad in the year 1261.

Who were the Fatimid?

The Fatimid were a North African Muslim dynasty. After defeating the Abbasid governor in Tunisia, the first Fatimid caliph (A.D. 910) was called al-Mahdi ('Guided One'). They conquered Egypt, built Cairo, and made it their capital. The Fatimid expanded their rule to Palestine, Syria and North

Arabia. They were *Shiah* in doctrine, believing that the caliphate should be elected on the basis of descent from Muhammad's family. They were related to another *Shiah* sect, the Druz, who are unduly esoteric in their religious beliefs and practices. Today they live primarily in Lebanon, Syria, Israel and Jordan. Moreover, they believe the claim made by the sixth Fatimid caliph that he was divine. As stated above, al-Hakim is known for his severe and cruel persecution of Christians. In 1171 the famed Sunni Muslim commander Saladin al-Ayyubi, who defeated the Crusaders, proclaimed the end of the *Shiah* Fatimid rule and established the Ayyubid state.

How many sects are there in Islam?

Not too many people realize the numerous divisions that exist among Muslims. While there is much that all have in common, nevertheless, most differ in some very important aspects of faith and practice.

The following charts show some of these divisions:

Sunni			
A member of the larger Muslim sect that encompasses approximately ninety per cent of Muslims. 'Sunnah' means 'path', 'way', or 'law'. The Sunni acknowledge the first four caliphs. Their Islamic beliefs and practices are based on the Quran and the traditions rather than devotion to the imams, as the case is in *Shiah* Islam.			
Wahhabiyah	Hanbalites	Kharijites	Murjites
A religious fundamental, traditional and puritanical movement which has impacted on all aspects of life. It was founded by al-Wahhab	Founded by Ahmad Hanbal (780-855). They recognize no sources other than the Quran and the *Sunnah* of the prophet.	The name means 'went out' and refers to the time when they went out leaving Ali, the fourth caliph, and assassinated him. The most	They disagreed with the Kharijites about the extent of punishment of apostasy *(irtidad)*. They were moderate and pacifist and

Sunni			
(1703-1792). He called for a renewal of Islam by the removal of all innovations *(Ar. bida)*. Today it is the dominant tradition in Arabia. Modern Saudi Arabia began in the eighteenth century with the alliance between al-Wahhab, the founder of the Wahhabi movement, and Muhammad Ibn al-Sa'ud, who accepted al-Wahhab's doctrine and practice.	They are hostile to speculative theology, innovations and Sufism.	radical sect within this movement was the Azraqi, who held that an apostate Muslim should be killed with his wives and children.	emphasized faith over works.
Shafites	**Hanafites**	**Ibadites**	**Mutazilites**
Founded by Imam al-Shafii (767-820), He was an enemy of the scholastic divines, and wrote to contradict the absurdities of their teaching. He was the first to reduce the science of jurisprudence into a system and to make a systematic collection of traditions.	A school of religious law and practice named after Abu Hanifa (d.767). He is considered very liberal in his interpretation of the law.	An offshoot of the Kharijites, founded by Ibn Ibad (d.680). It rejected the extreme practices of the Kharijites and held a different view of the Quran.	Disagree with other schools about the nature of the Quran and the question of sin and apostasy.

Sunni			
Malikites	**Asharites**	**Ahmadyya**	**Lahoris**
Named after Malik Anas (715–795), who considered the tradition of the prophet as binding and authoritative, superseding all human judgements.	Another school of theology, founded by al-Ashari (873–935). He rejected rationality and declared that the Quran is eternal and uncreated. He was an extreme fatalist in his understanding of Allah.	A sect started in India based on the teaching of Ghulam Ahmad (1835–1908). He claimed to be a prophet. His followers conduct vigorous missionary activity, particularly in the West.	
			Qadians

Sufi
In medieval times, a sect within Islam called Ismailis stressed the inner meaning of the sacred texts of the Quran that goes beyond the literal interpretation. They feared that the Sunni schools of law were concentrating too much on tradition and the external elements of religion. The Ismailis, and later the Sufis, devoted themselves to seeking purification of the heart through the mystic life.

Suhrawardiah	Dervishes	Qadiriah
A Sufi school of thought founded by Ahihab Al-Din, who emphasized the divine gift of knowledge.	Naqshbandiah	Another religious Sufi order founded by Qadir, an ascetic preacher.

Sufi		
Khalwatiah	Rifaiyah	Nimatullahiah
Their founder is thought to be Umar al-Khalwati (d. 1397)	Sheikh Ahmad al-Rifa'i (d. 1182) is the sheikh from whom the Rifa'i order is derived.	Named after its founder, Nur al-Din Ni'matallah Vali, known as Shah Ni'matallah. Although originally a Sunni order, it became Shi'i in the sixteenth century.
Rahmaniah	Bektashiah	Sanusiah
	A heterodox and eclectic Sufi order founded by Bektash in 1337, assimilating Christian and Shiite elements.	

Chistiah

Khwaja Moinuddin Chishti was the founder of the Chistiya order, which is prominent in India and Pakistan and has spread (in various forms) to the West. The body is thought to be made of the material elements — fire, earth, air and water — and to have five external senses — sight, hearing, smell, taste and touch — and five internal faculties — discursive thinking, imagination, doubting, memory and longing. All these powers — that is, both the external senses and the internal faculties — serve the heart. By the 'heart' they do not mean the physical organ which pumps the blood, and which is possessed by both man and animals. Rather the 'heart' refers to the divine spark which distinguishes man from the animals.

Shadhiliya

The Shadhiliya order is named after Abu al-Hasan al-Shadhili (d. 1258). The *Tariqa Shadhiliyya* is the way of the person who forgets all things and returns back to the truth as in the beginning; a child in the presence of God. You cannot see more than him or hear of any other place. You cannot speak without him. You are with God, in God, to God in the origin of all things.

Sufi	
Tijaniah	**Darqawi**
The *Tariqa Tijaniyya*, named after Shaykh Ahmad al-Tijani (1737-1815), is a path, a way *(tariqa)* and method of studying and putting into practice Islamic Spiritual Science *(Tasawwuf)*. The latter has at times been misleadingly called mysticism. However, in Islam it is a regular science, with its set laws and a fully detailed scheme. It is based on definite experiences that can be reproduced, just as in any other science. Every person passes through the same stages in their spiritual journey as did the masters before them. Even the humblest learners can at least aspire to develop a living sense of the presence of Allah and acquire an increasing control over their passions and desires for worldly things.	**Alawi**
	Isani

Shiah
In contrast with the Sunni, the Shiah sect of Islam, also called the party of Ali (the son-in-law and cousin of the prophet Muhammad), recognizes Ali and his descendants as the only legitimate leaders of the Islamic community. They reject the first three caliphs and accord great reverence and authority to the descendants of Ali.

Ismailiah	Ithna Ashariah (or Twelvers)
A medieval sect within Islam that stressed the inner meaning of the sacred texts of the Quran which goes beyond the literal interpretation. They feared that the Sunni schools of law were concentrating too much on tradition and the external elements of religion. The Ismailis, and later the Sufis, devoted themselves to seeking purification of heart through the mystic life.	The imam whom they recognized as the 'twelfth' was the last of those descended from Ali, the cousin and son-in-law of Muhammad. They held that the office of the imam is infallible.

Shiah		
Druz	Nizariyah	Imamiyaha
A secret, exclusive sect that traces its name back to Muhammad al-Darazi (d.1019). They reject two of the pillars of Islam, namely fasting and pilgrimage. They hold that the Fatimid caliph al-Hakim was a manifestation of Allah and believe in the transmigration of souls. They are found in Lebanon, Israel and Syria.	An offshoot of Ismailiah who gave loyalty to Nizar, son of the Fatimid caliph Mustansir (d. 1094). They emphasized outward piety and the esoteric meaning of religious writings.	A branch of the Ithna Ashariah who held a high view of the imam, who was the religious and political leader viewed as being Allah's deputy on earth.
		Nusayriah
		Also called Alawis. Their leader is Ibn Nusayr (d.873). Their religious practice is more secret than that of other sects and is believed to incorporate some syncretistic elements from Shiites and Christians. The majority live in Syria, Lebanon and Turkey.

Tayyibiya	Zadiyah
The result of a further split among the Ismailiah. A mystical sect, based in the Alamut Valley in Iran. Like other Muslim schools of thought, they developed their own interpretation of law and theology, giving the imams the critical role.	Followers of Zayd Ibn Ali (d. 740), the fifth Shiite Imam. While they disagree with the Sunni on the matter of the succession, they are the closest to them in recognizing the Quran and the *Sunnah* as the basis for life and theology. They oppose Sufism. Mostly they live in Yemen.

Shaykhyah

An Iranian religious movement founded by al-Ashai (1753-1826). He claimed to be the hidden imam, but that he would arise again as a messianic deliverer of Islam.

Shiah

Usuliyah

A dominant Shiite school in Iran which emphasizes deductive reasoning in religious matters. It paved the way for the Ayatollah Khomeini as the supreme jurist whose *fatwa* is binding.

Akhbariah

Contrary to the Usuliyah, Akhbariah were more traditional. They held that religious and legal opinions should be based on the *Sunnah* of Muhammad and the imams.

2.
Questions about West-East encounters

What were the Crusades?

The Crusades, *al-Houroob al-Salibiah* (الحروب الصليبيّة), undertaken between the eleventh and thirteenth centuries, were a complex drama in the history of the church and its relationship with Islam. Historians tell us that, although the Crusaders had economic and political reasons for fighting, the primary grounds on which the church justified the wars of the Crusades were religious. The Western church felt the immediate threat by Muslims at home several centuries prior to the Crusades, when Muslim armies invaded Spain in A. D. 711 and endangered the very existence of the church in Western Europe. The Fatimid in Egypt, as we noted in chapter 1 (see p. 55), ruled the Holy Land during the brutal reign of al-Hakim, the neurotic Caliph of Egypt, who destroyed the Church of the Nativity and curtailed the freedom of worship for Christians in the Holy Land. While other caliphs were relatively more tolerant, al-Hakim now threatened the very life of Middle-Eastern Christianity, which traced its roots to the Christ of Bethlehem and the early apostolic church.

The first Crusades (A. D. 1095–1099) accomplished their goal by recapturing Jerusalem. However, by the end of the second Crusade (1147–1149), the celebrated Muslim general Saladin embarked on a *jihad* that managed to recapture Jerusalem. In 1187, King Richard I of England led a third Crusade. The Christians won some battles, but Saladin was able to cling on to Jerusalem. Finally, the two sides negotiated a truce that allowed the Muslims control of the Holy Land, but gave Christians freedom to visit their shrines.

What were the results of the Crusades?

The goals of the crusading wars were mainly religious — to free the Holy Land, to restore freedom of worship and to provide a safe environment for pilgrimages to the Christian sites. The popes also hoped to extinguish all dissension and division in Christendom, east and west.

However, these goals were embedded in unbiblical views of the nature of true conversion and of the church, and of what constitute appropriate methods for achieving them. By the time of the eventual defeat of the Crusaders, after 200 years of wars, not only had these aims not been realized, but a deep and lasting stain was left on the reputation of the professing Christian church.

The wars of the Crusades are still vivid in the minds of Muslims in general and fundamentalists in particular. They often, incorrectly, equate the Crusades with both the Christian faith and Western cultural and political power.

What should we think about the Crusades today?

The term 'crusades' is widely used, abused and misunderstood today. When President Bush used the term 'crusades', pointing to the moral duty to fight the evil of terrorism, he was criticized by the media in America and also in several Muslim nations. They alleged that such a usage evokes in the minds of Muslims negative memories associated historically with the term. Osama Bin Laden declared war against the 'Jews and the Crusaders'; Campus Crusade for Christ uses the same term as they endeavour to spread the good news — the message of God's grace around the world. Furthermore, the legacy of the Crusades, *Salibioun* (الصليبيون), still lingers in the minds of Muslims, as they mistakenly associate it with the core message of the gospel. Some today are calling on Christians to apologize for the wars of the Crusades. How are we to make sense of all of this? The following questions need to be asked:

1. Were the Crusades a justified Christian holy war based on biblical principles, or an enterprise intimately connected with that of the popes?
2. Were the Crusades justifiable on the basis of the defence of the Christian ideal, plus the freedom and protection of Christians from persecution?
3. Were the harshness and devastation that characterized the Crusades justified?
4. Are Muslims correct to equate the Crusades with their holy war *(jihad)*?
5. Did the church gain by the Crusades?
6. Did the Crusades have a permanent negative effect upon Muslims?

Stephen Neill, perhaps the greatest church historian of modern times, gives us criteria as to how we should approach the issue of the Crusades: 'There have been faults on both sides, and these we can leave for the judgement of God. What is essential that we should understand [is] the dark shadow which has been cast everywhere on the Muslim mind by the wanton aggressiveness of the west. Like the Jew, the Muslim may forget his own faults in the contemplation of ours; we may leave him to this occupation, and welcome only the service that he has rendered in calling our attention to our own. Memories are long in the east. To us the Crusades are very ancient history; to the Muslim they are as though they had happened yesterday.'

Who were the Ottomans?

The Ottoman Turks (1342–1924) are named after their first sultan, Othman I. They were the longest-enduring Muslim dynasty in Islamic history, with their centre of power in what is now modern Turkey. Their expansion to the heart of Europe sent a wave of fear through the courts of European monarchs. The dynasty expanded as far west as Hungary, and later even to the gates of Vienna, east to Persia, north to Azerbaijan and south to Egypt. Ottoman expansion reached its zenith when they wrested control of Constantinople from the Byzantine Empire in the year 1453. Since that time, the former capital of the once-great Byzantine Empire has been in the hands of Muslims. It was renamed Istanbul and has remained the capital city right up to the present time. Suleiman the Magnificent (1494–1566) was one of its most accomplished leaders. After Ottoman power reached its height in the sixteenth century, and after they had failed for the second time to capture Vienna, corruption and serious disintegration set in during the eighteenth century. Turkey became known as 'the sick man of Europe', and began to lose most of its territory after siding with Germany in the First World War.

How did Muslims react to Western colonialism?

At the end of the Ottoman Empire after World War I, most of the Arab and Muslim lands fell into the hands of Western powers, mostly French and British. The bulk of the Arab states resented the Ottomans — even though they were Muslim rulers — for their ruthlessness, stagnation and lack of innovation. Suddenly, they found themselves under other occupying colonial Western powers that shared very little, if any, of their values and way of life, and they could not do anything about it. This further subjugation of Muslims fuelled their frustration and antagonism, though the colonial powers have contributed to their advancement in learning and industry.

Additionally, the introduction of Western-style schools, vigorous Christian mission activities and proselytizing, or *tansir* (تنصير), publications of Christian literature that questioned the credibility of Islam, have augmented Muslim antipathy towards the West. Furthermore, while Muslims understood that the battle with Western colonialism was fundamentally a conflict of values, they also saw it as an imperialistic political and economical undertaking.

During the colonial period Arabs vehemently resisted the attempts of the colonialists to replace Arabic — the language of their holy book — with the English or French language. Islam and the Arabic language are two major foundations maintaining a strong sense of Arab nationalism. They are considered as two inseparable aspects of the same thing.

In short, losing their civilization, which had once been so advanced — particularly in the Middle Ages — to the hands of the colonialists, has contributed to Muslim estrangement from Western powers and antipathy to Christianity, which Muslims incorrectly associate with these colonial powers. This kind of attitude became a fixation and was a prelude to the resurgence of modern-day Islamic fundamentalism.

What is modern-day Islamic fundamentalism, and how does it influence Muslims?

The *Oxford Dictionary* succinctly defines fundamentalism as a 'strict adherence to traditional orthodox tenets ... opposed to liberalism and modernism'. Such a definition might apply to the Christian fundamental movement in our modern day because it is basically characterized by religious motives. None the less, Islamic fundamentalism is far more complex, for it enshrines a number of religious themes and socio-political sources of discontent, as we shall see in the following brief historical sketch.

Perhaps the first pioneer of Islamic fundamentalism, and still the most influential today, was Jamal al-Din al-Afghani (1838–1897). His call for Pan-Islamic unity against the imperial conquest by the West, particularly after the Napoleonic invasion of Egypt in 1798 and that of the British in 1882, became very popular among Muslims. He infused religious Islamic themes into his political activism, appealing to the growing resentment against foreign domination. He also called for the overthrow of rulers who are submissive to foreign power.

Another influential fundamentalist was Hasan al-Banna (1906–1949). He was influenced by the thinking of al-Afghani. However, he founded a new movement in Egypt, still in operation today, called 'The Society of Muslim Brethren', which became the first modern strict and militant fundamentalist movement. The society engaged in a series of assassinations that included non-Muslims and judges, plus an attempt on the life of Egypt's president, Gamal Abdel Nasser. Al-Banna himself was killed, and Abdel Nasser suppressed the Society of Muslim Brethren ruthlessly, but they continued to operate in Egypt and other countries in the Middle East.

Another extremist leader in Egypt was Sayyed Qutb. After the death of al-Banna, he assumed the leadership role and succeeded in inspiring Islamic Jihad organizations by revitalizing anti-Western sentiments. Violence at tourist attractions in

Egypt in recent years is an example of the fundamentalists' hostility towards Westerners, while at the same time they attempt to destabilize what they maintain is a secular government.

A well-known fundamentalist who was the first successful revolutionary was Ayatollah Khomeini (1902–1989). He emphasized revolution to overthrow secularized Islamic governments. His seizure of the US embassy in Teheran and capture of American hostages was an indication of his deep resentment of Western values. He understood that the conflict with the West, under the leadership of America, is more than just political. Rather, it is religious and cultural and based on the idea that the Western powers represent the real enemies of Islam.

After the 1967 Six Day War, in which Arabs suffered a shameful defeat at the hands of Israel, Islamic fundamentalism flourished. Fundamentalists turned defeat to their own advantage, moving the masses by appealing to their history and deciphering their frustration. They contended that the Arabs had lost the war because they had lost their faith in Islam. They claimed that the real reason for defeat was the secularism and departure from the true Islam that characterize most Arab regimes.

Fundamentalists are ardent in their emphasis that the Allah of Islam is the Allah of absolute power. The very make-up of Islam is power. They assert that the reason Islam has lost its glory and power is because its followers have lost their religious bearings. They insist that the only way of survival is a return to a system of beliefs based on the Islamic *Shariah* law, as taught in the Quran and implemented by Muhammad. For them, Islam provides the only answer. Recapturing the lost power and sense of history necessitates a true *'jihad'*, based on total religious commitment and sacrifice, including martyrdom.

In short, Islamic fundamentalism, which is nourished by appealing to the religious and socio-political sentiments of

Muslims, will remain a threat and continue to surge forward unless real democratic reforms are established in the Arab and Muslim world, the Arab-Israeli conflict is resolved and, perhaps, Islam is rethought and diverted into a new course, as some Islamic thinkers are trying to do.

What is Wahhabism?

Al-Wahhabiyyah (الوهابيّة), or Wahhabism, is an unyielding Islamic persuasion and revivalist movement begun in Arabia by Muhammad Ibn Abd al-Wahhab (1703–1792). He called for a strict interpretation of Islamic theology, as practised by Muhammad a thousand years earlier. When opposed by certain tribes, he allied himself with the modern founder of Arabia, the tribal chief Muhammad Ibn Saud. Both declared a *jihad* to purify the land from the infidels and un-Islamic practices. By the death of Abd al-Wahhab in 1792 Wahhabism had grown to be the dominant power in Arabia and it continues today in the hands of the Saudi clan. While Wahhabism is not the dominant sect in Islam worldwide, nevertheless it exercises immense power in the world. Saudi Arabia has more than one quarter of the world's oil reserves. The oil industry not only dominates the local economy, but, unfortunately, influences the world economy and the foreign policy-making of other countries.

As an adherent to Wahhabism, Saudi Arabia heads the *Open Doors World Watch List* as the world's worst persecutor of Christians and for its abuse of religious liberty. Saudi Arabia makes no secret of such policies. On 10 March 2003 Associated Press Network reported: 'Saudi Arabia, as the birthplace of Islam, will not allow churches to be built on its land, according to Defense Minister Prince Sultan. Islam is the only accepted religion in Saudi Arabia, home to the faith's holiest shrines in Mecca and Medina. "This country was the launch pad for the prophecy and the message, and nothing can contradict this, even if we lose our necks." '1

Moreover, according to the *US State Department's Annual Report on International Religious Freedom* published in the year 2000, 'Freedom of Religion does not exist [in Saudi Arabia]. Islam is the official religion, and all citizens must be Muslims. The Government prohibits the public practice of other religions. Private worship by non-Muslims is permitted. The Government has declared the Islamic holy book the Koran, and the *Sunna* (tradition) of the Prophet Muhammad, to be the country's Constitution. The Government bases its legitimacy on governance according to the precepts of a rigorously conservative form of Islam. Neither the Government nor society in general accepts the concept of separation of religion and state. Conversion by a Muslim to another religion is considered apostasy. Public apostasy is a crime under *Shariah* (Islamic law) and punishable by death. Islamic practice generally is limited to that of the Wahhabi order... Apostasy is a capital offence under the *Shariah* Islamic law, as when a Muslim converts to another religion.'2

Nothing has changed to date. According to a number of human rights organizations, persecution, imprisonment and deportation of any who are suspected of being practising Christians are regular occurrences.

Among the modern-day extremist Wahhabi followers who hold grotesque interpretations of religious values are Bin Laden and the now defunct Taliban, who were not originally Wahhabis.

How did Arabs react to the birth of the state of Israel?

In 1917, Chaim Weizmann (1874–1952), Zionist leader and first president of Israel (1948–1952), was able to procure from the British government what is known as the Balfour Declaration. It included a pro-Zionist statement for the establishment of a Jewish state in Palestine. After World War I, the League of Nations ratified the declaration, and in 1922 appointed Britain to rule in Palestine. Thousands of Jews began immigrating to Palestine, particularly as a means of escaping from persecution in Germany.

In 1947, the United Nations General Assembly passed the partition plan for Palestine, creating a Jewish and a Palestinian homeland. The Jewish religious leaders vehemently objected to this partition, hoping to rule all Palestine, and later engaged in a series of militant activities against the British and Arabs, while Arabs in Palestine stepped up violence against Jews.

On 14 May 1948, however, the interim government of Israel announced the birth of the state of Israel. Arab nations remained staunchly opposed to the declaration. The 'land of milk and honey' became the land of militancy and hostilities. On 15 May 1948, five Arab armies entered Israel and the first Arab-Israeli war began. The Arab armies were composed of nearly 80,000 men. Israel, however, mobilized a greater number of well-trained fighters. The invading Arab armies failed, and Israel gained more territories. After its victory, Israel expected the Arabs to concede and accept its independence. This did not happen until 1979, when President Anwar Sadat of Egypt signed a peace treaty with Israel. Syria opposed Sadat's visit on the grounds that any lasting peace with Israel should be comprehensive, including all concerned parties. While time has proven that this was a wise assessment, nevertheless Sadat was eager to travel to Israel, leaving other neighbouring countries in a state of war with the country they still regard as an enemy.

While Sadat has become very popular in the international community, he was opposed in the Arab world for a variety of reasons. His bold and courageous stand led to his death, when members of an extremist Muslim brotherhood organization assassinated him in 1981.

What is the attitude of Western Christians towards the national state of Israel?

To answer this question, we must ask another: 'What is the nature of the church and her relationship to Israel?' There are various answers given to this question in evangelical Christian circles today, but they fall into two main categories. We shall consider two representative, and very dissimilar, views: the Dispensationalist and the covenantal.

What is Dispensationalist theology's understanding of the plan of salvation, the nature of the church and its relationship with ethnic Israel?

Certainly we can highlight only the major points here. Dispensationalism, by definition, is a theological stance that outlines a particular method of interpreting Scripture about God's way of salvation, Israel, the church and eschatology (i.e., the study of the end times). Dispensationalism partitions the history of salvation into periods, or dispensations, in which God deals with man in seven distinct ways:

1. 'The dispensation of innocence'

This relates to Adam prior to the Fall. Though he was warned not to eat of the fruit of the tree, his disobedience led to his fall. Thus this dispensation ends in failure and God provides another one, called 'the dispensation of conscience'.

2. 'The dispensation of conscience'

Man is aware of his guilt and operates through a system of sacrifices. Again, man fails this test and is offered another dispensation, designated 'the dispensation of government'.

3. 'The dispensation of government'

This covers Genesis 8:15 – 11:32. Man fails to govern the
earth and establish a righteous society. God rejects the Gentile world and establishes Israel as the recipients of his bless-
ings. Another failure ensues, and God provides another test
which is called 'the dispensation of promise'.

4. 'The dispensation of promise'

God chooses Abraham and enters into a gracious covenant
with him. Again, when man manipulates God and his test,
another dispensation is offered, named 'the dispensation of
law'.

5. 'The dispensation of law'

This encompasses the period from Moses to Christ. God sup-
plies the Israelites with his law, mediated through Moses,
which they repeatedly break. Ultimately the supreme test
comes as God sends his Son, whom they refuse and crucify,
thus failing utterly in this test; another dispensation begins,
that of 'grace'.

6. 'The dispensation of grace'

This dispensation commences at the Day of Pentecost. When
Israel rejects her Messiah, God produces a Gentile church un-
til the 'millennial kingdom'. When the church fails her test,
God once again raises up ethnic Israel.

7. 'Dispensation of the millennial kingdom'

This entails a thousand-year reign of Christ on earth centred
on Jerusalem.

We notice that the common thread in each dispensation is
designed to test man: obedience to the will of God. When one

fails, another is introduced. This raises the question: 'Who is in charge here, man or God?'

As far as the nature of the church and its relationship with Israel and the end times is concerned, we refer to a succinct doctrinal statement from Dallas Theological Seminary (perhaps a standard representative of this school of theology):

> We believe that all who are united to the risen and ascended Son of God are members of the church which is the body and bride of Christ, which began at Pentecost and is completely distinct from Israel.

> We believe that the period of great tribulation in the earth will be climaxed by the return of the Lord Jesus Christ to the earth as He went, in person on the clouds of heaven, and with power and great glory to introduce the millennial age, to bind Satan and place him in the abyss, to lift the curse which now rests upon the whole creation, to restore Israel to her own land and to give her the realization of God's covenant promises...

Thus Dispensationalism makes a clear differentiation in its central doctrine between God's plan for Israel and God's plan for the church. It follows that Dispensationalism sees Israel as an earthly people with earthly promises given to them in the Old Testament — promises which will be literally fulfilled in the national state of Israel in Palestine.

What is covenant theology's understanding of the plan of salvation, the nature of the church and its relationship with ethnic Israel?

Another compelling theological position — which is gaining increasing momentum today is 'covenant theology'. It is much older than Dispensationalism. Though covenant theology is based on the Scripture, it was systematized during the

Reformation of the sixteenth century. It centres around two covenants: first, the 'covenant of works' or the covenant with Adam, as representative of all humanity, and consisting of, on the one hand, the promise of eternal life in full fellowship with God in the garden upon the condition of obedience, and, on the other, punishment of death upon disobedience (Gen. 2:15-16; Rom. 10:5; Gal. 3:12); secondly, the 'covenant of grace'. God made a gracious covenant after the Fall by giving the first Messianic promise (Gen. 3:15), and this was sovereignly set in motion by the covenant of promise made to Abraham (Gen. 12; 15).

Dispensational theology makes a clear distinction between ethnic Israel and the church, which its proponents believe commenced on the Day of Pentecost. In contrast, covenant theology maintains that, from the beginning, the church *(ecclesia)* of Jesus Christ is one church, one people redeemed by Christ. The Israel of the Old Testament is in fact the Old Testament church (Acts 7:38; cf. Col. 1:18, where the same Greek word is used). This church, according to the teaching of the New Testament, embraces both Jews and Gentiles. The church is called 'the Israel of God' (Gal. 6:16), sharing the same Saviour, the same faith and the same covenant.

The Encyclopaedia of the Reformed Faith delineates the major points addressed in the question:

> The Covenant of Grace, beginning with the call of Abraham (Gen. 12; 13; 15; 17:1-7), lies at the heart of Scripture. Frequently mentioned in the Psalms (Ps. 89; 105) and the prophets (Jer. 31:31-34), it was given a new form and richer meaning by Jesus Christ (Matt. 26:28; Mark 14:24; Luke 22:20; 1 Cor. 11:25). Appearing often in the epistles (2 Cor. 3:6; Heb. 8-10; 12:24; 13:20), the teaching of the covenant that God established with the people of God and sealed with the blood of Jesus Christ is a major NT [New Testament] theme, just as its fundamental idea was at the centre of

Israel's religious life. It runs throughout the two Testaments as a golden chain holding them together, with Jesus Christ the connecting link. Thus Paul saw both OT [Old Testament] Israel and believers in his day as bound together in Christ. That was God's intention with the call of Abraham; the covenant made with him was eventually to include Gentile nations. In Abraham all families of the earth would be blessed. This promise Paul recalled in Gal. 3:7-9,14,27-29. The continuity of the two covenants, Old and New, is portrayed by Paul through the figure of an olive tree. Some natural (Jewish) branches were broken off; Gentile branches were grafted in. The tree itself, spanning both dispensations, is the continuing community of those who know and serve God (Rom. 11:17-24). Jesus' parable of the wicked husbandmen (Matt. 21:33-46) teaches the same truth, climaxing with Jesus' words to Jewish leaders: 'The kingdom of God will be taken away from you and given to a nation producing the fruits of it' (v. 43). That nation, or people (alternative translation), can be none other than the Christian church which is now God's covenant community. The new covenant, that is, the new form of the old covenant with Abraham, has been established with it. In Jer. 31:31-34 God promises a new covenant with God's ancient people. In Hebrews 8, that passage is quoted to teach that the covenant promised to Israel has been given to the church. The author clearly understood the Christian church to be the covenant people of God. Jesus had instituted the Lord's Supper before his crucifixion by saying, 'This is my blood of the new covenant which is shed for many for the remission of sins' (Matt. 26:28). Thus the author wrote that 'for this cause he is the mediator of a new covenant' (Heb. 9:15; cf. 7:22). So, Paul reminded the Corinthians that Christ had made them 'ministers of a new covenant' (2 Cor. 3:6). New Testament writers

were aware that the new form of the old covenant had
been promised to Israel and claimed that this promise
had been fulfilled in the church. This is the uniform NT
teaching. Since Christ has come and established the
new form of the covenant, distinctions formerly prevail-
ing in Israel are no longer binding. The old dietary laws
became obsolete (Acts 10:28,34-35). One is not a Jew
who is one outwardly; the real Jew is the person whose
heart is right with God (Rom. 2:28-29). The 'dividing
wall of hostility' that once separated Jews and Gentiles
is said to have been removed. Gentiles are no longer
'alienated from the commonwealth of Israel, and
strangers to the covenants of promise, but fellow citizens with the saints and members of the household of
God, built upon the foundation of the apostles and
prophets, Christ Jesus himself being the cornerstone, in
whom the whole structure is joined together and grows
into a holy temple in the Lord' (Eph. 2:11-21). The
temple is the church which traces its descent from
Abraham, the father of all the faithful. Believers in the
Lord Jesus Christ are the Israel of this age.[3]

What are some of the implications for evangelizing Muslims and for Arab Christians?

There is little doubt that Dispensationalism can be characterized as pro-Israel for humanitarian, historical and, most importantly, theological reasons. Jews across the centuries have been
scattered throughout the world and persecuted. As was re-
marked earlier, perhaps this was the main reason why Zionist
leader Chaim Weizmann (1874–1952) was able to procure
from the British government the Balfour Declaration for the
establishment of a homeland for the scattered Jews. Dispensationalists, however, see the promises given to Abraham in
Genesis 12-18 as being peculiar to ethnic Israel. These include,

firstly, the promise of land; secondly, the promise of a continuing national existence, past, present and future; and, thirdly, the promise of punishment for those who oppose Israel. It must be said that most Dispensationalists are strong evangelicals who attempt to safeguard the basic tenets of the gospel in the face of the liberals and so-called 'Higher Criticism'. However, as a theological movement, Dispensationalism has been criticized strongly. Some have gone so far as to call it a heresy, although George Ladd feels that this characterization is a little strong. Charles Ryrie, a well-known defender of Dispensationalism, finds himself asking this question in his book *Dispensationalism: Is Dispensationalism Help or Heresy?* At any rate, we must return to our question.

Media evangelists such as Hal Lindsey, Jimmy Swaggart, Jerry Fallwell, Pat Robertson, Jack Van Impe, Oral Roberts, Kenneth Copeland and, most recently, the *Left Behind* book series popularize Dispensational eschatology today, including its emphasis on modern-day Israel and its relationship with its Arab neighbours. Their unreserved theological commitment to ethnic Israel has given a *carte blanche* endorsement of the state of Israel in its conflict with the Palestinians, and by so doing overlooked the genuine human needs of others and the requirement for justice which is commanded by the Word of God.

Thus, it is not surprising to hear perplexing questions both from Palestinian Christians and from Arab Muslims, who ask, 'Why do these Christians impugn us and unconditionally ally themselves with Israel, denying us our basic human rights?' In his book *I Am a Palestinian Christian*, Rev. Mitri Raheb, a pastor of the Evangelical Church in Bethlehem, passionately cries for justice and calls for a balanced Christian approach to the conflict.

In *The Israel of God* Palmer Robertson gives a balanced and persuasive biblical view, answering many questions regarding the relationship between Israel, the church and the modern state of Israel. His conclusions must be heard, not only by Christians in the West, but by millions of Arab Christians, who have for a long time felt abandoned by their Dispensationalist brothers.

Robertson's concluding 'propositions' are worth serious consideration:

1. The church of Jesus Christ, embracing the elect of God from both Jewish and Gentile backgrounds, is a part of the messianic kingdom of Christ, even though the church does not exhaust the dimensions of Christ's kingdom.

2. The modern Jewish state is not a part of the messianic kingdom of Jesus Christ. Even though it may be affirmed that this particular civil government came into being under the sovereignty of the God of the Bible, it would be a denial of Jesus' affirmation that his kingdom is 'not of this world order' (John 18:36) to assert that this government is a part of his messianic kingdom.

3. It cannot be established from Scripture that the birth of the modern state of Israel is a prophetic precursor to the mass conversion of Jewish people.

4. The land of the Bible served in a typological role as a model of the consummate realization of the purposes of God for his redeemed people that encompasses the whole of the cosmos. Because of the inherently limited scope of the land of the Bible, it is not to be regarded as having continuing significance in the realm of redemption other than its function as a teaching model.

5. Rather than understanding predictions about the 'return' of 'Israel' to the 'land' in terms of a geopolitical re-establishment of the state of Israel, these prophecies are more properly interpreted as finding consummate fulfilment at the 'restoration of all things' that will accompany the resurrection of believers at the return of Christ (Acts 3:21; Rom. 8:22-23).

6. No re-established priesthood and no reinstituted sacrificial system ever will be introduced that would serve to provide a proper supplement to the currently established priesthood of Jesus Christ and his final sacrifice.

7. No worship practices that place Jewish believers in a category different from Gentile believers can be a legitimate worship-form among the redeemed people of God.

8. The future messianic kingdom shall include as citizens on an equal basis both Jewish and Gentile believers, even as they are incorporated equally into the present manifestation of Christ's kingdom.

9. The future manifestation of the messianic kingdom of Christ cannot include a distinctively Jewish aspect that would distinguish the peoples and practices of Jewish believers from their Gentile counterparts.

10. The future messianic kingdom will embrace equally the whole of the newly created cosmos, and will not experience a special manifestation of any sort in the region of the 'promised land'.

11. Gentile believers should diligently seek a unified ecclesiastical fellowship with Jewish believers, rejoicing when Jewish believers are regrafted into Christ and consequently bring immeasurable blessing to the world.

12. Jewish believers should diligently seek a unified ecclesiastical fellowship with Gentile believers, rejoicing in God's purpose of bringing additional Jews to faith in Jesus as their Messiah by moving them to jealousy through the blessing of Gentile believers.

Unquestionably, all true Christians are obliged to 'pray for the peace of Jerusalem' (Ps. 122:6) and aspire to ensure Israel's security in the midst of increasing religious fanaticism. Still, it has been said, 'Christians who stand with modern-day Israel are not necessarily standing with God.' The ultimate security of Israel hinges on their response to the question: 'Is Jesus Christ the Messiah?' Our task as Christians is to love both our dear Jewish and Arab friends. We are obligated to herald the gospel 'both to Greeks and non-Greeks ... because it is the power of God for the salvation of everyone who believes: first for the Jew, then for the Gentile' (Rom. 1:14,16). Heralding the gospel takes priority over any political stance. We are called by God to build a spiritual kingdom. While we need to pray for the peace of Jerusalem, we need to ponder the words of our Lord: 'My kingdom is not of this world. If it were, my servants would fight to prevent my arrest by the Jews. But now my kingdom is from another place' (John 18:36). In the parable of the tenants, Jesus clearly told the Jews that by rejecting him they have forfeited their privileges and that 'the kingdom of God will be taken away from you and given to a people who will produce its fruit' (Matt. 21:43). The Israel of God is the church of Jesus Christ — one, holy, catholic and apostolic church embracing God's children from both Jewish and Gentile backgrounds. They are to bring forth the fruits of the gospel.

This is not only a New Testament theme. The book of Hosea is a vivid reminder of God's covenantal relationship with a people who are unfaithful to him. At the same time, Hosea discloses God's covenant love for the Gentiles in these words:

> I will show my love to the one I called 'Not my loved
>   one'.
> I will say to those called 'Not my people', 'You are my
>   people';
>   and they will say, 'You are my God'
>   (Hosea 2:23).

Paul, in the epistle to the Romans, clarifies this relationship further by declaring Abraham to be the spiritual father of all who believe in Jesus Christ (Rom. 4:11). Furthermore,

Abraham's descendants are not promised an inheritance of real estate in Palestine, but are the inheritors of the whole world — his body, the church of Jesus Christ. Paul clearly affirms this glorious fact and today we see its fruition across the globe: 'It was not through law that Abraham and his offspring received the promise that he would be heir of the world, but through the righteousness that comes by faith' (Rom. 4:13; cf. Rom. 11). Indeed, God's wonderful grace has brought the blessing of salvation both to Abraham's descendants and to the nations of the earth, just as he promised in Genesis 12.

3.
Questions about faith and practice

What does the term 'Islam' mean?

The word Islam (اسلام) has at least three shades of meaning. In the first place, it is derived from the Arabic verb aslama (اسلم). When a combatant surrenders his weapon in defeat, the expression 'aslama' is used, indicating that 'he submits'. Secondly, the general usage of the term refers to the religion founded by Muhammad, signifying the religion of submission, or resignation — presumably to the will of Allah. Thirdly, the noun form, 'Islam', refers to the total belief system introduced by Muhammad, including the practices of the religion. Followers of Islam are known as Muslims (مسلمون), sometimes spelled 'Moslems'.

It is interesting that an increasing number of Muslims, particularly in the West, allege that the term 'Islam' is also derived from the root word for 'peace', salam (سلام). This is incorrect. Although the two words are similar in inflection, this claim is not borne out by the etymological derivation, as can be seen in the definition of each given by the authoritative Arabic Al-Munjid Dictionary. The Arabic term 'salema' (سلم) means 'to be delivered or safeguarded' (i.e. at peace). However, as noted above, 'aslama' (اسلم), is a military designation, meaning to embrace Islam by surrendering to the religion, as well as to the will of Allah.

What do Muslims believe?

Muslim belief, known as *iman* (ايمان), is normally divided into five categories: Allah, angels, the Quran and previous revelations, prophets, and the Day of Judgement.
    Let us look at each of these briefly:

1. Belief in Allah

There is a definite emphasis on the oneness, or *Tawheed* (توحيد), of Allah, who has no partners. This emphasis took root in the mind of Muhammad largely as a reaction to misconceptions about the authentic Christian teaching on the Trinity, as we saw in chapter 1.

Apart from the aesthetic design of Islamic geometric architectural patterns, they also carry a religious significance. These complex, unending, repeated units reflect the Islamic emphasis on the unbroken unity of Allah.

2. Belief in angels

Muslims believe that angels are created from light by Allah, and serve his purposes as part of his invisible macrocosm. There are other kinds of invisible creatures made of fire, called *'jinn'* (cf. English 'genie'), which possess exceptional power. Some are good, others evil, and both can influence human affairs.

Let's investigate

The biblical teaching about angels goes still further. The central role of angels in the New Testament is to advance the work of redemption of the Lord Jesus Christ. We read of angels participating in the three great salvation events: the incarnation (Matt. 1:20; Luke 1:26), the death and resurrection of Christ (Matt. 28:2; Luke 24:4) and the culmination of the work of redemption when the truth of God's kingdom will in the end triumph over the forces of evil (Rev. 8-10).

3. Belief in the Quran and previous revelations

These are divided into four categories: the books of Moses, known as *Tawrat* (توراة), the book of Psalms, or *Zabur* (زبور), the Gospels, referred to as *Injil* (إنجيل), and the Quran (قرآن), which Muslims claim is the final and authentic revelation from Allah. Muslims have charged both Christians and Jews with falsifying their Scriptures, and believe that the Quran has abrogated the previous revelations, thus replacing them.

Let's investigate

There are several reasons why Muslims charge both Christians and Jews with falsifying their Scriptures:

First, there is vexation among Muslims over the Jews' and Christians' rejection of their prophet, on the grounds that neither the Old nor the New Testament predicted the coming of Muhammad. Muslim scholars reacted to such affirmations by attempting to find allusions or references to Muhammad in the Bible.

Secondly, there are intellectual objections to certain biblical pronouncements. The argument goes something like this: 'We Muslims do not understand or accept the Christian teaching on the Trinity, or on Jesus as the Son of God; nor do we accept that God would allow Jesus to die an appalling death on a cross.'

Thirdly, Muslims deduce that the use of several different versions of the Bible by Christians today is a proof of its inaccuracy.

It suffices to say that not being able to understand the mysteries of God spoken of in the Bible is not a valid reason for rejecting its teaching. That is like saying, 'I do not accept the Bible because I don't understand it and I don't like what I read.' Our likes or dislikes are irrelevant. Just because the Bible does not predict Muhammad and contains some difficult teaching, we cannot say it must be corrupted and therefore needs another book, such as the Quran, to replace it. This logic is self-defeating.

Sad to say, because such allegations and misconceptions have been ingrained in the minds of Muslims throughout their history, many of them have dismissed, or at least doubted, the gospel message.

Here are eight questions Muslims must address before they challenge the authenticity of the Bible:

1. How can both Jews and Christians have conspired to alter their sacred books without anyone knowing about it?

2. Did they succeed in amassing all the written copies of the Scriptures, from each and every geographical location, in order to perpetrate such a forgery, without

even a single charge being levelled against them by anyone except for Muslims, who only came on the scene six hundred years later?

3. Can Muslims produce one shred of evidence to demonstrate that the Bible has been altered?

4. Is God unable to keep his Scripture from being changed?

5. Can Muslims tell us when it was altered?

6. Can Muslim scholars tell us why both Christians and Jews would decide to alter their most sacred Scriptures? What would they gain by defying its commands which specifically prohibit them from doing so?

It is important in this connection to look at what the Bible teaches about its authority and inerrancy, and how it warns anyone who attempts to alter it: 'And the words of the LORD are flawless, like silver refined in a furnace of clay' (Ps. 12:6). 'Sanctify them by the truth; your word is truth' (John 17:17). 'All Scripture is God-breathed and is useful for teaching, rebuking, correcting and training in righteousness' (2 Tim. 3:16). 'For prophecy never had its origin in the will of man, but men spoke from God as they were carried along by the Holy Spirit' (2 Peter 1:21). 'You shall not add to the word which I command you, nor take from it, that you may keep the commandments of the LORD your God which I command you' (Deut. 4:2, NKJV). 'Your word, O LORD, is eternal; it stands firm in the heavens' (Ps. 119:89). 'Do not add to his words, or he will rebuke you and prove you a liar' (Prov. 30:6). 'The grass withers and the flowers fall, but the word of our God stands for ever' (Isa. 40:8). 'For assuredly, I say to you, till heaven and earth pass away, one jot or one tittle will by no means pass from the law till all is fulfilled' (Matt. 5:18, NKJV). 'Heaven and earth will pass away, but my words will never pass away' (Matt. 24:35). 'I warn everyone who hears the words of the prophecy of this

book: If anyone adds anything to them, God will add to
him the plagues described in this book' (Rev. 22:18).
'Whatever I command you, be careful to observe it; you
shall not add to it nor take away from it' (Deut. 12:32,
NKJV). 'Do not let this Book of the Law depart from
your mouth; meditate on it day and night, so that you
may be careful to do everything written in it...' (Josh.
1:8).

7. Does the Quran contradict itself when it authenticates biblical infallibility from the following references?
'We gave the children of Israel the Scripture and the
Command and the Prophethood' (45:16). 'We verily
gave Moses the Scripture; so be not ye in doubt of his
receiving it; and we appointed it guidance for the Children of Israel' (32:23). '... and we caused Jesus, son of
Mary, confirming that which was revealed before Him,
and we bestowed on Him the Gospel, wherein is guidance and a light, confirming which was revealed before
it in the Torah, a guidance and admonition' (5:46).

8. Why does the Quran admonish Muslims who are
in doubt to approach both Christians and Jews for assurance and guidance? Is the Quran advising Muslims
to trust Scriptures that have been changed when it says,
'And if thou art in doubt concerning that which We revealed unto thee, then question those who read the
Scripture before thee'? (10:94).

No one can with a clear conscience attest that the Bible
has been changed. History provides no evidence of this —
not even the Muslim sacred book. Muslims must come to the
Bible, read it, understand it and see what it says about God,
man and salvation.

4. Belief in prophets

On the basis of a saying *(Hadith)* by Muhammad, Muslims believe that Allah has sent over 120,000 prophets, *anbiya* (أنبياء), to mankind over the millennia of history, but no one can identify who they all are. However, some of these prophets include figures from the Bible, such as Adam, Noah, Abraham, Moses and Jesus. Muslims add Muhammad to this list, calling him the 'Seal of the Prophets', *Khatim al-Anbiya'* (خاتم الأنبياء).

Let's investigate

Several of the accounts found in the Quran about these major prophets parallel the biblical narratives. Nevertheless, a cursory reading of the Quran reveals a significant amount of reconstruction and raises historical questions. Some of these will be discussed in the section: 'Questions we must ask about the Quran' (see below, pp. 101-5).

5. Belief in the Day of Judgement

There are some similarities and also some inconsistencies between Islam and Christianity about eschatology in general, and the Day of Judgement in particular. The Quran emphasizes the idea of resurrection of the body and the final judgement, in which the wicked will be consigned to eternal hellfire, while believers will receive their final reward in Paradise. The Day of Judgement *('youm al-din')* will be preceded by great cosmic conflicts similar to those described in the book of Revelation. The Antichrist *('Al-Dajjal')* will appear and will cause much devastation and moral corruption. Afterwards the Mahdi (literally, 'Guided one'), will appear to bring justice, wealth and peace. This Mahdi, however, is believed to be Jesus Christ, who will descend (some say to Damascus, some to Palestine) to kill the Antichrist and judge non-Muslims.

Let's investigate

It is important for our discussion to take time here to consider some of the critical differences between Islam and Christianity concerning the Day of Judgement. In Islam the basis on which people are judged at the Last Day is firmly grounded in personal merit. In the day of reckoning, a person's evil and good deeds are put in the scales. Whichever category is greater outweighs the lesser and determines the person's *'kismet'* (i.e., fate), either in eternal heaven or eternal hell.

In his clash with the Pharisees, however, Jesus warned against trying to gain merits by a righteousness of one's own. The Pharisees, who were the orthodox core of Judaism, laid excessive emphasis on external piety. Their adherence to the meticulous details of the letter of the law and their reverence for tradition became their basis for morality, spirituality and their hope of final salvation. But Jesus insisted that '... out of the heart come evil thoughts ...' (Matt. 15:19). The final judgement is based upon the fact that the holy and just God must punish sin; therefore, sinners must face the penalty. It is those who trust in Christ, the sinless Son of God who took upon himself the penalty due to them, who are saved from God's judgement. Therefore, final judgement is determined on the basis of a person's relationship to Jesus Christ. God is 'just and the one who justifies those who have faith in Jesus' (see Rom. 3:21-26). Thus the ground on which God accepts the person as righteous is by faith alone in Christ alone.

Another difference with regard to the Muslim concept of Paradise, *Fardous* (فردوس), is that the Islamic Paradise is described in sensual and physical terms. The Quran is replete with details about the pleasures that await believers in Paradise. These include beautiful virgins, luscious fruit, wine and other meat and drink, dishes and goblets made of gold — in other words, their hearts' desire (*surahs* 37; 56; 74; 83).

In contrast, the Bible speaks of heaven as the eternal abode of the triune God. It is a holy place, where God's

people experience to the full the enjoyment of perfect fellowship with him and of seeing him face to face. It is a place of
utter beauty prepared for those who love God:

> No eye has seen,
>   no ear has heard,
> no mind has conceived
>   what God has prepared for those who love him
>   (1 Cor. 2:9).

It is a place characterized by holiness, love, joy and eternal
praise and service to God the Father, God the Son and God
the Holy Spirit (Isa. 35:8; 1 Cor. 13:13; Heb. 12:2; Rev.
22:3).

What are the religious duties required of Muslims?

There are five religious obligations, identified as 'pillars',
arkan (أركان), or foundations:

 1. *Profession* — *Shahadah* (شهادة.). The first pillar
acknowledges that 'There is no god except Allah, and
Muhammad is the messenger of Allah.'
 2. *Prayer* — *Salat* (صلاة). This includes the regular
observance of five daily prayers.
 3. *Alms* — *Zakat* (زكاة). *Zakat* is an obligatory payment to be used for charitable giving.
 4. *Pilgrimage* — *Hajj* (حج). This trip to Mecca is
usually taken during the twelfth Islamic lunar calendar
(see chapter 1, pp. 37-45).
 5. *Fasting* — *Sawm* (صوم). Muslims who are in good
health must observe a fast during the ninth month of
Ramadan according to the Muslim calendar.

Adhan, or *Athan*, is the Muslim call to prayer. The *muathen* (caller) summons Muslims to the mosque for the five daily mandatory prayers.

Let's investigate

By way of contrast, the central and most distinctive aspect of the gospel is that salvation comes through Christ Jesus, who offers his own life as a substitute for the guilty. His death alone makes eternal life possible. The guilt of those who trust in him is removed, and they are adopted into God's family as 'heirs of God and co-heirs with Christ' (Rom 8:17).

Not so in Islam. Islam is a religion of law and acts to its very core. The five duties become the Muslim way of salvation. Orthodox Muslims structure their lives by a series of 'dos and don'ts' and by rigidly revering, and adhering to, the traditions and the law.

The Pharisees were in many respects analogous to Muslims. They were captivated by the tyranny of legalistic obligations. They were convinced that observing the requirements of the ceremonial law and the tradition of the elders was meritorious and constituted the way to righteousness. Jesus called them 'blind' (Matt. 23). Because they conditioned their hearts with morality, their misinformed consciences excused their actions even when they were harassing and plotting to kill the Lord. If they were sincere, they were sincerely wrong. Their moral dilemma, which they did not recognize, was that, instead of allowing their guilt to drive them to God, they rebelled against him.

Paul, after being dramatically delivered from the encumbrance of legalism, recognized that a righteousness based on works denies justification by grace through faith in Jesus Christ alone. His letter to the Galatians warns against the teaching of the Judaizers, which is based on legalism. In responding to such teaching, the apostle Paul insisted that a man is justified only through faith on the basis of Christ's finished work (Gal. 2:1-10). His message aroused vehement opposition. Paul called his opponents' teaching (which they claimed to be superior to the gospel of Jesus) 'turning to a different gospel — which is really no gospel at all' (Gal. 1:6-7).

What is the Quran?

The Quran is the sacred book of Islam. *Quran* (قرآن) is an Arabic name which means 'reading' or 'recitation'. It contains what Muhammad claimed to be the final disclosure of Allah's revelation given to him audibly and verbatim in the Arabic language via the angel Gabriel. Muhammad is said to have begun receiving these revelations when he was forty years of age, and then to have done so continually over a period of twenty-three years till his death in A.D. 632. Muhammad was a contemplative man, often retreating to a cave on Mount Hira, near Mecca (see p. 36). While in a state of trance he heard a voice commanding him to read, notwithstanding the fact that he was illiterate. However, Muslims claim that Muhammad's being miraculously enabled to read and recite authenticates the revelation and his status as a prophet. Moreover, Muslims believe that Muhammad had nothing to do with the actual composition of the Quran; he was only an instrument, a conduit through which Gabriel transmitted a revelation from Allah in the original Arabic language. Muslims believe that the Quran is inscribed in heaven on tablets which are eternally preserved. Other names are given to the Quran, including *al-Furkan* (الفرقان), meaning 'demarcation', and *al-Huda* (الهدى), meaning 'guidance'.

What does the Quran contain?

The Quran is somewhat smaller than the New Testament. It contains 114 chapters, known as *surahs* (سورة), revealed to Muhammad over a period of twenty years. Unlike the Bible, the Quran is not arranged either logically, chronologically, or by theme or genre. The *surahs* were put in order after the death of Muhammad, according to their length, and include a variety of themes and subjects, such as the oneness of Allah, his wrath if he is not heeded, stories analogous to many of the Old and New Testament narratives, and laws and regulations about religious and social life.

Let's investigate

The overwhelming majority of the Quranic accounts, including those relating to creation, the prophets and elements of faith, have their antecedents in the Bible and rabbinic traditions. Not only does the Quran derive most of its content from the Bible, but it acknowledges the Bible's authority by recognizing the 'Torah' (the first five books of Moses), the 'Zabur' (the book of Psalms) and the 'Injil' (the Gospel narratives concerning Jesus). However, even a cursory reading of the Quran reveals significant reconstruction of some of these accounts.

Questions we must ask about the Quran

One can appreciate the fact that the majority of Muslims are sincere about protecting the Quran, believing it to be the inerrant revelation of Allah. However, as I read the Quran, and glean from the analysis of it by other scholars — both Muslims and non-Muslims — I find that a number of critical questions are raised, which demand forthright answers:

1. How can both the Quran and Allah be eternal?

Muslims hold that the Arabic Quran is the exact replica of tablets the prototype of which are eternally preserved in heaven, and the content of which was communicated verbatim to the prophet Muhammad (Quran 43:3; 85:21-22; 56:76-77).

The view that the Quran is divine and is the very words of Allah has given rise to controversy even among Muslim scholars. One such is Faruqi, who recounts 'the controversy that raged under Ma'mun [an Abbasid Caliph who reigned from 813–833], when he appointed Ibn Abu Daud as chief justice. That jurist belonged to the Mutazilah school, which held the Quran to be the created word of God because it feared that the contrary (namely that the Quran is the eternal word of God) would compromise the divine unity. Ibn Abu Daud used his position to promote his view, and he was opposed by Ahmad Ibn Hanbal who led a popular resistance against the Mutazilah position. The opposing populace correctly perceived that to declare the Quran created is to subject it to space and time and all the conditioning of history, to divest it of its holiness and thus to liberate the Muslim consciousness from its determining power and normativeness. The upshot was the downfall of the Mutazilah school and repudiation of its doctrine. The Quran emerged victorious, and the masses accepted it as uncreated not only in its meaning or content but also in its form, in the Arabic words in which it is composed.'[1]

Perhaps the dispute was settled, but the dilemma is not. Certain questions must be asked:

- How can it be alleged that two distinct eternal entities exist together — one of them material in nature (i.e. the Quran, which is said to be written on tablets, according to 85:21-22), and the other spiritual (i.e. Allah)?
- How can we account for such dualism? How can a material object exist coeternally with Allah without being created by him?
- Does this mean that the Quran exists independently, without being contingent upon Allah? If this is the case,

then we must conclude that Islam teaches that matter is eternal.

- Can we conclude, then, that Islam is, at least in part, congruent with Greek thought and with the theory of evolution, which teach that matter is the basic stuff, or raw material, from which everything else is composed?

- How can Islam accept that these two distinct entities exist eternally side by side and at the same time reject the biblical teaching of the eternal Trinity, or the one triune God existing in three persons — Father, Son and Holy Spirit, who are equal in essence and glory? Is not this triunity much more logical and reasonable than the two distinct eternal entities in Islam?

Scholars agree that these questions and others demand answers, and that they will continue to dog Muslim claims about the Quran unless and until they are cogently answered.

2. Is the Quran inerrant?

As cited above, most traditional and fundamentalist Muslims believe that the Quran is 'uncreated not only in its meaning or content but also in its form, in the Arabic words in which it is composed' — therefore it must be inerrant. However, an increasing number of learned voices among Muslims oppose such a view. For example, Mohammed Arkoun, in his scholarly book, *Rethinking Islam*, calls for re-examination of Islamic tradition, including its sacred book, the Quran. Let us return once more to the matter of Muslim claims of inerrancy for the Quran, and raise a few further questions:

Firstly, how can the Quran, which is revealed, as Muslims claim, in the pure Arabic language (26:193-195), contain many foreign words from the surrounding region? The following are only a few examples:

The word	The reference	The language
Abariq (ewers)	56:18	Persian
Adam	2:30-34	Akkadian
Allah (God)	1:1	Assyrian
Adn (Eden)	9:72	Persian
Firdaws (Paradise)	18:107	Syriac
Injil	57:27	Greek
Jinn	51:56	Persian

Secondly, how can the Quran be inerrant if it contains the following historical errors, which contradict not only the biblical account, but also archaeological and historical evidence?

1. We read in 28:8,38 that Haman was Pharaoh's minister. History tells us that Haman was the minister of King Ahasuerus in Persia while Pharaoh was the King of Egypt. How can this be reconciled?

2. In 20:85-88 we read that the Samaritans made the golden calf. The problem is, how could a Samaritan have made a golden calf for the Israelites if Samaria did not exist when the Israelites came out of Egypt? It was built several centuries later by Omri who made it his capital.

3. How is it that the Quran calls Abraham's father by the name Azer, when his name was Terah? (Gen. 11:27).

4. Mary, the mother of Jesus, was the daughter of Heli (Luke 3:24). Why does the Quran say she was the daughter of Amram, the father of the prophet Moses (66:12). Roughly 1,400 years separate Mary from these Old Testament figures.

5. In Quran 10:90-92, we read that Pharaoh was delivered from drowning. Yet the Quran also says in

28:38-40 that Pharaoh was plunged into the sea because he was an evildoer. How can the Quran contradict itself and the Bible, which asserts that Pharaoh indeed drowned in the Red Sea? (Exod. 14:27-28; Ps. 136:15).

How are people converted in Islam?

The Muslim confession, or 'Shahadah', says, 'There is no Allah except one Allah and Muhammad is the messenger of Allah.' If a person believes this statement and makes a formal verbal declaration to that effect in the presence of two Muslim witnesses, he automatically becomes a Muslim.

Let's investigate

Conversion, as expounded in the Word of God, is entirely incompatible with Muslim belief. It is imperative, however, to emphasize the biblical teaching in this connection. It is inaccurate to say that conversion according to the gospel is a change of affiliation from one religion to another, as many of our Muslim friends are led to believe. Conversion, according to the Word of God, is a profound and wonderful divine intervention in the life of a sinful man, by which God enables him to turn away from wickedness and the dominion of Satan to his marvellous light. Sin is the moral corruption that entered the world as a result of the disobedience of our representatives in the garden, namely Adam and Eve. Sin, therefore, is not, as Muslims assume, a weakness, or lapse, or mistake. It is the condition of alienation from the holy God. The Bible speaks of sin as 'lawlessness' (1 John 3:4). Moreover, we need to differentiate between original sin, which Islam denies, and actual sin, which we commit by virtue of being born in a state of rebellion against God. The Bible maintains that sin and guilt, seen in the light of the Fall, cannot be expunged by

performing good works, obeying the law, or believing in a
creed or dogma. There must also be an ultimate standard by
which we measure all ethical and moral behaviour (Rom.
3:10-20; Titus 3:5-7; Heb. 9:9).

We cannot speak of conversion without speaking of sal-
vation, redemption and sanctification. The Bible says, 'All
have sinned,' whether Jew or Gentile, Muslim or Christian.
Therefore, all need salvation from sin (Rom. 1:18 – 3:18,23).
This salvation comes only through the redemptive work of the
Lord Jesus Christ, and is the result of what he has done.

Two things must take place prior to true conversion: faith
and repentance. There are three elements of saving faith,
leading to true conversion. The first is intellectual: the mind is
opened to the truth of God's Word. The second is emotional:
the heart is gripped by the truth through the working of God
the Holy Spirit. The third element is trusting the Lord Jesus
Christ in steadfast obedience. Likewise, there are three elements of true repentance, in some ways parallel to the elements of saving faith. The first is intellectual: we acknowledge
our state of sin. The second is emotional: we are genuinely
sorrowful for our sin. The third is the inner motivation of the
will to turn from sin and ask for forgiveness through Jesus
Christ.

Accordingly, any religious preoccupation with rituals will
never absolve a person's sin. 'Zeal without knowledge' is
nothing more than an attempt to suppress nagging guilt feelings by resorting to endless acts designed to gain a righteousness of one's own — acts which, as we shall continue to see
(see especially ch. 6), are 'not able to clear the conscience of
the worshipper' (Heb. 9:9). This is the case in Islam.

What is the Sunnah?

The Sunnah (سُنَّة) — from an Arabic word meaning 'path',
'way,' 'custom' or 'law' and referring to Muhammad's

practices and Islamic tradition — found its background in the earlier traditions and was skilfully developed, first by Muhammad and later by his companions, or *sihaba* (صحابة), who made the sayings and deeds of Muhammad the principal foundation for most aspects of Islamic tradition. In the centuries that have followed, the *Sunnah* of Muhammad has become the core of Islam itself.

From the beginning, the *Sunnah* came to be second only to the Quran as the sacred and authoritative source for Islam in faith and practice. While Muslims believe that the Quran was revealed by Allah, they also hold that it is complemented and interpreted by the sayings and customs of Muhammad. The *Sunnah's* authority is considered binding on all Sunnite Muslims. They attribute to it a semi-divine status, and cite the Quran to support this position. For example, *surah* 59:7 reads: 'I am giving the Quran and the like of it' (i.e., the *Sunnah*). Another *surah* (3:113) says, 'We have sent down to you the book and the wisdom' (i.e. the *Sunnah*). Thus, divine approval is said to have been given to the *Sunnah*. Nevertheless, it was Muhammad and his *sihaba* who made it the measuring rod for all aspects of Muslim life and thought.

Who are the Sunni?

A Sunni (سني) is a member of the Muslim sect that encompasses approximately ninety per cent of Middle-Eastern Arab Muslims, who claim that they represent orthodox Islam (see chart, pp. 59-61). The Sunni acknowledge the first four caliphs, the successors of Muhammad. While the Sunni do not believe that the caliphs attained to Muhammad's status as a prophet, they do maintain that they extended his political and spiritual authority. Sunni beliefs and practices are based on the Quran and the traditions rather than on devotion to the imams, as is the case in Shiah Islam.

What is the *Shariah*?

The *Shariah* (شريعة) — meaning 'path', 'track', or 'passage-way' — is the Islamic law and is based on four sources: the Quran, the *Sunnah*, the *Qiyas* (the analysis, or assessment, of past traditions and their application to modern cases), and the Consensus (the agreement of the prophet's companions on various points which had not been settled earlier, resulting in a consensus for the community). The *Shariah* is described by the well-known Islamic scholar Schacht as an 'all-embracing body of religious duties, the totality of Allah's commands that regulate the life of every Muslim in all aspects; it comprises on an equal footing ordinances regarding worship and ritual, as well as political and legal rules.'² While the *Shariah* is practised by some Islamic nations, the majority balance their Islamic laws with secular codes. Such practice has energized a new movement of Islamic radical fundamentalism calling for a return to the fundamental tenets of Islam *('al-Usoliat')*, as we shall discuss in more detail later.

Who are the *Shiah*?

The *Shiah* (شيعة), a sect of Islam, are also known as the Partisans of Ali (who, as we saw in chapter 1, was the son-in-law and cousin of the prophet Muhammad). The *Shiah* recognize Ali as the only leader of the Islamic community and reject the other caliphs, thus conferring great reverence and authority on Ali's descendants, whom they consider to be the only legitimate leaders in Islam. The majority of *Shiah* live in Iran and Iraq; there are other pockets in Lebanon, Syria and Turkey. In contrast to the *Sunni*, the *Shiah* have developed their own corpus of law and a system of theology. The *Shiah* have split into different divisions: the Twelvers are those who recognize twelve imams, while the Fivers recognize only five.

Another division, the Ismailis, is also known as 'the Seveners'. They believe that a seventh imam will emerge some time in the future to establish a new order.

What is the *Hadith*?

The *Hadith* (حديث) is a tradition traced back to the speeches and conversations of the prophet of Islam, and including a variety of comments covering most aspects of life. Believing that Muhammad was incapable of doing wrong, his followers scrupulously recorded his sayings and followed them to the letter. During his lifetime, his sayings and actions were considered a living example and normative standard for all believers, *al-Momenoun* (المؤمنون). It was not until the third century after Muhammad's death, however, that an effort was made to write them all down. Among the traditionalists whose collections of the *Sunnah* have become authoritative is al-Bukhari (d. A.D. 870). The *Sunnah*, as mentioned above, is basically deduced from the *Hadith*, and became second in authority only to the Quran.

Here we must add two points.

First, there is no way of knowing which are the authentic saying, or *Hadith*. Muslims developed a science of *Hadith* criticism in order to distinguish the 'sound' *(sahih)* from the 'weak' *(dhaif)*. This resulted in the production of six major collections, which were all later accepted by Sunni Muslims. The most significant is that of al-Bukhari.

Secondly, in addition to the six collections of *Hadith*, the Shiah produced the sayings of their imams (Muslim leaders descended from the fourth caliph, Ali), and made them normative for all aspects of life.

What is the influence of the *Hadith* and tradition upon the followers of Islam?

After the Quran, the *Hadith* became the most influential factor in shaping the ethical, social, political, liturgical, religious and legal systems of Muslims, particularly those of the Sunni sect. In considering this question we should avoid passing judgement on the motives or the sincerity of this mode of behavioural control, for it is inevitable that in any educational process — secular or religious — certain values and attitudes will be infused. For this reason, however, education must be guided by the right moral principles. Otherwise, any wrong mode of indoctrination from the early stages of childhood has the potential to force the mind to change its orientation, ultimately enslaving the conscience in a way that leaves little room for correct beliefs or values.

Muhammad gave absolute and concrete meaning to every detail of the rituals of worship and of religious practice. The vast majority of the pieties, both personal and corporate, which govern the ritualistic acts of worship and daily life of his followers have been modelled on his example. The ceremonies which he customarily adopted continue to be observed by his followers without any modifications or change. For example, they observe the ritual of prayer, in its content, time and the manner of its performance, exactly as it was practised and prescribed by the prophet. The Quran reinforces the importance of this habitual practice (2:110; 11:114; 17:78-79). Thus, both the symbols and the contents become deeply embedded in the consciousness, and therefore in the conscience, of every worshipper.

How do the *Hadith* and tradition contrast with the gospel?

Islam is a religion, but a religion of law to its very core, encompassing all facets of spiritual and temporal matters of the community, *al-Ummah* (الأُمَّة). Thus, the faith, or *iman* (إيمان), of Islam is more than creeds and doctrine. For a devout Muslim, particularly one of the Sunni sect, faith primarily means the ordering of one's life according to a conscious imitation of the actions of Muhammad. Certainly, this strong orientation towards law makes Islam appealing to the natural man, who thinks that he can gain worthiness through his own efforts and his own goodness. Pascal made a keen observation in this connection: 'Mahomet a pris la voie de réussir humainement; Jésus-Christ celle de périr humainement' (Muhammad chose the way of human success; Jesus Christ that of dying a human death). Conformity and intense bondage to the law as a means for salvation have left a deep impression on the religious psyche of most Muslims, particularly the Sunni.

Moreover, this impression has been produced by concrete acts of religious symbolical significance that have coloured their religion and social ethics, as will be seen in the following discussion. Jesus attacked the legalism of the Judaizers and the Pharisees for missing the real intent of the law by being enslaved to the letter of it. They were entangled in the snare of works-righteousness, which had become the foundation of their faith. Such an orientation, which fails to be motivated by love and spurns the grace of God, becomes a tragic religiosity consumed by a destructive zeal, which is not based on knowledge (cf. Gal. 1:13-14; Rom. 10:2). Only grace, which is the distinctive feature of the gospel, can fulfil the demands of the law and emancipate the believer to live not according to the flesh, but by the Spirit (cf. Rom. 8:1-4).

What influence does Muhammad have over his followers?

Apart from the fact that Muhammad was an astute political leader and a dogmatic religious commander, his followers firmly believe that he was divinely guided. His claim to be the recipient of divine revelation reinforces this assertion: 'Obey Allah and obey the messenger and those in authority from among you, and if you quarrel about anything, refer it to Allah and the messenger' (*surah* 4:58). Abu Hurrairah, one of the prophet's companions, quotes Muhammad as having said, 'He who obeys me obeys Allah, and he who disobeys me disobeys Allah.'[3]

The influence of Muhammad's religious orientation continued to capture the hearts and souls of his followers and inspired the jurists to establish the *Sunnah* as normative for all generations, and it is still a potent force controlling the minds and hearts of Muslims today.

How does Allah of Islam compare with the God of the Bible?

Much has been said in recent days about the Allah of Islam in connection with the God of the Bible. A number of questions are raised: 'Is the Allah of Islam the same as the God of the Bible?' 'To what extent does Allah of Islam correspond to the God of the Bible?' Is the Christian understanding of God the same as the Muslim concept of Allah, as set out in the Quran? Which are more important — the common factors, or the differences? What does the Bible say? What does the Quran say? What does the historical church say? These are weighty questions, pregnant with theological and missiological implications. Nevertheless, we must tackle them briefly.

Is the Allah of Islam the same as the God of the Bible?

From what has been said earlier, it is evident that Islam is indeed a modified mixture of Judaism and Christianity. Moreover, in its main belief, Islam is very much a theocentric, or more accurately, an 'Allah-centric' religion. It is undeniable that Muslims sincerely worship one God, Allah (الله), and place great emphasis on his oneness. However, their perception of the nature of Allah is different — and in my judgement, far removed — from the Christian understanding of God.

The name 'Allah', as referring to the God of the Bible, was popularized among Middle-Eastern Christians via the excellent 'Van Dyck' translation of the Arabic Bible completed in 1864 by able Bible scholars and experts in philology and linguistic sciences. The same word-form is also used in the Quran. None the less, the two terms are loaded with different theological meanings.

In Arabic and Islamic usage, the term 'Allah' is a contraction of *el* (ال) and *ilah* (إله), i.e., 'god', which was a common term in the pre-Islamic pagan pantheon, as discussed in chapter 1 (see p. 19). Some Muslim scholars today try to connect the term 'Allah' with the biblical name for God, 'Elohim', while others argue that the term is purely Arabic. In any case, Muhammad was undoubtedly a revisionist who took the pre-Islamic name and loaded it with new meaning borrowed from pre-Islamic ideas, and also from the Old and New Testaments, thus introducing Allah as a 'high god'. The testimony of the Quran itself leaves no doubt that the worship of *'al-ilah'* was an integral part of the worship system of the pre-Islamic pantheon (29:65; 31:31; 26:61-63). The ninety-nine traditional Islamic names for Allah are attributes of Allah, most of which can also be found in the Bible, although there are some crucial omissions and additions.

To what extent does Allah of Islam correspond to the God of the Bible?

The ancient Arabian tribes were familiar with the concept of a 'high god', *allahu al-mutali* (الله المتعالي). As we have just seen, Muhammad took this same concept and loaded it with new meaning, thus introducing Allah as a 'high god' who bore some similarities to the God of the Jews and Christians. Perhaps being able to unite all the tribes around the worship of the one god was one of Muhammad's strengths.

In order to deduce how the Muslim concept of Allah contrasts with the God of the Bible, we need to look at their holy book. The Quran introduces Allah in a number of ways that are contrary to the biblical teaching, thus raising questions about his nature and moral character. The following are representative:

1. Allah is absolute unity and never triune

One finds a number of references in the Quran such as, 'Your Allah is one Allah' (2:163). Islam is strictly and radically a monotheistic religion. The Muslim *Shahadah* (شهادة) — i.e. 'witness' — known as the First Pillar in the Islamic creed, reads: 'There is no god but Allah and Muhammad is his apostle.' The doctrine of *Tawheed* (توحيد) — i.e. oneness — is considered the core and kernel of Islamic theology and worldview, and is the basis for morality. Muslims claim to be the only true Unitarians. This insistent emphasis on the oneness of Allah is embedded very deeply in the religion and the subconscious of most Muslims and is often reflected in their art, architecture and calligraphy.

Furthermore, the Quran seems to deny the Christian doctrine of the Trinity: 'So believe in Allah and his messenger, and say not Three' (4:171). Though a number of Christian apologists argue that Muhammad was actually attacking the pagan polytheists of his day, nevertheless, Muslims still deny the Trinity. For a fuller examination of this point, refer to chapter 1 and the question: 'Where does the confusion in Islam about the Trinity come from?' (see pp. 19-21).

2. Allah as 'the best of schemers'

In the Quran we read, 'And they [disbelievers] schemed, and Allah schemed and Allah is the best of the *makereen*' (الماكرين), (3:54). The scholarly Arabic dictionary *al-Munjid* correctly defines the Arabic word *'makereen'* as 'deceivers'. Moreover, elsewhere in the Quran, Allah is called 'the best deceiver', or 'cunning' (8:30). Allah beguiles people (4:90); 'Allah misleadeth whom he will and whom he will he guideth' (14:4). So far, I have not seen a cogent Muslim explanation for these disturbing pronouncements.

3. Predestination or fatalism

This leads us to another related theme connected with the nature of Allah, namely predestination, or fatalism. The Bible speaks consistently of God's sovereignty and his plan of predestination, but never in fatalistic terms. Most Christians assert the fact that the sovereignty of God does not destroy the free will of man. For example, the *Westminster Larger Catechism* states: 'God from all eternity, did by the most wise and holy counsel of His own will, freely, and unchangeably ordain whatsoever comes to pass yet so, as thereby neither is God the author of sin, nor is violence offered to the will of the creatures... God hath endued the will of man with natural liberty, that it is neither forced, nor by any absolute necessity of nature, determined to good or evil' (cf. Eph. 1:11; James 1:13; Acts 11:23; Matt. 17:12; James 1:14; Deut. 30:19).

Not so in Islam, where we shall discover that all events and the will of man are predetermined in such a way that all human efforts are irrelevant. While an increasing number of Muslim scholars today are attempting to present this doctrine in a better light, nevertheless, they cannot escape the fact that the concept of fate — *kadaa* (قضاء), *kismet* (قسمة) and *qader* (قدر) — is embedded deep in Muslim theology, which is rooted in the absolute and unconditional surrender to Allah's decrees.

Everything is determined by the will of Allah, so that the will of man is rendered futile. The Quran declares: 'Say: "Nothing will happen to us except what Allah has decreed for us..."' (9:51). 'Nor can a soul die except by God's leave, the term being fixed as by writing' (3:145). 'And with Him are the keys of the unseen treasures — none knows them but He; and He knows what is in the land and the sea, and there falls not a leaf but He knows it, nor a grain in the darkness of the earth, nor anything green nor dry but [it is all] in a clear book' (6:59). 'Say: "For myself I have no power to benefit, nor power to hurt, save that which Allah willeth"' (7:188).

4. Allah unjustly predestines the fate of every soul

We read in the Quran: 'The guiding of them is not thy duty, but Allah guideth whom He will' (2:272). 'Whatever is in the heavens and whatever is in the earth is Allah's; and whether you manifest what is in your minds or hide it, Allah will call you to account according to it; then He will forgive whom He pleases and chastise whom He pleases, and Allah has power over all things' (2:284). 'Do you not know that Allah — His is the kingdom of the heavens and the earth; He chastises whom He pleases; and forgives whom He pleases and Allah has power over all things...' (5:40-41). A Muslim critic would say, 'But predestination is also found in the Bible.' What is forgotten here is the fact the God of the Bible acts in a way that is consistent with his goodness, grace and justice. His election is not capricious and he is not the author of sin, nor does it violate the will of men. This is not the case in Islam, as we shall see below.

5. Allah causes people to err, and some people are made for hell

The following quotations from the Quran advance the notion that Allah is the author of error: 'Do you wish to guide him whom Allah has caused to err? And whomsoever Allah causes to err, you shall by no means find a way for him' (4:88). 'Whomsoever Allah guides, he is the one who follows the right way; and whomsoever He causes to err, these are the losers. Many are the *Jinns* and men we have made for Hell' (7:178-179). 'My counsel will not profit you if I were minded to advise you, if Allah's will is to keep you astray...' (11:34). 'And the Word of thy Lord hath been fulfilled: Verily I shall fill hell with the *jinn* and mankind together' (11:117-119).

The following Quranic pronouncements show the enigmatic character of Allah: 'Allah leads astray whomsoever He will and guides whomsoever he will' (14:4). 'Such is Allah's guidance, wherewith He guideth whom He will. And him whom Allah sendeth astray, for him there is no guide' (39:23). 'And he whom Allah guideth, for him there can be no misleaders. Is not Allah Mighty, Able to Requite? If Allah willed some hurt for me, could they remove from me His hurt...?' (39:37-38). 'He whom Allah sendeth astray, for him there is no protecting friend after Him. He whom Allah sendeth astray, for him there is no road' (42:44, 46).

6. Allah predetermines human wills

When we read the following verses from the Quran in the context of the characteristics of Allah described above, we ascertain the fact that the human will is predetermined and fixed by fate, leading to the resignation to one's future *kismet* with a sense of its inalterability, leading to fear and uncertainty: 'Let any who will, keep it in remembrance! But none will keep it in remembrance except as Allah wills. He is the fount of fear' (74:55-56). 'This is an admonition: Whosoever will, let him take a [straight] Path to his Lord. But ye will not, except as Allah wills' (76:29-30). 'Unto whomsoever of you willeth to walk straight. And ye will not, unless [it be] that Allah willeth, the Lord of Creation' (81:28-29).

What does the *Hadith* say about predestination / fatalism?

Presuming that Muhammad is the final and supreme prophet of Allah, his followers scrupulously recorded his sayings (the *Hadith*) and followed them to the letter. His sayings and actions were considered a living *Sunnah* and a normative standard for all believers — particularly the Sunnite sect of Islam. The following are representative of his sayings about human free will and predestination (quoted from the two collections of Muhammad's sayings recognized by the majority of the Muslim world: *Sahih Muslim* and *al-Bukhari*):

> Adam and Moses argued with each other. Moses said to Adam, 'O Adam! You are our father who disappointed us and turned us out of Paradise.' Then Adam said to him, 'Do you blame me for [an] action which Allah had written in my fate forty years before my creation...?' (*Hadith*, vol. 8, no. 399).

> Hudhaifa b. Usaid reported directly from Allah's Messenger that he said, 'When the drop of [semen] remains in the womb for forty or fifty [days] or forty nights, the angel comes and says, "My Lord, will he be good or evil?" And both these things would be written. Then the angel says, "My Lord, would he be male or female?" And both these things are written. And his deeds and actions, his death, his livelihood; these are also recorded. Then his document of destiny is rolled and there is no addition to and subtraction from it' (*Hadith*, book 033, no. 6392).

Ali reported that one day Allah's Messenger [Muhammad] was sitting with a [piece of] wood in his hand and he was scratching the ground. He raised his head and said, 'There is not one amongst you who has not been allotted his seat in Paradise or Hell.' They said: 'Allah's Messenger, then, why should we perform good deeds, why not depend upon our destiny?' Thereupon he said, 'No, do perform good deeds, for everyone is facilitated in that for which he has been created' (book 033, no. 6400).

Abu al-Aswad reported that 'Imran b. Husain asked him, "What is your view — what the people do today in the world, and strive for, is it something decreed for them, or preordained for them, or will their fate in the Hereafter be determined by the fact that their Prophets brought them teaching which they did not act upon?" I said, "Of course, it is something which is predetermined for them and preordained for them." He [further] said, "Then, would it not be an injustice [to punish them]?" I felt greatly disturbed because of that, and said, "Everything is created by Allah and lies in His Power. He would not be questioned as to what He does, but they would be questioned." Thereupon he said to me, "May Allah have mercy upon you. I did not mean to ask you but for testing your intelligence." Two men of the tribe of Muzaina came to Allah's Messenger (may peace be upon him) and said, "Allah's Messenger, what is your opinion — that the people do in the world and strive for, is it something decreed for them, something preordained for them, and will their fate in the Hereafter be determined by the fact that their Prophets brought them teachings which they did not act upon. And thus they became deserving of punishment?" Thereupon, he said, "Of course, it happens as it is decreed by Destiny and is preordained for them" ' (book 033, no. 6406).

I said, 'O Allah's Apostle! Why should a doer [the person carrying out the actions] try to do good deeds?' The Prophet said, 'Everybody will find [it] easy to do such deeds as will lead him to his destined place for which he has been created' (*Sahih Al-Bukhari,* vol. 9, book 93, no. 641).

Aisha, the mother of the believers, said that Allah's Messenger (may peace be upon him) was called to lead the funeral prayer of a child of the Ansar. I said, 'Allah's Messenger, there is happiness for this child who is a bird from the birds of Paradise, for he committed no sin nor has he reached the age when one can commit sin.' He said: 'Aisha, peradventure, it may be otherwise, because God created for Paradise those who are fit for it while they were yet in their father's loins and created for Hell those who are to go to Hell. He created them for Hell while they were yet in their father's loins' (*Sahih Muslim,* book 033, no. 6436).

What does the biblical revelation say about God?

Fairness calls us to acknowledge that the majority of Muslims have a high view of their absolute deity — Allah. The term *Allahu Akbar* (الله أكبر) or *'al-takbir'* ('Allah is most great'), which is uttered frequently by Muslims in routine daily prayers and on other occasions, coupled with their recitation of some of the most excellent names for Allah, including his mercy and benevolence, is a reflection of their devotion to him. A problem arises as we thus come to encounter Allah in a different light from the capricious terms described above. I will leave to Muslim scholars the burden of reconciling the lack of harmony in these conflicting accounts. In the meantime, let us contemplate the God of the Bible as he has revealed himself, by tracing some of his perfections throughout the Scripture, particularly those that are relevant to our discussion of the Allah of Islam.

The God of the Bible is distinctive and great in at least two ways:

1. He is absolute and totally other than his creation

God is totally other in a number of attributes, which, according to Louis Berkhof, are incommunicable — i.e., not shared by any human being. These include the following:

- He is 'self-existent': God is independent from any causation.
- He is 'unchanging': God's perfection is unalterable; he cannot increase or decrease, for he does not need any improvement, nor is he subject to deterioration, being infinitely unchangeable.
- He is 'eternal and infinite': God exists from all eternity; he is the first cause of everything that exists, and is unlimited by time and space.
- 'The unity of God': there is only one God. He is not composed of different parts or essences, but is one essence in his state of blessed triunity.

There are other attributes that set God apart from creation:

- 'He is spirit and invisible': not composed of matter, and not possessing physical nature, nor can he be confined by time and matter.
- 'He is the Creator': while distinct from all creation, he is the creator of everything that exists.
- 'He is all-knowing': the nature of his knowledge is perfect; nothing in the past, present or future escapes his perfect awareness.
- 'He is all-powerful': yet his power is conformed to his infinite goodness and never employed capriciously.

- 'He is sovereign': there is no limit to his absolute authority over the universe and humanity. Nevertheless, his sovereignty is the ground for the believer's confidence, for his sovereignty is an extension of all his perfections, including his goodness and righteousness.
- 'He is great': 'For the LORD your God is God of gods and Lord of lords, the great God, mighty and awesome, who shows no partiality and accepts no bribes' (Deut. 10:17).

2. God is personal, immanent and approachable

He graciously shares certain attributes with man in a limited measure. To these we shall now turn, keeping in mind how they contrast with Allah as he is described in specific passages in the Quran and the *Hadith*, which we have discussed previously.

The God of the Bible is holy

While the term 'holy' is mentioned only once in the Quran in connection with Allah, the Bible attributes holiness to God more than ninety-two times. It is at the centre of God's perfections, the essence of his moral character. God alone is holy and all-righteous; morality finds its origin in him. God always acts in ways that are consistent with his moral purity. 'His works are perfect, and all his ways are just. A faithful God who does no wrong, upright and just is he' (Deut. 32:4). 'His way is perfect' (Ps. 18:30). His 'eyes are too pure to look on evil; [he] cannot tolerate wrong' (Hab. 1:13). Consequently, sin and iniquity are foreign to him and provoke his holy indignation.

The God of the Bible is trustworthy and faithful

He never leads anyone astray, nor entices any to do wrong: The Lord is 'abounding in love and faithfulness' (Exod. 34:6). 'All the ways of the LORD are loving and faithful for those who keep the demands of his covenant' (Ps. 25:10). 'God is faithful; he will not let you be tempted beyond what you can bear' (1 Cor. 10:13). 'Those who know your name will trust in you, for you, LORD, have never forsaken those who seek you' (Ps. 9:10).

The God of the Bible is truthful

One of the disturbing descriptions of Allah in the Quran is this verse: '... and Allah schemed and Allah is the best of schemers' (3:54). On the other hand, one of the most encouraging attributes of God is his truthfulness. He can never be misleading, whimsical or arbitrary, but is always consistent and faithful to all his promises: 'You know with all your heart and soul that not one of all the good promises the LORD your God gave you has failed. Every promise has been fulfilled; not one has failed' (Josh 23:14). God 'does not lie or change his mind; for he is not a man, that he should change his mind' (1 Sam. 15:29). 'For the word of the LORD is right and true; he is faithful in all he does' (Ps. 33:4); 'God is truthful' (John 3:33).

The God of the Bible is loving

The Bible's distinct teaching on love finds its justification in the character of God. While this emphasis is practically absent from Islam, it is built intrinsically into the very nature of the biblical God. The Bible says, 'God is love' (1 John 4:8). As far as I know, the Greek term 'agape', used in the Bible in connection with the unconditional love of God, is an exclusively Christian concept; it is not established clearly in other religions, including Islam. Nothing in us attracts God to love us.

We are fallen, sinful and rebellious people and nothing lovable and worthy is found in us. God's supreme demonstration of this love was expressed on the cross, entirely by his grace. God is good. The Word of God says, 'O LORD ... you are good, and what you do is good'; 'How great is your goodness, which you have stored up for those who fear you' (Ps. 119:65,68; 31:19). It is plain that God, unlike man, has goodness inherent in himself, for he is eternally good. Unlike other deities, the God of the Bible is never vindictive and unpredictable. His justice is consistent with his holiness, mercy, compassion, graciousness, wisdom, longsuffering and patience.

The God of the Bible is gracious

The basis for God's love is his nature and grace manifested in history in the life, death and resurrection of Jesus Christ. God's grace reverberates throughout the Bible: 'But God demonstrates his own love for us in this: While we were sinners, Christ died for us' (Rom. 5:8). In Exodus 34:6 God is proclaimed to be: 'The LORD, the compassionate and gracious God, slow to anger, abounding in love and faithfulness, maintaining love to thousands, and forgiving wickedness, rebellion and sin.' The New Testament echoes the grace of God in these words: 'For it is by grace you have been saved, through faith — and this not from yourselves, it is the gift of God' (Eph. 2:8-9). Thus at the heart of the gospel is God's redemptive grace, which is undeserved: 'All this is from God, who reconciled us to himself through Christ and gave us the ministry of reconciliation' (2 Cor. 5:18).

In Islam, however, grace ('Nemah') is not understood in a redemptive sense; rather, it is connected with common grace, benefiting all mankind and connected with the idea of bounty and material blessing and benevolence. It is true that the idea of common grace is also found in the Bible — God cares, sustains his creation and restrains human society from destroying itself by evil: 'He causes his sun to rise on the evil and the good, and sends rain on the righteous and the unrighteous' (Matt. 5:45). None the less, this grace is not sufficient for salvation; that must come by God's special grace, through his redemptive work in Christ by which we are redeemed. God's grace is always sufficient and efficient; nothing can frustrate its purpose of saving all those who embrace the Saviour.

The God of the Bible is knowable

Muslims do not hesitate to assert that Allah is an absolutely incomprehensible unity, who cannot be described by human language or by human perception (Quran 42:11; 6:103). Furthermore, according to Muslims, the multiple names for Allah are not meant to describe Allah's essence, but to show that there is no simplistic notion of Allah. Languages, categories and conventions cannot delineate his nature. The phrase 'Allah Akbar' ('Allah is great'), which summons Muslims to prayer, is meant to remind believers of his absolute transcendency. Allah has made his will known on the pages of the Quran, and to a certain extent by the creation, but he remains hidden, inaccessible to personal knowledge.

The Bible, however, describes God in a distinctive way. We are told that God is a personal being and has created man in his own image; it seems most reasonable to believe that he would have communion and fellowship with the beings he created. This affirmation is echoed in numerous passages in Scripture:

God made himself known to us

'Then the man [Adam] and his wife [Eve] heard the sound of the LORD God as he was walking in the garden' (Gen 3:8). 'The LORD said to Abram: "Leave your country, your people and your father's household and go to the land I will show you"' (Gen. 12:1). 'I know you by name' (Exod. 33:17). 'Before I formed you in the womb I knew you, before you were

born, I set you apart…' (Jer. 1:5). 'But now that you know
God — or rather are known by God — how is it that you are
turning back to those weak and miserable principles?' (Gal.
4:9).

God is known by his miraculous works

'Has any god ever tried to take for himself one nation out of
another nation, by testings, by miraculous signs and wonders,
by war, by a mighty hand and an outstretched arm, or by
great and awesome deeds, like all the things the LORD your
God did for you in Egypt before your very eyes?' (Deut.
4:34).

Come and see the works of the LORD…
Be still and know that I am God …
   I will be exalted in the earth

(Ps. 46:8,10).

Come and see what God has done,
   how awesome his works on man's behalf!
He turned the sea into dry land,
   they passed through the waters on foot —
   come, let us rejoice in him'

(Ps. 66:5-6).

God is known by his creation

'O LORD, our Lord, how majestic is your name in all the
earth!' (Ps. 8:1).

The heavens declare the glory of God;
   the skies proclaim the work of his hands.
Day after day they pour forth speech;
   night after night they display knowledge

(Ps. 19:1-2).

What may be known about God is plain to them, because God has made it plain to them. For since the creation of the world God's invisible qualities — his eternal power and divine nature — have been clearly seen, being understood from what has been made, so that men are without excuse. For although they knew God, they neither glorified him as God nor gave thanks to him, but their thinking became futile and their foolish hearts were darkened (Rom. 1:19-21).

God is known by his written Scripture

'All Scripture is God-breathed and is useful for teaching, rebuking, correcting and training in righteousness' (2 Tim. 3:16). 'The law of the LORD is perfect, reviving the soul' (Ps. 19:7). 'And we have the word of the prophets made more certain, and you will do well to pay attention to it, as to a light shining in dark place, until the day dawns and the morning star rises in your hearts. Above all, you must understand that no prophecy of Scripture came about by the prophet's own interpretation. For prophecy never had its origin in the will of man, but men spoke from God as they were carried along by the Holy Spirit' (2 Peter 1:19-21).

God is made known in Christ

Conceivably, the heart of the gospel is outlined in one verse: 'The Word became flesh and made his dwelling among us. We have seen his glory, the glory of the One and Only, who came from the Father, full of grace and truth' (John 1:14). There are at least three main reasons why Christ came in the flesh.

First, *he came to show us the Father.* 'Don't you know me, Philip, even after I have been among you such a long time? Anyone who has seen me has seen the Father' (John 14:9). 'No one knows the Son except the Father, and no one knows the Father except the Son and those to whom the Son chooses to reveal him' (Matt. 11:27). 'Jesus answered ... "I and the Father are one"' (John 10:25,30). It is plain that Jesus claimed that in him alone God is perfectly revealed. The *Westminster Shorter Catechism* asks the question: 'What is God?' It then gives the answer: 'God is a spirit, whose being, wisdom, power, holiness, justice, goodness, and truth are infinite, eternal, and unchangeable.' This definition is now personified in Jesus Christ. Such a manifestation and full revelation of the Father at once sets to rest all abstract conceptions about God, making the gospel the only viable and clear disclosure of God to man.

Secondly, *he came to reconcile us to God*. Reconciliation presupposes enmity. Genesis 3 demonstrates the dawn of fear and guilt and alienation from God because of man's rebellion against him. When Adam and Eve sinned, they realized their shame and guilt, and hid from God, experiencing objective guilt, which can be removed only by God's own initiative. And, while the biblical account asserts that Adam's sin of disobedience resulted in the total depravity of human nature and carried with it far-reaching consequences, it also provides the remedy. The New Testament says of Christ: 'He is the image of the invisible God... For God was pleased to have all his fulness dwell in him, and through him to reconcile to himself all things, whether things on earth or things in heaven, by making peace through his blood, shed on the cross' (Col. 1:15,19-20). This change of attitude from hostility to harmony is the central doctrine of redemptive history. Christ took upon himself the penalty that we deserve in order to assuage the holy justice of God and restore our broken relationship with him. Hence, we are released from a state of sin and fear to grace and freedom; for 'God was reconciling the world to himself in Christ, not counting men's sins against them' (2 Cor. 5:19).

As far as the gospel is concerned, nothing in all religious practices — no matter how intense, passionate and sincere they may be — can remove man's guilt and bring him to a right relationship with his Creator. Samuel Zwemer described Islamic religious practices as 'barren formalism'. The majority of Muslims see their salvation as depending upon total obedience to the sacred law and on meticulous performance of religious duties. Such practice results in inner crises which, according to Hebrews 9:9, will never clear the conscience. Legalism contradicts the heart of the Christian message of reconciliation, which can only come through faith in Jesus Christ.

An increasing number of adherents to Islam find themselves troubled by tradition and are moving away from legalism to a more mystical and personal way of worship. The Sufi sect is very fascinating and worthy of much study. By stressing certain themes, it has evolved to become a new 'way', or *Tarikah* (طريقة), within Islam, moving away from blind obedience to tradition to a more personal relationship with God. Some of these ideas overlap with Christian ones. Among these are the inward search for God, the love of God, the

Unlike other Sunni Muslims, the Sufis dance ecstatically and perform other rituals as part of their mystical path, in an attempt to gain closer knowledge of Allah.

immediacy of God (in contrast with his absolute transcendence in traditional Islam), grace (not necessarily the Christian understanding of grace), humility, love for one's neighbour and personal communion with God in the form of chanting, dancing and repetition of certain liturgical formulas.

Thirdly, *Christ came to destroy the works of the devil.* The Word of God clearly says, 'Dear children, do not let anyone lead you astray. He who does what is right is righteous, just as he is righteous. He who does what is sinful is of the devil, because the devil has been sinning from the beginning. The reason the Son of God appeared was to destroy the devil's work' (1 John 3:7-8). Certainly, the devil succeeded in separating man from his fellowship with God in the Garden of Eden. However, as we have seen above, the reconciling work of Christ has defeated the devil's schemes and work. Hope, forgiveness, cleansing from sin and fellowship with God become possible in Christ. The promise of crushing the devil's head in Genesis 3:15 is now fulfilled through Christ's victory on the cross of Calvary. Jesus Christ achieves what human religions were unable to accomplish. 'Therefore, there is now no condemnation for those who are in Christ Jesus, because through Christ Jesus the law of the Spirit of life set me free from the law of sin and death. For what the law was powerless to do in that it was weakened by the sinful nature, God did by sending his own Son in the likeness of sinful man to be a sin offering. And so he condemned sin in sinful man' (Rom 8:1-3).

The Quran seems to describe Christ in a number of conflicting ways. Some passages, however, would appear to substantiate the biblical narratives. For example, the Quran refers to Christ as the 'Messiah' (3:45) and advocate to God (3:45), and acknowledges his virgin birth (3:47). Another important designation of Jesus is the 'Word' (cf. John 1:1). As we saw in chapter 1, *surah* 3:45, translated literally, is: 'O Mary! God giveth thee glad tidings of a Word from Him: his name will be Christ Jesus.' George Sale translates this verse from the original Arabic as follows: 'O Mary! God sendeth thee good tidings, that thou shalt bear the Word, proceeding from Himself; his name shall be Christ Jesus.'[4] The 'Word, proceeding from Himself' seems to correlate with John's affirmation of Christ, the eternal Word, being incarnated as Jesus the Messiah.

Martin Luther says about this: 'Just as a man has a word in his heart, so also God in His eternal majesty and Deity has a thought, a word in his own heart, with himself. This word, which God the Father has, is so entirely one with Him, so that there is nothing in God which does not also belong to the Word, so that when we see the Word we see God.' John illustrates a great theological truth: Jesus belongs to a timeless eternity. As Augustine says, 'He is in the beginning which has no beginning.'

The God of the Bible is approachable

In answering the question, 'Is God knowable in other religions?' it will suffice to say that the concept of deity varies from one religion to another. For some, the supreme deity remains hidden, austere, inflexible and capricious; for others, he is an abstract void, which cannot be known; for some he is always silent, vague and impersonal.

In contrast, the Bible sketches for us a beautiful portrait of God being knowable and accessible. Moses asks the rhetorical question: 'What other nation is so great as to have their gods near them the way the LORD our God is near us whenever we pray to him?' (Deut. 4:7).

The LORD is near to all who call on him,
    to all who call on him in truth.
He fulfils the desires of those who fear him;
    he hears their cry and saves them
                                (Ps. 145:18).

'Blessed are the pure in heart, for they will see God' (Matt. 5:8). 'But when you pray, go into your room, close the door and pray to your Father, who is unseen. Then your Father, who sees what is done in secret, will reward you' (Matt. 6:6). 'Therefore, since we have been justified through faith, we have peace with God through our Lord Jesus Christ, through whom we have gained access by faith into this grace in which we now stand. And we rejoice in the hope of the glory of God' (Rom. 5:1-2). 'Come near to God and he will come near to you' (James 4:8).

God is known experientially by fellowship with him in Christ and the Holy Spirit

One of the unique teachings of the Bible, in contrast with other religions, is the fact that salvation and regeneration are exclusively the work of the triune God. Salvation is anchored in God's sovereign purposes made visible in the incarnation of Christ and his atonement and the work of God the Holy Spirit, who draws us to Christ. This experiential act of redemption makes it possible to know God through Christ, who said, 'I am the good shepherd; I know my sheep and my sheep know me' (John 10:14).

The God of the Bible is Father

Here it will suffice to quote the following Bible verses which use anthropomorphic language about the fatherhood of God that sets him apart from all other deities, while at the same time giving believers unshakable comfort and confidence in him: '... you, O LORD, are our Father, our Redeemer from of old is your name' (Isa. 63:16). 'Moreover, we have all had human fathers who disciplined us and we respected them for it. How much more should we submit to the Father of our spirits and live!' (Heb 12:9). 'Every good and perfect gift is from above, coming down from the Father of the heavenly lights, who does not change like shifting shadows' (James

1:17). 'For you did not receive a spirit that makes you a slave again to fear, but you received the Spirit of sonship. And by him we cry, "Abba, Father." The Spirit himself testifies with our spirit that we are God's children. Now if we are children, then we are heirs — heirs of God and co-heirs with Christ, if indeed we share in his sufferings in order that we may also share in his glory' (Rom. 8:15-17).

To sum up

While the majority of Muslims and some Christians contend that both Christians and Muslims worship the same God, such a claim is rather naïve, to say the least. According to the dictionary, the word 'same' means: 'being the very one, identical, alike in kind, quality, amount, or degree'. The Bible, as we have seen above, answers many of our questions concerning the nature of God. Indeed, Scripture demonstrates God's uniqueness; there is no doubt about the dissimilarity between Allah of Islam and the God of the Bible. I am aware that this testimony collides with the increasing clamour of today's politically correct, multi-cultural, relativistic world-view. None the less, the Bible, being the Word of God, maintains an exclusive absolute truth which, by its nature, transcends all human claims. To bypass the Bible's claims for the sake of political and religious expediency is, in fact, to abandon its validity. As Charles Colson observes, 'When truth retreats, tyranny advances.'

How can we know that certain revelation is genuine?

Loraine Boettner said it well: 'Granted that any person has received a revelation, it would also follow that he should be able to give some proof to his fellow men that he does possess such a revelation. Otherwise he would not be believed.' In our relations one with another at the human level, whenever someone comes to us claiming to represent another person or institution, we demand that he present his credentials. We have a right to demand them, and they must be of such a nature that no other person can duplicate them. Likewise, the prophet who comes with a message from God must be able to show his credentials, and they must be of such a nature that they cannot be duplicated. They must accredit him as a true representative of the court of heaven. Hence, it seems very reasonable to expect that in the course of God's dealings with the human race certain men would be accredited as his messengers and would be given power to do works of a supernatural order.

The Bible gives us certain criteria by which we can examine the authenticity of any revelation.

1. Miracles

Firstly, the prophets and apostles not only worked miracles, but also possessed the gift of inspiration and wrote books which we acknowledge to be the Lord's Word to the people. *Revelation and miracles go together.* This gift is not possessed by present-day ministers. The apostle John wrote, 'Jesus did many other miraculous signs in the presence of his disciples, which are not recorded in this book. But these are written that you may believe that Jesus is the Christ, the Son of God, and that by believing you may have life in his name' (John 20:30-31). Again, the writer of the Epistle to the Hebrews tells us that the message of salvation, 'which was first announced by the Lord, was confirmed to us by those who heard him. God also testified to it by signs, wonders and various miracles, and gifts of the Holy Spirit distributed according to his will' (Heb. 2:3-4). Miracles were an integral part of God's plan of redemption as that plan was made known to a lost and unbelieving race. Miracles are not to be put on a level with the tricks of a magician. It is not a question of miracles being liable to happen at any time, or of just anyone being able to perform them.

It is important to point out that, apart from their evidential value, certain miracles, such as the incarnation and resurrection, enter into the very substance of Christianity to such a degree that apart from them there is no such thing as Christianity. We know, for instance, that many miracles occurred which have not been recorded in the Bible, and readily acknowledge that some of those that have been recorded might have been omitted from the record without seriously impairing the Christian belief-system. But such miracles as the incarnation and resurrection of Christ are so vital to that system that their omission would leave us with a radically different religion. For, by the incarnation, God was enabled to enter personally into the human race and, as the God-man, Jesus Christ, took upon himself the penalty due to us for sin, suffering and dying for us on the cross and thus redeeming us. Also as the God-man, in his capacity as the federal head and representative of his people, subject to all the trials which befall human nature, he overcame all temptation and perfectly kept the moral law (which our former head and representative, Adam, had failed to keep) and thus earned for us eternal life. And by the resurrection he, as federal head and representative of his people, triumphed over death, came forth from the grave with a glorious body and calls his people to a life of eternal happiness and joy. Paul spoke only the solemn truth when he declared, 'And if Christ has not been raised, our preaching is useless and so is your faith... And if Christ has not been raised, your faith is futile; you are still in your sins' (1 Cor. 15:14,17). Consequently, the miracles of the incarnation and resurrection are such vitally important parts of the Christian system that if they are omitted, what we have left cannot rightly be called historic Christianity.

2. The fulfilment of prophecy

Another way in which God can accredit a revelation to man is
through the foretelling of events, or predictive prophecy. This,
in reality, is a miracle in the realm of knowledge, a supernatural unfolding of future events. The principal value of a
miracle worked in the physical world is to accredit a revelation immediately to the people to whom it is given, while
the principal value of prophecy is to accredit the revelation to
people who live years later and who see its fulfilment. The
Lord alone is able to declare the end from the beginning, and
to make known the things which are yet to come. By prophecy, in the sense of foretelling events, we are not talking of
mere general statements or shrewd guesses, such as a person
might make by closely observing present tendencies. In every-
day conversation the term is sometimes used in that sense,
but not properly so. Here we mean the foretelling of events in
such detail that only the hypothesis of supernatural knowledge can adequately account for their fulfilment.

Today, for instance, the political observers with the best
intellect and keenest insight and most advanced technology
are not able to predict with any accuracy what the political
fortunes will be during the next four years; much less can they
predict what these fortunes will be during the next four hundred years. What person one hundred years ago could have
predicted in detail the two World Wars, or the rise of Fascism,
or Nazism? Or who today would dare to prophesy in detail
the political conditions of the world twenty-five years from
now? And yet we find that the Old Testament prophets did
this time after time. Some of the events which they prophe-
sied were not to be fulfilled until centuries after the prophecies
were written, and they were set forth in such detail that they
cannot be accounted for by anything less than supernatural
revelation. We know, for instance, that the Scriptures of the
Old Testament were written centuries before the time of
Christ. Consequently when we find prophecies foretelling the

very town in which he should be born, the virgin birth, numerous things about his manner of life and public ministry, and many prophecies which were fulfilled in detail at the time of his crucifixion and resurrection, we have convincing proof that the Scripture writers had supernatural knowledge and that the messages which they gave really came from God.

4.

Questions about cultural themes

We have seen previously that the formative period of Islam played a pivotal role in shaping the identity and sustaining the ethos of Islamic culture. For example, the tradition of the *Sunnah* has provided a concrete regulative standard embracing the whole of religious, moral, social and political life.

Culture plays a potent role in shaping society and its members. The absorption of a culture is a kind of indoctrination, particularly when it is integrated with religion. One of the distinctive features of Islam is the dominant role religion plays in shaping all facets of socio-cultural and political life. This is because every orthodox Muslim is under an obligation to conduct his entire life in accordance with the dictates of the Quran and the *Sunnah*. The cultural themes that will be discussed in this chapter are all coloured by the religion of Islam.

What is culture?

Culture is a way of life, embracing all its material, spiritual and intellectual aspects. The *Willowbank Report* of the Lausanne Committee provides a good and thorough definition of culture:

'Culture is an integral system of beliefs (about God, or reality, or ultimate meaning), of values (about what is true, good, beautiful and normative), of customs (how to behave, relate to others, talk, pray, dress, work, play, trade, farm, eat, etc.), and of institutions which express these beliefs, values and customs (governments, law, courts, temples or churches, family, schools, hospitals, factories, shops, unions, clubs, etc.), which bind a society together and give it a sense of identity, dignity, security, and continuity.'[1]

What are some influential cultural themes in Arab Islamic culture?

Some of the themes selected for discussion here are thought to be most influential, not only in shaping the Arab Muslim personality, but also in furnishing the moral content for both collective and individual standards of behaviour. This provides the ground for further analysis and appraisal of Arab Muslim culture. The aim is to present these themes objectively and to avoid any stereotyping or generalization that will not serve the cause of the gospel.

What part does the concept of ethnicity play in Islamic culture?

There is no doubt that the concept of ethnicity in Islamic culture is a powerful unifying force and arouses a sense of superiority that often creates a resistance to conversion. The idea of ethnicity is deeply embedded — particularly in the consciousness of Arab Muslims. When we study Islam, we are introduced to the concept of the Islamic community, or *Ummah* (أُمَّة). In verse after verse, the Quran emphasizes the primacy of bonds created through Islam, reinforcing the shared identities of kinship, descent, region and language. The Arabic term

Al-Asabyiah (العصبية) describes this ethnic idiosyncrasy and social grouping of Arabic culture from ancient times. The Quran reinforces this belief (3:103; 8:63; 9:71) and so does the *Sunnah*.[2] It is important to emphasize that the Arab Muslim's awareness of a strong sense of belonging is not only rooted in a cultural heritage shared by the group, but is also reinforced by divine claims.

From the beginning of his mission, the prophet of Islam recognized the importance of ethnic feeling among the Arabs and used it to promote his new-found faith. As we have seen earlier, Muhammad adopted all the powerful pre-Islamic Arab traditions, including tribal solidarity, and demonstrated his ability to unite the Arabs under the banner of Islam by playing the role of an arbiter of disputes among the tribes. Step by step, he acquired religious authority, not only by uniting disputing tribes, but also by infusing in them a sense of religious superiority and destiny — *kismet*. Thus, he inculcated in them the idea of religion as the basis for identity and social cohesion. This idea, which is reinforced in the Quran, continues to provide Arab Muslims with a deep sense of calling as a people chosen for the propagation of Islam: 'Thus we have appointed you [Arab Muslims] as a middle nation, that you may be a witness against mankind, and the messenger may be a witness against you' (2:143).

What does the concept of the family involve in Islam?

Generally speaking, the term *aelah* (عائلة), meaning 'family', expresses the idea of the basic social unit. In Islam, however, the term denotes the basic social unit of a religious society, an idea that includes the social as well as the sacred. The term is comprehensive and includes not only the nuclear family, but also the grandparents, uncles, aunts and cousins. In its broadest sense, the term corresponds with the concept of *Ummah*

(أُمَّة), used to indicate the bond of Muslim society under the banner of Islam. The family in Islamic society in general, and Arab Sunni society in particular, established the moral foundations that have become deeply and indelibly fixed in the consciousness of its members.

The Arab family today, however, is facing new challenges. Modernization, technological advances and Westernization are some of the themes that are under discussion among the Islamic educators, *ulama* (علماء), concerned about the state of traditional Islamic values.

The Arab Muslim family, as a basic relational and social unit, is very influential in the formation of the individual conscience from the earliest stages of life. In her account of family life in Islam (emphasizing the traditional Arab family), Muslim scholar Fatima Heeren gives the Islamic view of the subject: 'Family life with all its aspects concerning not only husband, wife and children, but all other relatives too, is firmly established by tradition as well as by religious law... This is due to the Islamic injunctions which have not at all become obsolete in the course of modern techno-industrial developments but [are] taken seriously by Muslims up to this very day, because they are fully aware of their role as God's vice-regent and because they feel contentment in fulfilling their religious duties, thus achieving God's good pleasure... Non-Muslims may wonder how a religion can still exercise such a powerful influence over people in modern times ... it is the firm structure of Islamic family resting on the Quranic regulations and the traditions from the life of the prophet Muhammad, handed down from generation to generation.'[3]

What is the relationship between husband and wife?

In the events leading up to marriage, the parents typically play a major role in the selection of the spouse. Arranged marriages are still current practice. Today, however, the man and woman have a greater say in the selection of a spouse.

Among numerous references in the Quran to the position of women in relation to men, *Surah Al-Nisa* 4:34 clearly speaks of the superiority of men over women in both position and function: 'Men are in charge of women because Allah hath made the one of them to excel the other... So good women are then obedient, guarding in secret that which Allah hath guarded. As for those from whom ye fear rebellion, admonish them and banish them to beds apart, and scourge them. Then if they obey you, seek not a way against them.' Quranic injunctions such as this one have historically been detrimental to the position of women and form the basis of the patriarchy that still prevails in Arab society. In contrast to the Arab world, Western society places a greater emphasis on parenthood, stressing the roles of both father and mother and the duties of parents. This reflects in some ways the idea of God's fatherhood and his relationship to his children, an idea that is basically absent from Islamic theology. In the traditional Arab Muslim family, it is the man who makes and enforces the rules of the home.

Halim Barakat describes this patriarchal role as follows: 'The father continues to wield authority, assume responsibility for the family and expect respect and unquestioning compliance with his instructions. Thus the continued dominance of the family as the basic unit of social organization and production has contributed to the diffusion of patriarchal relations and to their application to similar situations within other social institutions. In all of these, a father figure rules over others, monopolizing authority, expecting strict obedience, and showing little tolerance of dissent.'4

Thus this paternal image leaves little room for the other members in the family, including the wife, to exercise a significant role in the decision-making process. This role of subordination has been, and still is, largely assigned to women in Arab society. Some reformist voices today are calling for reinterpretation of the Quranic injunctions concerning the role and position of women. This continued dominance by a single male leader provides the basis for the husband / father to wield unquestioned leadership in fulfilling the central aim of the Quran, which is to establish a viable social Islamic order that begins in the home.

What do the Quran and the *Hadith* say about the position of women in Islam?

The Bible describes man and woman as equal in the eyes of the Lord. The first chapter of the Bible declares that both were created in the image of God. Jointly they were given the mission of being fruitful and having dominion over the earth (Gen. 1:27-28). In marriage both become one flesh, an expression of union, love and fidelity (Gen. 2:23-24). The Decalogue gives honour to both father and mother (Exod. 20:12). Likewise, contrary to the ethos of his day, the Lord Jesus Christ gave women a place of honour. The Scripture tells us that in Christ there is no difference between male and female (Gal. 3:28). While the role of spiritual leadership was given to the husbands, they are commanded: 'Husbands, love your wives, just as Christ loved the church and gave himself up for her' (Eph. 5:25). In contrast with all other faiths, past and present, there is no doubt that the Bible portrays women as equal companions to men, though they have a different role.

In contrast, the *Oxford Encyclopaedia of the Modern Islamic World* argues that the position of women in early Islam was improved in comparison with the pre-Islamic period; none the less, it admits that women are given less status than men: 'Quranic verses do assign women's testimony half the value of men's; permit men to unilaterally divorce their wives; deny women custody rights over their children after they reach a certain age; permit polygamy; and favour men over women respecting inheritance.'[5]

It must be kept in mind that conflicts between traditional and fundamentalist Muslims on the one hand and reformists on the other are continuing today. The traditional majority still hold on unyieldingly to a literal interpretation of the teachings of the Quran and the *Hadith* (the sayings of the prophet Muhammad) concerning the position and role of women, while the reformists take a more liberal position. The following extracts are representative of the teaching about women in the Quran and the *Hadith* taken from Muhammad Pickthall's translation:

The Quran

The rights of women

Concerning women's rights the Quran says, 'And women shall have rights similar to the rights against them, according to what is equitable; but men have a degree over them...' (2:228). 'To the male a portion equal to that of two females...' (4:11).

The testimony of two women equals the witness of one man

'And get two witnesses out of your own men, and if there are not two men, then a man and two women such as ye choose, for witness' (2:282).

Husbands are permitted to scourge their wives

'Men are in charge of women, because Allah hath made the one of them to excel the other. As to those women on whose part ye fear disloyalty and ill-conduct, admonish them, refuse to share their beds, scourge them...' (4:34).

Polygamy is allowed

'Marry of the women who seem good to you, two, or three, or four; and if you fear that ye cannot do justice [to so many] then one ...' (4:3). Muhammad was allowed to marry unlimited wives, according to the Quran (33:50).

Women as objects of pleasure

'Your women are a tilth [soil prepared to be cultivated] for you, so go to your tilth as you will...' (2:223).

Divorce

A husband may divorce his wife for any reason he seems fit; however, for the divorce to be lawful, he must twice repeat verbally to his wife his intention to divorce her: 'Divorce must be pronounced twice' (2:229-230).

The Hadith

Very essential for an understanding of the position and role of women in Islam are the sayings of Muhammad. Sahih Al-Bukhari narrates the following maxims about women. I shall not read anything into the text, but these teachings certainly call for adequate explanation by Muslim scholars:

Mohammed asked some women, 'Isn't the witness of a woman equal to half that of a man?' The women said, 'yes'. He said, 'This is because of the deficiency of the woman's mind' (Sahih Al-Bukhari, vol. 3:826).

Mohammed said, 'I was shown the Hell-fire and that the majority of its dwellers are women' (vol. 1:28, 301; vol. 2:161; Sahih Al-Bukhari, vol. 7:124).

Mohammed said, 'Bad omen is in the woman, the house and the horse' (*Sahih Al-Bukhari*, vol. 7:30).

Aisha narrated that the prophet married her when she was six years old and he consummated his marriage when she was nine years old (*Sahih Al-Bukhari*, vol. 7:64).

What are the customs associated with the birth of a child?

From the very first day, the child is surrounded by Islam. Shortly after birth, he or she is presented to a gathering of relatives and priests. The priest then recites a prayer close to the child's left ear, followed by recitation of *al-Fatiha* (الفاتحة) — literally, 'the opening' — which is memorized by the majority of Muslims around the world. The *Fatiha* is the first *surah* in the Quran and corresponds to the Lord's Prayer in the Bible. It reads: 'In the name of Allah, the Beneficent, the merciful. Praise to Allah, Lord of the Worlds: the Beneficent, the Merciful: owner of the day of judgement. Thee alone we worship; thee alone we ask for help. Show us the straight path: The path of those whom thou hast favoured; not [the path] of those who earn His anger nor of those who go astray' (1:1-7).

When the child is named, two goats are offered for a boy and one for a girl. The goats must not be over a year old and must be without spot or blemish. The child is named on the seventh day. The name is chosen carefully. Most Arab Muslim names carry a religious or ethical significance, a practice found also in the Jewish tradition. The inclusion of the word 'Allah' in the first name is common. Names such as, for example, Abd-Allah (Slave of Allah), Abd-Alatif (Slave of the Subtle One) and Abd-Alsamad (Slave of the Eternal) are derived from the ninety-nine Islamic most excellent names for

Allah. The name Muhammad and its derivations, such as Ahmad, Mahmood, Hamid, Hamdoon and Hamdi, are chosen with the hope that the child will receive Allah's favour as he strives to model his life and conduct on the character of the prophet. The *Hadith* says, 'Call your children after your prophet' (i.e., Muhammad).[6] Thus, in a real sense, the name given is basically a religious and moral contract between the family, the child and, ultimately, Allah.

How are children reared?

From the earliest stage of his cognitive development, the child is systematically taught the religious doctrines of Islam. When able to talk, or at the age of four years, four months and four days, he is taught to memorize the *Bismillah* (بسملة) — literally, 'In the name of Allah, the Beneficent, the Merciful'. This phrase is used at the beginning of every *surah* in the Quran and is repeated often in the daily lives of most Muslims.

A boy is circumcised between seven and twelve years of age, and occasionally in the first week after birth, although the Quran is silent on this issue. But the custom of circumcision is widely observed, having its roots in the practice of ancient Semitic peoples, including the Hebrew people. The Arabic word for circumcision is *khitan* (ختان), meaning 'to seal'. This borrowed practice came to signify total identification with Islam as the final revelation that supersedes all previous religious traditions. According to Muslim tradition, Abraham, Christ, Adam, Lot and Muhammad were circumcised. Circumcision in Islam is the counterpart to baptism in Christianity, the new believers being circumcised as a sign of reception into Islam.

Thus circumcision, for children and adults alike, becomes a permanent physical reminder throughout the whole of life of belonging to Islam. The Quranic declaration, 'This day have I perfected your religion for you and completed my favour unto you, and have chosen for you as religion Al-Islam' (5:3), is often quoted by Muslims, reinforcing the individual's attachment to his faith.

A great emphasis is placed in the Arab Muslim family on the unconditional obedience of children to their parents, particularly to their father. Two Arabic proverbs reflect the close association between the father's role in the family and that sanctioned by religious imperatives. The first is: *Riddha al-Abb min riddha ar-Rabb* (رضى الأب من رضى الرب) — 'The father's satisfaction is part of Allah's satisfaction.' The other is: *Ghadab al-Abb min ghadub ar-Rabb* (غضب الأب من غضب الرب) — 'A father's anger is part of God's anger.' A greater understanding of the implication of these proverbs is gained from a consideration of the Islamic doctrine of God. Allah is described in absolute terms, making Islam a theocentric, or more accurately, an 'Allah-centric' religion of the highest degree. The father's authority is thus reinforced by religious tradition and sanctioned by the approval of Allah.

Margaret Nydell, an Arabist and expert in Middle-Eastern social life, makes this observation concerning the approach to discipline in Arab Muslim society: 'It is significant that an Arab child is conditioned to feel shame rather than guilt. He is made to feel ashamed because others see him as having acted wrongly, not because he inwardly regrets having done wrong and judges himself accordingly. In such conditioning, the capacity for self-criticism is not cultivated; instead a reflex to social pressure and criticism is developed. Shame is formed by what the individual thinks others think of him, rather than by what he thinks of himself.'[7]

What are some of the implications of such a method of child-rearing?

The continuous pressure exerted by parents for perfect compliance with Islamic standards is often augmented by the pressure exerted by the child upon himself to obey and please his parents and to conform to society's expectations of him. As such, behavioural conditioning becomes inevitable. The interplay between conscience as a God-given inner enforcer of discipline and parents as external enforcers of discipline shapes the life of the child from early childhood through adulthood. In his book *The Protestant Temperament*, Philip Greven insists that what made most children of evangelical families in the early years of the American church behave properly — whether or not any adult was around to notice — was their continuously active conscience, which governed their lives from early childhood through adulthood, monitoring, checking, censuring and controlling their thoughts, feelings and behaviour. For this a powerful conscience was essential, and the methods of child-rearing characteristic of evangelical families were designed to ensure the formation of such conscience based on biblical principles.[8]

But what happens when patterns of child-rearing, particularly in the process of teaching values, are not based on biblical principles, or, worse still, are based on anti-biblical principles, as is the case in Islam? In this case the content of conscience — internalized rules that mirror the parents' standards — provide the child with his moral standards. When such a process continues throughout life, it no doubt leaves a lasting and profound impact upon the individual; he will never be entirely free from it. Conscience is not meant to function only according to principles determined by social norms. Conscience plays a crucial role in stirring up our rebellious inclinations (i.e., producing an awareness of guilt that drives us to God). Conscience is not meant to be 'a kind of computerized morality. You feed the data into the machine and conscience selects the pertinent norm.'[9]

We need to make a distinction between conscience as a God-given faculty and its content, which is mainly derived from surroundings. When parental and cultural influences are applied to child-rearing, particularly in religious matters, as we shall see below, it undoubtedly becomes an even more potent factor in the process of shaping, not only the character of the child, but his whole moral and ethical direction. Moreover, these influences provide the basis on which his conscience operates. The tragic prospect is that the very conscience that was meant to drive a person to faith in Christ becomes conditioned to drive him away from Christ. We shall see more of this effect later.

What religious training is given to children?

Given the impact of the factors observed above, it is necessary to note several religious directives that are historically found in a typical Arab orthodox Muslim home. The first pertains to the religious training of children within the home. At the age of adolescence, the child is expected to adhere to and observe the religious rites of Islam. Prior to this time, the parents are responsible for teaching him the prayers and the memorization of the Quran. 'The mother cares for the children', and '... the father who according to the patriarchal nature of Islam, is an Imam ... upholds the tenets of faith and his authority symbolizes that of God in the world.'[10]

The Muslim scholar Alhlag Al-Jalali gives the following description of the instruction of children in religious matters: 'For the mind of the child is like a clear tablet, equally open to any inscription. Next to that, he should be taught the institutes of religion and rules of propriety. Thus, at the age of seven, we are told by the traditions to enjoin him merely to say his prayers; at the age of ten, if he omits them, to admonish him by blows. By praising the good and censuring the bad, we should render him emulous of right and apprehensive of wrong.'[11]

We see here that the goal of the child's education in the home is to produce nothing less than a child who is a *bona fide* Muslim. The disciplinary perspective mobilizes parents to

Historically, the child has always been trained not only through internalizing theoretical and abstract moral principles, but also by engaging in religious practices.

instil a religious character that is capable of thinking in a way that is thoroughly Islamic. In a survey of one hundred orthodox Muslims, I found that approximately 72% of the respondents have been practising Islam regularly in their homes. Consequently, when this scenario persists throughout life, the conscience becomes, as it were, immunized against, and the mind conditioned to exclude, any other religious and moral options. This becomes one of the most potent reasons why Muslims at first contest the gospel.

How does this contrast with Christian education?

While the ultimate goal of Christian education is to assist the individual to discover and appropriate for himself a personal Saviour, the emphasis in Islamic education is to assist him to assimilate a system that requires the individual to conform to its demands by performing external religious acts of piety. Thus the Islamic educational process is fundamentally legalistic. Herein lies the core distinction that explains the major difference between Islam and Christianity, at least in terms of the function of religious education in particular and the religious law in general.

In her book, *I Dared to Call Him Father*, Bilquis Sheikh explains how her conscience was conditioned in relation to the Bible by means of her home training as a young child: 'I found myself picking up the Koran out of a sense of duty, and eagerly turning to the Christian book, dipping into it here and there to look into the confusing new world I had discovered. Each time I opened the Bible a sense of guilt filled me. Perhaps this stemmed from my strict upbringing. Even after I became a young woman, father would have to approve any book I read.'[12]

Bilquis' strict upbringing is not unusual in orthodox Muslim Sunni society. The process of learning in Islam is always inseparable from religion. The aim of education, as we shall see below, is the education of the total personality within the Islamic world-view.

What is the Muslim principle of 'halal'?

Two concepts closely related to the Muslim ethos, constituted as it is by pervasive beliefs, are those of *halal* (حلال) — that which is 'lawful / kosher' — and *haram* (حرام) — that which is 'forbidden'. Both concepts are an integral part of the religious and ethical system of Islam.

The principle of *halal* is considered an important and integral part of the total Islamic codes of ethics. In his introductory remarks to his work on the Islamic law, or *Shariah* (شريعة), Abdur Ruhman makes the following remark in connection with the subject at hand: 'Islam is a religion and way of life based on the commandments of Allah contained in the Holy Quran and the Sunnah of the prophet. Every Muslim has to observe at every step the distinction between what is right *(Halal)* and what is wrong *(Haram)*.[13]

The concept of *halal*, however, is not peculiar to Islam. The codes relating to what is *halal* and *haram* find their roots in the Old Testament (in particular, Leviticus), which addresses matters relating to laws and regulations concerning dietary matters, purity, sexual relations and ethical injunctions. However, in Islam something which is *halal* is permitted as long as it does not contradict the basic list of what is *haram*. In this case, the individual is directed to exercise judgement by observing a list of regulations that determine what is right and wrong. Certainly, this course of action is appealing to people, particularly in order to assuage their nagging consciences.

What is the principle of haram?

According to the Quran and the *Sunnah*, *haram* (حرام) means declaring something unlawful. The Quran provides a list of unlawful practices, such as animals which are forbidden for food (6:145), marriages which are proscribed (4:22-24), wine (5:91), gambling (5:91) and usury (2:275-276). The *Sunnah*, however, is more detailed concerning these injunctions, describing what is both permissible and unlawful in the areas of purification, practices in the mosque, prayer life, fasting, marriage, *jihad*, divorce, buying and selling, cultivation of the land, wills and inheritance, food and drink, sanitary laws and ethics. Thus, what is lawful is not for the individual to decide. For the most part, it is the Quranic and *Sunnah* codes that regulate the ethical and religious life of individuals and communities.

What are some of the implications of the laws of *haram* and *halal*?

Since its inception, Islam has been intolerant of antinomianism. As a consequence, those who choose to free their consciences from legalism encounter serious opposition, as the following account demonstrates: 'Some of the prophet's companions in Syria (the most eminent among them being Abu Jandal), who did not let the Quran interfere with their drinking, justified their transgression with the following Quranic verse (5:93): "Those who believe and do good works are not regarded as sinful on account of what they eat as long as they place their trust in God, believe, and do good works." No wonder that Umar, a strict caliph, had them flogged for this liberal interpretation.'[14]

In his evaluation of the legal practices in Islam, Goldziher, an eminent Muslim scholar, makes these surprising remarks: 'The predominance, in religious learning, of the tendency to search into law, using the methods of casuistry ... gradually resulted in impressing upon the teaching of Islam the stamp of a quibbling legalism. Under the influence of this tendency, religious life itself was seen from a legal point of view. This was not likely to strengthen true piety, the devotion of the heart. A faithful adherent of Islam is thus, even in his own consciousness, under the governance of man-made rules.'[15]

Goldziher is not too far from the truth. For law without grace becomes 'quibbling legalism', as we have already seen. For any spiritual life which is accepted by God must be demonstrated by a life of righteousness imparted by the grace of God. Since God is righteous, he will deal with man only according to his plans for righteousness. Man cannot gain righteousness, but he can be declared righteous. This is done by the grace of God through Jesus Christ. The sinner is no longer reckoned a sinner, because he places his faith in Jesus Christ and his faith is counted for righteousness (Rom. 4:5-8). This is the core of the gospel message — an inward righteousness, imparted by God through Christ, manifesting itself outwardly.

How does the concept of shame manifest itself in Muslim society?

We must now turn our attention to another cultural theme which is a distinctive feature of Arab Muslim society, namely that of shame. According to Patai[16] and Nydell,[17] Arab Muslim society may be called 'the shame society'. The idea conveyed is that the concept of shame is rooted in the consciousness of the Arab Muslim ethos.

In order to see how this concept relates directly to individual ethics, it is important to see first of all how it relates to the collective morals. Shame is connected with the Arab moral imperative of self-respect, *Ihtiram al-nafs* (احترام النفس), which is rooted in the ancient Arab tribal codes of ethics.

It is customary practice for a man as he enters a building or climbs the stairway (as used to be the case where I lived at one time) to announce his coming by repeating the phrase: '*Tasataru ya harem*' ('Veil [or "Cover"] yourselves, women'). This gives the women who are normally chatting in the hallways with their neighbours a chance to cover their faces. In traditional Muslim society, exposure of the face is considered a shameful sign. When caught uncovered, the woman rushes indoors, overcome with shame, while repeating certain religious expressions in the hope of expiating the psychological guilt that arises from the recognition that she has offended against the social norm.

The concept of shame is multi-faceted and cannot be reduced to a single illustration. However, the instance cited above helps us to see how a sense of shame bears on the idea of morality. In this context, shame is the result of running counter to the cultural standards that inform the conscience.

An increasing number of Muslim women in the West wear the *hijab*. The name *hijab* (حجاب) comes from the Arabic word *hajaba* (حجب), meaning 'to hide from sight'. Apart from the fact that the Quran commands women to wear the hijab (33:59), it is primarily intended to safeguard the honour of women.

The whole idea of strict codes of dress, including veiling, is connected closely with family honour. In contrast with the Western emphasis on individual responsibility and accountability, the conduct of the individual in Arab Muslim society has a direct relationship on the reputation and honour of the group. Any dishonourable conduct brings what is called *tasweed al-wajeh* (تسويد الوجه) — literally, 'the blackening of the face' — against the nuclear, and also the extended, family.

Thus, in such a close-knit culture, all means are employed to minimize the occurrence of shame. The veiling of women is only one of the means introduced by the customary practices of early Islam to keep both sexes from the risk of falling into sexual encounters which would bring shame and disgrace to both individuals and their families. This idea finds its roots in pre-Islamic society. However, the Quran and the *Sunnah* intensify the fear of shame by giving specific rules and regulations, prohibitions and punishments.[18]

What are some of the implications of shame?

Bruce Thomas puts his finger on a fundamental truth in connection with the idea of a misplaced sense of security and shame in the Muslim society: 'Perhaps the greatest need felt by Muslim people is not need for assurance of salvation from sin, but deliverance from the tyranny of being in a near constant state of defilement. Every element in their daily lives is ordered by this insecurity.'[19]

Thomas goes on to ask some probing questions in this regard. Do general and special revelation teach us something about the defilement of man? Is man's defilement an integral part of his sinfulness? Is shame related to defilement in the same way that guilt is related to sin? Does Christ's death atone for man's defilement as well as his sin?[20] In attempting to give a preliminary answer, Thomas suggests that we contextualize the term 'depravity' by using the term 'defilement' instead — which makes more sense to a Muslim. But, more importantly, he asks another question: does the Muslim's preoccupation with an endless cycle of ritualistic cleansing point to another human problem? Perhaps a part of the answer to Thomas's question is found in the nature of all legalistic religions. Man is religious by his very nature, but, being sinful, his conscience operates to convict him when he violates the law of God as he perceives it. Thus the Islamic preoccupation with rituals is nothing more than an attempt to suppress the nagging guilt feelings by resorting to endless attempts to secure a righteousness by one's own efforts — acts which, as we have already seen and shall see again in chapter 6, are 'not able to clear the conscience of the worshipper' (Heb. 9: 9).

The biblical concept of shame is grounded in the transgression of God's standards (cf. Jer. 7:19; 31:19; 2 Tim. 2:15). Hence, true shame must drive the guilty to repentance. True shame is not embarrassment at having been caught out, or regret because of what Paul calls 'worldly sorrow' (2 Cor. 7:10). Instead, it is the conscious acknowledgement of having done that which is wrong in God's sight, and of having incurred actual, objective guilt before him, that imparts a sense of deep shame which at the same time leads to repentance from the sin: 'Godly sorrow brings repentance that leads to salvation and leaves no regret... See what this godly sorrow has produced in you: what earnestness, what eagerness to clear yourselves, what indignation, what alarm, what longing, what concern, what readiness to see justice done' (2 Cor. 7:10-11).

What role does the code of honour play in Muslim society?

Honour is another notion that occupies a prominent place in the ethical ideals of Arab Muslim society. This idea, however, also finds its roots in pre-Islamic tribal codes of ethics. Though the Arab tribes lived in a state of perpetual war, their hostilities were conducted according to a strict code of honour. The object of the Arab warrior was not so much to win the war as to gain glory. Patai concludes that since 'there is a correlation between honour and group survival, the honour concept is easily extended from the individual, the family, and the tribe to the nation as a whole'.[21]

The furore in recent years over Salman Rushdie's book *The Satanic Verses* illustrates this point. His book is viewed by the majority of Muslims as an insult to Islam and a direct attack against the character of its founder. This feeling evoked an angry response in the Muslim world. Ayatollah Khomeini of Iran issued a special *fatwa* (فتوة) — i.e. a ruling on a point of religious law — declaring Rushdie's attack against Islam to be an act of blasphemy, a crime that is punishable by death according to the law of apostasy in Islam. Furthermore, in Arabia, a group of Islamic foreign ministers took the issue very seriously. They denounced the book and also condemned Rushdie as an apostate. However, they refrained from calling for legal action. Al-Azhar, the leading Islamic religious and educational institution, also made a similar statement.

Such actions are characterized by modern secular Western standards as wrong, to say the least. However, for a Muslim, they are perfectly justified. The Rushdie affair was considered a direct assault on the honour and integrity of their prophet and the Muslim faith as a whole. What seems to others to be deplorable behaviour is for the Muslim's conscience nothing more than the right action generated by a sense of duty. Thus preserving the Islamic ideals, protecting the honour of the prophet and doing the will of Allah, as pronounced in the Quran and *Sunnah*, are non-negotiable moral imperatives.

One of the distinctive features of Islam is the close correlation between its theological and cultural themes. For example, the cross, which is the dominant symbol of redemption and victory in Christianity, is seen in Islam in relation to their cultural themes. For a Muslim the cross is a symbol of shame and ignominy. Thus it is no surprise that among the reasons for the rejection of the cross by Muslims is that it is seen as violating the honour of Allah.

Another word used for 'honour' is *sharaf* (شرف), 'character'. It has to do with the reputation of the individual and his family in relation to society. One of the most dishonouring types of behaviour, at least among Muslim Arabs, is the act of adultery, zina (زنى). The customary punishment is one hundred lashes, a practice that is based on the Quran (24:2-5).

What is the impact of religious education on Islamic society?

During the war on terrorism, much has been said about the Taliban's Islamic school, or madrasah (مدرسة), in Afghanistan, where Islam ruled in every aspect of education and the school system. Such schools were intended not only to educate, but also to indoctrinate the children with certain religious beliefs and values. The results were devastating. In neighbouring Iran, where the Shariah law is also practised, we find a similar situation.

From the early stages of Islamic development in the seventh century right up to the eighteenth, the schools were predominantly religious in nature. It was not until the colonial period and the arrival of missionaries from the West that these schools were influenced by external factors. However, the Quranic higher religious schools are the basic educational institutions. These schools stress memorizing, reading and writing the Quran. Memorization, however, does not necessarily mean comprehension. The very fact that the Quran is memorized brings spiritual satisfaction. As mentioned earlier, this practice starts at home with the first stages of the child's cognitive development. The chanting recitation of the Quran, tajweed (تجويد), has been developed to an important artistic science called ilm al-tajweed (علم التجويد), or 'the science of articulation'.

Among the most famous schools are Al-Azhar in Cairo, the Suleymaniye in Istanbul, Qaraniyini in Fez, Zaytunah in Tunis and various mosques, including the religious schools (madrasah) in Mecca and Medina in Arabia. These stand out in the Sunni world. These schools have continued to play an influential role right up to our own day.

What are some of the implications of such religious training?

Perhaps a more significant factor contributing to the antipathy towards Christianity is that the masses had been trained in an educational system that for the previous twelve centuries had revolved around the sacred book by providing the foundations for the Islamization of knowledge. Accordingly, in Muslim minds the content and the form of education are inseparable and neither can be replaced. Education has everything to do with the core moral principles of Islam.

It is notable that the purpose of Islamic religious education is to mould the person's character in such a way that he sees the world only through the prism of Islam. The paramount goal becomes imparting knowledge that is based on religious axioms organically integrated into the Islamic world-view. The spiritual and the intellectual aspects go hand in hand. Training imparted to a Muslim must be such that faith is infused into the whole of his personality and must create an emotional attachment to Islam which enables him to follow the Quran and the *Sunnah* and to be governed by the Islamic system of values. Thus, when Islam becomes the sole religious authority, suppression of alternative beliefs is naturally justified. Moreover, when this procedure is adopted as the conclusive educational norm, it inevitably has an impact on the legitimate operation of the conscience. Conscience, as was mentioned earlier, is not infallible; it can lapse because it is culturally conditioned. When a coercive authority (particularly an erroneous one) is applied without allowing the student a free use of his own moral judgement, it inevitably leads to his conscience being brought into captivity.

What is the role of the mosque in Islamic society?

The place and the role of the mosque also contribute to the development and conditioning of the individual in Muslim society. It was suggested earlier that the integration of worship with social and political life was characteristic of the early Islamic community. The first centre for worship in Islam was the mosque of Muhammad at Medina. The importance accorded to this sacred site derives from the fact that the Quran commands all Muslims to turn their eyes and hearts towards it: 'Whencesoever thou comest forth, turn thy face toward the Inviolable Place of worship' (2:150). Moreover, the third caliph, Uthman, said, 'I heard the messenger of Allah say: whoever builds a mosque desiring thereby Allah's pleasure, Allah builds for him the like of it in paradise.'[22]

In addition to its important historical and religious role, Muslims have paid special care to the social and intellectual significance of the mosque as a place from which the message of Islam emerges. In a recent film by the Smithsonian World with the title *Islam*, the narrator made a perceptive remark in describing the significance of the architecturally flat design of the mosque in contrast to the towering sanctuary of a church: 'The word "mosque" means a place of prostration; that is what Muslims do. They hug the earth — they are earthbound, their concern is focused on the here and now. The horizontal design of the mosque is indicative of this earthly concern. This is a very different idea architecturally from the upward reach of the cathedral. This is important to understand, for Islam is a religion that seeks to establish its rule here on earth rather than wait for the eschaton. The mosque and the marketplace are always together.'

Furthermore, from the beginning of Muhammad's mission he used the mosque as a place for religious indoctrination. His pedagogy was based on the absolute authority of the Quran and the tradition. Later generations followed Muhammad's model by establishing the Sunni religious schools *(madrasah)*, as we mentioned earlier (see pp. 161-2), which are connected closely with the mosques. Among such schools is the renowned Al-Azhar in Egypt, which continues to be the voice of the Muslim conscience and the seat of religious learning throughout the Muslim world.

How are Muslims instructed in the mosque?

The Friday sermon in the mosque, or *khutbah* (خطبة), delivered by the imam is usually crafted carefully and charged with a strong emotional appeal to Islamic principles. However, it often addresses the current political and social issues facing the Muslim community both locally and globally. Among the recurring themes in the Friday sermons are the legacy of Muhammad, the supremacy of Islamic ethics over those of the West, national political problems, the Palestinian situation,

appeals to the past glory of Islamic civilization and passionate calls for the rebuilding of the Islamic empire.

Since they are aware of the power and authority that the mosque exerts over the masses, it is not unusual for political leaders in our day to try to win the approval of the imams. Therefore, it is customary for heads of states in the Middle East to make occasional appearances in the mosques.

What is the sacred law?

Ellis Nelson, a noted writer and speaker on the issue of conscience, describes Protestantism after its break with the Roman Catholic Church as a 'religion of conscience'. It returned the responsibility for the Christian life to the individual.[23] By comparison, if Protestantism is a religion of conscience, Islam can be called a religion of law. As we observed earlier, Islam is both religion and law, encompassing all facets of both spiritual and temporal matters relating to the community, or *Ummah*.

From the early stages of its development, two main sources of authority were adopted: the Quran and the *Sunnah* of the prophet who served as God's spokesman, thereby performing the triple function of administrator, judge and executive.

As time progressed and Muslims found that the Quran and the *Sunnah* were no longer sufficient to address all the contemporary issues relating to the life of the community, two more authorities were introduced. The first is *ijma* (اجماع), meaning 'consensus'. It is based on the collective opinions of the 'jurists', *fuqaha* (فقهاء), and the 'learned', *ulama* (علامة). This branch was developed soon after the death of Muhammad, and continues to be a guiding principle for the application of the *Shariah*.

The second is analogical reasoning, or deduction, known as *al-qiyas* (القياس). These four sources (Quran, *Sunnah*, consensus and analogical reasoning) became the canonical pillars on which the sacred *Shariah* law stood.

What are the different schools of law in Islam?

Four orthodox Sunni schools of law were developed to ensure the correct application of the Quran and traditions (i.e,, the teachings of the prophet).

The first is the *Malikiyya* (مالكية), or Malikites, named after the Islamic jurist Malik Anas (d. 845), the Imam of Medina. He regarded the tradition of the prophet as binding and authoritative, superseding all human judgements.

The second school is the *Hanafiyyah* (حانفيّة), or Hanafites. It grew out of the teachings of Abu Hanifa (699–767). Like the other schools of Sunni Islam, the Hanafiyyah acknowledge the Quran and the deeds of the prophet as the primary sources of law.

The third school is the *Hanbalia* (حنبليّة), or Hanbalites, founded by Ahmad Hanbal (780–855). It recognizes no other sources than the Quran and the *Sunnah* of the prophet. It is hostile to speculative theology, innovations and Sufism.

Among Hanbal's work is the famed encyclopaedia of tradition
containing over 28,000 traditions.

The fourth is the school of Shafiiyya (شافعيّة), or Shafites. It
is connected with al-Shafii (767–820), a respected Islamic
imam and jurist. He was a great enemy of the scholastic di-
vines, and most of his writings were intended to contradict
the absurdities which they propounded. He was said to have
been the first to reduce the science of jurisprudence into a
regular system and to make a systematic collection of
traditions.

What are the implications of Muslim devotion to the law and tradition?

The Sunnis' preoccupation with preserving traditions and living by the letter of the law is not new. Several reasons might
be suggested to explain why this should be so.

In the first place, they are naturally conservative and traditional. These are two distinctive traits of Arabs, which can be
traced back to the pre-Islamic era, as we noted earlier.

Secondly, the majority of Muslims, particularly the Sunni,
believe that the Shariah law is sanctioned by Allah, demanding absolute and unconditional obedience to his decrees
(Quran 45:18). Thus, it is natural for a Muslim to equate allegiance to the Shariah with allegiance to Allah.

Bavinck argues that the tendency to religious legalism
gradually but ultimately pushes God out of our lives.[24] He
goes on to warn that 'This tendency to bury God under the
law appeared to be extremely strong in Israel in the period
after the exile. There then arose gradually the phenomenon of
Pharisaism that is well known to us... In Islam the danger of a
legalistic religion has been extreme from the beginning. The
Fikh [Muslim theology], the doctrine of duties, has for centuries constituted the very heart of Muslim theological
thought. Islam is characterized by a theocratic awareness, and

these theocratic ideals are accompanied by a strong emphasis upon the obligation of the believer. Anyone who has experienced this piety in practice knows how easily Allah is reduced to a distant, unapproachable concept... Also here again the word "I" threatens to engulf the full intensity of religion, and Allah remains only as the lawgiver and the final rewarder.'[25]

Thirdly, following the Jewish precedent, Islam is no different from most of the Semitic religions in its orientation and legalism.

A fourth reason can be found in Muslims' fixation with guidance as a means of salvation and with discerning Allah's will in order to be 'rightly guided' — a phrase repeated many times in the Quran.

Thus, an elaborate system of *Shariah* law, or legal system, is constructed out of the written and the oral traditions in order to provide concrete injunctions to guide the actions of Muslim Sunni believers and govern their religious, political and social life. This *Shariah* has become 'more than a set of rules; it entails a whole mentality and a way of life which when fully adhered to, permeates the minds, actions, and the feelings of the Muslims'.[26] This is because Muslims make no attempt to separate religion from state. Islam is not only a religion of the mind, soul and heart, but it also represents an all-encompassing culture. It enshrines a theocentric society in which all facets of life are focused on Allah. The call for the application of the *Shariah*, however, is not confined to fundamentalist movements, as we are led to believe by the media. The former Minister of Petroleum of Saudi Arabia, an orthodox Sunni and a scholar in the Islamic Sunni law, after asserting the absolute validity of the *Shariah*, charged the Muslim community with these words: '*Shariah* has a binding authority on every Moslem, and he is obligated to follow and employ it.'[27]

When this scenario persists it naturally becomes a binding force. Consequently, its influence goes beyond shaping the individual and collective moral and ethical decisions and has an impact on the will that ultimately stands behind these decisions.

An example from the history of Islam shows what happens when an individual endeavours to liberate his conscience from the bondage of law and tradition by calling people to find God in their own hearts rather than in tradition and dogma. Husein Ben Mansur (857–922), an Arab Muslim Sunni mystic and theologian known by the name al-Halaj, became a martyr for his convictions. He roamed Iraq preaching against the traditional religious establishment. He was imprisoned by the authorities and crucified like his hero Jesus, whom he considered the great liberator.

For the majority of Muslim Sunni, their sacred law, the *Shariah*, is the only religious, moral and ethical compass that man needs in this life. Such conviction results in definite consequences not only for the formation and education of the conscience, but also for the potential desensitization of it, particularly in relation to the message of the gospel.

Why is the Arabic language considered sacred?

The impact of the Arabic language upon both the individual and collective psyche is a topic that merits serious consideration. The relationship between the Arabic language and the Arabs is a phenomenon that must not be overlooked, particularly by those who wish to understand and relate to Arab Muslims.

The classical language of Arabic, which is known among the Arabs as *Lisan al-Arab* (لسان العرب), the Arabic tongue, has become one of the world's great languages. In a conference of the Arab Academies held in Damascus, the Arab linguist Ajlani addressed the delegates in the following words: 'Your work is not only a scientific-cultural task, but also a nationalist task. Today you are more than judges, because you are setting the foundation of the great Arab government *(dawlah)*.

Arabic calligraphy is more than artistic design. From the beginning Muslims used it on a spiritual level to transcend cultural boundaries. The Arabic calligraphy seen here represents the Muslim *shahadah* ('No god by Allah and Muhammad is his prophet') while depicting a person prostrating himself before Allah.

No one is able to separate the life of the language or its future from that of community *(Ummah)*. Our language, gentlemen, unites the message *(resalah)* of heaven with that of earth. In it are eternal glory, eternal prose, and the Quran. It is like a flag behind which soldiers march.'[28]

In the Arab world it has reached the position of absolute religious and cultural dominance. Muslims in general, and Arab Muslims in particular, claim that Arabic is the most sacred language of all. According to the Quran and tradition, the Arabic language is believed by Muslims to be not only the sole language of the Quran and the prophet, but also the one spoken by Allah and used in utterances to Muhammad by the angel Gabriel (cf. Quran 2:97; 26:193; 12:2; 16:103).

How does the Arabic language contribute to the national identity?

Most philologists agree that language constitutes a bond and fosters a sense of affinity among people who speak the same tongue. While this is true of Arab Muslims, it goes one step further. Stephen Neill rightly says that Arabic is 'one of the great bonds of unity in the Islamic world'.[29] Raphael Patai asserts that there is a pervading consciousness of being one nation, irrespective of the number of political units into which this one nation is broken up. He attributes this consciousness to the Arabic language: 'There can be no doubt that the Arabic language is the most potent factor in both the creation and the maintenance of the Arab nation, Arab unity and Arab brotherhood. In the non-Arabic-speaking world … there are several groups of countries in which one and the same language is spoken. However, only in the case of Arabic is the language the factor that defines and determines membership in the national aggregate.'[30]

This 'membership in the national aggregate' is determined, basically, by the Islamic world-view and the Arabic language. Islam and the Arabic language are the two axioms that determine the concept of *Ummah* as set out in the Quran. These two axioms are considered by the majority of Arab Muslims to be two inseparable aspects of one thing. For instance, Arabs during the colonial period vehemently resisted the attempts of the colonialists to replace Arabic — the language of their holy book — with the English or the French language. Although the Arab world was divided into several nations during the colonial period, and still is today, each has developed a national consciousness and possesses a cultural cohesiveness which is expressed in a common language. The famed Arab philologist Al-Tha'alibi (d. 1038) said, 'Whoever loves the prophet loves the Arabs, and whoever loves the Arabs loves the Arabic language in which the best of books was revealed. Whomsoever God has guided to Islam … believes that Muhammad is the best of prophets ... that the Arabs are the best of people ... and that Arabic is the best of languages.[31]

How does the Arabic language contribute to the cultural identity?

In addition to being a unifying factor on the national level, the Arabic language has continued to facilitate the development of culture in a unique fashion on the basis of the belief that the language itself has intrinsic sacred value. This deeply held belief is considered by non-Muslims to be incompatible with the view that languages are man-made.

This religious element (which will be discussed in more detail in the following pages) must be kept in mind as we consider the Arabic language in relation to its culture. Historically, for the Arabs, veneration of their language led to the veneration of the Arab culture itself, which was transmitted through the medium of language to become the culture of most of the Middle East and North Africa.

Perhaps no other peoples in the world manifest the same enthusiastic admiration for literary expression, and respond to the spoken or written word, as do the Arabs. Research shows that there is broad agreement among philologists, orientalists, and Arab scholars *(ulama)* that Arabic has a peculiar aesthetic stimulus upon Arabs, as perhaps no other language has upon people. The power of its rhetorical expression has gripped even some Western orientalists who learned it. Poets have enlisted it to fascinate their listeners, storytellers to grip their audience and politicians to sway the masses. The one who is able to master the Arabic language and the art of its delivery will ultimately captivate the masses.

An example of this phenomenon is the former President of Egypt, Gamal Abdel Nasser. His charismatic oratorical delivery of extemporaneous speeches using emphatic language and hyperbolic repetitions captivated millions of people throughout the Arab World. His skilled use of the language and his appeal to the emotions of the masses made him a national hero, which continued even after the disastrous defeat, for which he was mainly responsible, in the Six Day War with Israel in 1967.

In his novel, *Days of Dust*, Barakat made one of the characters say in an angry and reflective mood following the Arab defeat in the Six Day War, 'Words are the only weapon we know how to use. Our houses are of words, our castles are of dreams, our dreams are of words. Words are what we export. And we have an odd relationship with them: we invent them, but in the long run they gain control over us and recreate us as they wish. We eat words, we drink words. We live in words. We kill ourselves with words.'[32]

How does the Arabic language contribute to the religious identity?

From what has been said, it is apparent that the Arabs have distinguished themselves by the highest linguistic achievement. The Arabic language has become the measuring rod by which they have determined their national and cultural identity. Moreover, as this section will show, Arabic has come to be venerated to an even greater degree because of its close and intimate relationship with Islam. Abu Ubaydah (d. 825), the well-known Muslim philologist, made his famous remark, 'Whoever pretends that there is in the Quran anything other than Arabic language has made a serious charge against God.'[33] This intimate relationship between language and religion is a phenomenon unparalleled in other religions.

The fundamental distinction between Islam and Christianity is that the 'Word / Logos' is God's self-revelation in Christ — in other words, the incarnate Word and deity are intrinsically connected. The God of eternity became known in the

Christ of history. On the other hand, to the Muslim the revealer (i.e., Allah) remains hidden and the 'logos / Allah's
word' turned into nothing more than a set of rules and regulations written originally in Arabic on tablets kept in heaven.
As we have already seen, Muslims hold that the Arabic Quran
is the exact replica of a prototype of eternally preserved tablets in heaven. These tablets are said to have been communicated verbatim to the prophet Muhammad (Quran 43:3;
85:21-22; 56:76-77). This belief, along with the linguistic
flawlessness, rhetorical eloquence and literary style of the
Quran, is held by Muslims to constitute a miracle. Therefore,
no man can construct a book like it. It is considered authentic
only in its original Arabic language.

An Arab Muslim reveres the Quran because he believes it
to have been revealed directly from Allah in his own Arabic
tongue. He sees it as being more than the word of Allah and
more than a linguistic miracle that gave concrete expression
to, and protected, his mother tongue. It provides a code for
personal and collective conduct, the basis for religious, intellectual, social and political life and for a complete world-view.
I was once asked, 'What is this charm that some Muslims
wear?' Because of their belief that the Quran originated in
heaven, that it was inscribed in tablets that are eternally preserved and could not have been influenced by any earthly
culture, Muslims attach a divine power to its format including
the Arabic words in which it is written. Consequently certain
verses and words from the Quran are stitched into small
leather pouches sold to members of the public who believe
that the pouch contains magical powers to protect from ill-
ness, barrenness, danger, etc.

What are some of the implications?

We need to be aware of the deep attachment the Arabs have
to their language. In a recent conversation with an Arab

Muslim friend, his objection to the deity of Christ came to the fore. Among the many proofs that I attempted to present was Christ's ability to perform miracles. My friend suddenly interjected with deep conviction: 'But the Quran is the greatest miracle there is. No other miracles are needed.' Obviously to him the Quran is more than just a religious book. Although my friend appears to have adapted to Western life, beneath the surface lingers a belief that is ingrained deep in his own conscience from early childhood. Such conditioning makes it naturally inconceivable for him to accept any alternative.

Among the missionaries who went to the Arab countries the ones who saw the most conversions were those who recognized the crucial role that language played in the Arab psyche. Some of the notable men are W. H. Gairdner, Samuel Zwemer, Eli Smith and Van Dyck, who in 1866 published the first complete Arabic Bible. Communicating the gospel to Arabs in their own language can be an important aid for the missionary. Most Arab Muslims believe that the Arabic language is a divinely instituted religious medium, pattern of culture and source of national pride. Accordingly missionaries should aspire to use this medium for effective evangelism and as a means to unlock the minds and hearts of Arabs.

5.
Questions about sharing the faith

Is it true that Muslims are more resistant to the gospel than others?

The Bible says that all people are born resisting the things of God because of the persistent impact of man's sinful nature as a result of the Fall. The apostle Paul says in Romans 1-2 that while the knowledge of God is clearly seen in nature and in man's conscience, man suppresses this knowledge in unrighteousness. The point Paul is making is that man's dilemma results from his corrupted nature and the state of original sin in which he was born. This deviation from truth is a result of deviation from the true faith. However, as we have discussed previously, certain cultural and religious themes in Islamic society make the presentation of the gospel to Muslims more challenging. Thus, finding the right method of approach becomes of the utmost importance.

How did some of the notable missionaries explain Muslim resistance?

A historical survey of the literature from A.D. 675 (the date of the initial witness by John of Damascus to Muslims in the Middle East) to our own day shows two main causes of Islamic resistance to the gospel: religious and cultural / political factors. John of Damascus was perhaps the first to recognize the important role that religious factors play in Christian-Islamic relations. In *De Fide Orthodoxa*, he argued that Islam is a Christian heresy, and he proposed an apologetic model for refuting the theological objections of Muslims.

Following in the footsteps of John of Damascus, Peter Venerabilis, an abbot of Cluny in the twelfth century, took up his pen to defend Christianity against the theological scepticism of Islam. He was the first to translate the Quran into Latin, and demonstrated that the Quran testifies against itself. He challenged the church to defend the faith against Muslim attacks and to win Muslims by proving the integrity of the biblical truth. Furthermore, he assumed that a political reason lay behind the Islamic resistance to the gospel. His own words reflect how the Crusades contributed to the antagonism on the part of Muslims: 'I came to meet Muslims not with arms, but with words, not by force, but by reason, not by hatred but in love.' Up to this point, most of the contacts between Muslims and those claiming to represent Christianity had been in the context of war. According to most missionaries to Islam, including Raymond Lull, Samuel Zwemer, Kenneth Cragg and others, this historical tension makes it natural for Muslims to interpret the authentic message of Christianity in the light of the historical practices of the church.

It has also been suggested that the ailing theological and spiritual condition of the Middle-Eastern church from the time of the rise of Islam in Arabia to the nineteenth century was an added factor in the legacy of antagonism and mistrust between Islam and Christianity.

Raymond Lull's (1235–1315) approach to Islam reveals three assumptions underlying his understanding of Islamic resistance to the gospel. First, this resistance is based upon theological scepticism with regard to the claims of Christianity. Secondly, Lull insists that pervasive ignorance among Muslims about the Christian faith is a contributory factor. He therefore worked to produce Christian literature to promote greater awareness among Muslims about the true nature of the gospel. Thirdly, assuming the same position as Peter Venerabilis, Lull acknowledges the role of the Crusades in reinforcing the alienation of Muslims from Christianity.

In contrast with the previous assessments, W. H. Gairdner (1872–1928) and Samuel Zwemer (1867–1952), in their enquiry into the nature of Islamic resistance to Christianity, amplify the role of cultural factors, in addition to advancing religious and political reasons for this resistance. Gairdner's considerable writings show his commitment to understanding the ways of Muslims in relation to faith. He seeks to use apologetics to help Muslims see the error of their ways.

While Gairdner argues for a reconstruction of theology, Zwemer argues that it is the overwhelming Islamic religious system that is at the root of Islamic resistance. He insists that the real challenge to missionaries is how to make the gospel penetrate effectively Islam's rigid system of beliefs and practices.

Hendrik Kraemer (1888–1965) describes Islamic resistance to Christianity not in cultural or religious terms, but rather in socio-religious ones. Islam, he writes, excels all other religions in creating in its adherents a feeling of absolute superiority. From this self-consciousness of Islam is born that stubborn refusal to open the mind towards another spiritual world.

Although Kenneth Cragg (b. 1913) is more sympathetic and accommodating towards Islam than Kraemer, he agrees that the major factor that must be considered by missionaries in relating to Islam is 'the sense of being a Muslim' and 'the deep sense of Islamic past glorious history'. This deep sense of belonging to the same religious community and culture expresses itself deeply in the mind and soul.

Christy Wilson finds a multiplicity of reasons for Islamic resistance and for the relative paucity of conversions. He articulates seven reasons why Islam holds its members with a grip that is almost impossible to break:

> *1. Historical.* Muhammad took the blood relationship and devotion to the Arabic tribe, which was considered the most sacred and binding of all ties, and substituted the religious relationship in the tribe.
>
> *2. Ethical.* When a person became a Muslim, the Quranic law was accepted as authoritative and became the rule of life.
>
> *3. Social.* It has been noted among many students of Islam that it is a social system as well as a religious and political one.
>
> *4. Communal.* The community of Islam is a body, and if one member splits off, that member is considered 'dead'. Thus schism became a cardinal transgression and radical sin.
>
> *5. Psychological.* The great body of the population in the Muslim lands is satisfied with the status quo. They make no attempt to reach an understanding faith, but rather follow customs as they exist.
>
> *6. Irrational.* The urge of solidarity comes from a primitive social instinct rather than from reasoned lines of conduct.
>
> *7. Economic.* Any conversion to another religion means a loss of the means of livelihood and one's economic place in the community.[1]

To dialogue or not to dialogue?

Dialogue between Christianity and Islam is not new. As we saw in chapter 1, from the time of its inception, Islam was surrounded by a number of professedly Christian sects which were scattered through the land of Arabia. Unfortunately, these various factions contributed much towards Muslim misunderstanding and misconceptions regarding the nature of biblical Christianity.

However, a number of people were heavily engaged in dialogue with Muslims trying to undo the damage that had been done. Perhaps these dialogues can be described in three categories: the first, a clash of polemics; the second, a clash of swords; the third, a clash of concerns.

How do we define dialogue?

People define dialogue in different ways on the basis of their own particular commitments. However, generally speaking, dialogue includes communication between two disputing parties for the sake of clarification, learning and persuasion — though persuasion is not adopted all the time, as we shall see in the following examples. *The Evangelical Dictionary of World Missions* remarks that in dialogue on religious pluralism, conviction on its nature and use appear to settle into three positions: first, the pluralist position, which rejects traditional views on biblical revelation; secondly, extreme conservatism, which calls for the rejection of dialogue in favour of proclamation of the gospel; and, thirdly, the more centrist view which affirms dialogue as a means of understanding and communication without rejecting biblical revelation.

As Christians, how should we approach dialogue?

Indeed, relations between Christians and Muslims today are at a crossroads. In the last few years we have witnessed a dramatic increase in contact, at both religious and political levels, between Islam and some form of Christianity. Certainly, the modern media and the use of the Internet make interaction an unavoidable reality. The question is not whether or not to dialogue, but how. How can we safeguard the absolute integrity of biblical truth while engaging in dialogue? Several questions are raised here:

1. Can this be accomplished by focusing on finding common ground with other faiths, and by exploring some co-operative ways to face the social, political and moral problems in the world? Can we say with certainty that dialogue which confines itself to the establishment of goodwill and healthy social relations is a Christian distinctive? Is it true that any social organization can attempt to perform the same task without having to be called a Christian organization? Is this compatible with Jesus' Great Commission (Matt. 28:18-20), or with the biblical instruction to 'contend earnestly for the faith which was once for all delivered to the saints' (Jude 3, NKJV), or the warnings against those who deny the gospel truth? (see 2 John 7-11).

2. How can we enter into an effective dialogue with other religions, such as Islam, which denies the core distinctives of the Christian faith, including the nature of God, the way of salvation, the cross, the death of Christ, the resurrection, the Trinity and the deity of Christ? Moreover, Islam is more than a religion that is concerned about the moral state of man and his destiny. It is a total system of life that strives to offer laws and regulations in all areas of life — socially, economically, politically and religiously. Do these non-

negotiable commitments make any attempt at dialogue a futile endeavour?

3. How can we enter into an effective dialogue with a religion such as Islam, which claims to be the only valid and final revelation from Allah? To what extent can we expect its adherents to suspend or surrender such beliefs?

4. How can we apply Proverbs 26:4-5 in dialogue? It tells us:

> Do not answer a fool according to his folly,
>   or you will be like him yourself.
> Answer a fool according to his folly,
>   or he will be wise in his own eyes.

5. Can we lose sight of the biblical distinctives without being led into syncretism (i.e., assimilating different and antithetical doctrines)?

6. Consider the examples of Christ in John chapters 3 and 4, the apostle Paul in Acts 13 and 17 and Peter in Acts 2 and 10. When they encountered those of other faiths, were they not consistently mindful that the objective of dialogue must ultimately be the proclamation of the truth?

7. The Bible points us to the most potent weapon in our arsenal as we encounter other religions: 'The Word of God is living and active. Sharper than any double-edged sword, it penetrates even to dividing soul and spirit, joints and marrow; it judges the thoughts and attitudes of the heart' (Heb. 4:12). We are forced to ask, can dialogue downplay this central element in our warfare? If so, would proclamation be more effective than dialogue in connection with this biblical promise?

A cursory reading of these questions might lead some to assume that the writer disputes the validity of any forms of dialogue. Of course, this is not the case. On the contrary, because of the peculiar nature of Islam and its culture, as we have already seen, it becomes incumbent upon us to understand this target group in order to communicate the gospel more effectively. This necessitates learning, listening, respect and forbearance. History tells us that those claiming to represent Christianity and Islam have often met on the battlefield. Such encounters resulted in countless sufferings, misconceptions and longstanding antagonism. More specifically, in the words of Hendrik Kraemer, 'Through all the ages Islam has been, in relation to the missionary efforts of the Christian Church, the teacher of patience.' Our manner, as we speak with Muslims, should reflect the biblical maxim: 'A gentle answer turns away wrath, but a harsh word stirs up anger' (Prov. 15:1).

While 'speaking the truth in love' (Eph. 4:15) must be our objective, this entails commitment. There is more to truth than articulation. Truth demands living and obeying, commitment to Christ and God's absolute truth. Such a commitment must penetrate and inspire all of our activities, including sometimes asking serious questions, as has been suggested above. The divine model of communication and dialogue is redemptive in nature. The incarnation and death of the Lord Jesus Christ is the outworking of God's purpose to reconcile men to himself by dealing with their personal sin, which involves the removal of their objective guilt.

What are some of the barriers to Muslim evangelism?

While only the Holy Spirit can penetrate the heart, the truth of the gospel must proceed via the mind. It must have a road map through which the presenter can articulate the truth convincingly and effectively. We shall therefore briefly examine the following questions: 'What occurs in the mind of the Muslim when he is exposed to the gospel? What are the barriers and objections that hinder the transmission of the gospel?' Although a brief allusion has already been made to this discussion, the treatment of it in the following pages is more systematic and representative.

1. Religious barriers

The word for 'religion' in Islam, *Din* (دين), basically means 'absolute submission'. In *Surah* 16:52 we read, 'Religion is his [Allah's] and it is to him that submission must always be made.' As a system of belief, Muslims are warned not to accept any other religion except that of Islam (Quran 3:83,85). A number of factors are ingrained in the minds of Muslims including the following:

Islam as the final word from Allah

One of the inconsistencies of Islam is that, while it adopts many ideas and theological truths from Judaism and Christianity, Muslims are convinced that they have nothing to do with these 'People of the Book' (Christians and Jews), except for what has been written about them in the Quran. From the beginning of his mission, Muhammad was convinced of the total reliability of the Torah and the Gospels (3:50; 5:68; 10:94). This was one of the reasons that Muhammad believed in all the prophets of the Bible (3:84; 3:3-4). However, Muslims claim that Muhammad is the final messenger, *Rasul* (رسول), and prophet, *Nabi* (نبي).

The claims of Muhammad to be the final authority (4:65) come into direct collision with the Christian affirmation that, 'in these last days', God 'has spoken to us by his Son, whom he appointed heir of all things, and through whom he made the universe' (Heb. 1:2). Nevertheless, the Quran asserts in the clearest terms that Jesus is the mighty apostle of God. Muslims hold Jesus in the highest reverence, and the Quran describes him as having been miraculously born of a virgin, as a miracle-worker and as being sinless.

Islam as a way of life

We have seen earlier that Islam is all-encompassing. It permeates the religious, social, judicial and political systems of its adherents. While Christianity proclaims the revelation of a divine Saviour, the person Jesus Christ, Islam proclaims the revelation of the divine law and will. This revelation enshrines all institutions of society. Although there is a progressive tendency on the part of some Islamic states to move away from strict application of the Islamic law, the fact remains that for a Muslim to accept Christ is, in the final analysis, to reconstruct his whole life and adopt a totally new world-view. This radical adjustment is not an easy task. To ignore the relationship between religion and the state would be a grave risk in a culture where every facet of life is regulated by religious laws.

Religious saturation

We have seen earlier the powerful influence of the religious education of children in the Muslim world. It suffices to say, however, that this religious tutelage continues until the age of maturity. Once the child has learned the basic Islamic practices, he is expected to be loyal to the faith and defend it with all his might. Islam becomes a way of life; a person forgets that he is anything but a Muslim. Freethinking is strongly discouraged. For a Muslim to question his or her faith is almost unthinkable and is considered a sign of rebellion not only against the social norm, but against the will of Allah.

Simplicity of creed and faith

Muslims claim that one of the strengths of Islam lies in the fact that it is a religion without any mythology. They allege that the teachings of the Quran are very simple, intelligible and rational. For Muslims these characteristics are the reason why Islam is appealing. The basic articles of faith reflect this alleged simplicity (see the question, 'What do Muslims believe?', pp. 90-97). Muhammad's goal was a simple and appealing religion, oriented to a salvation which can be achieved by one's own works.

Atonement in the gospel is the gracious sovereign act of God to deal with the cardinal human problem — our sin against the holy God, which shattered the relationship between the Creator and his creation. God accomplished the way of restoration through the death of Christ. However, Islam claims that man is created good by nature and able to atone for his mistakes and sins by following the guidance given in the Quran and by performing certain duties: i.e., confession, prayer, giving, fasting and the pilgrimage to Mecca. Thus the whole concept of the need for, and the way of, salvation is new to Muslims and is often approached with a considerable degree of unease.

The view of Christianity as being an outdated religion

The advent of Muhammad is explained in the Quran as that of a messenger sent by Allah to restore all other religions to their original state, namely Islam. Thus the claim that Islam is the final religion abrogates the earlier revelations. This indoctrination makes it natural for a Muslim to question the validity of other religions, including the teaching of the Bible.

2. Family and social barriers

The foregoing discussion of certain cultural themes shows the potency of these factors in relation to the gospel. From early childhood, youngsters are encouraged to cultivate a strong loyalty to their immediate family. This home-centred focus is more than just a biological and social unit; it is more or less a religious community. Therefore, this strong family affinity demands a unified religious allegiance. Consequently, any conversion from Islam to Christianity is considered by the Muslim community as a serious matter and often results in harsh persecution.

It is not often realized that national Christians, born into Christian families and belonging to a regional church, which may possibly date back to the early Christian era, have a legal right to live in an Islamic state as Christians. Muhammad tolerated them to some extent as 'the People of the Book'. But for converts who have forsaken Islam there is no mercy. Allah's law, the *Shariah*, demands their punishment. They may be offered the opportunity to repent and return to Islam under the guidance of a Muslim religious leader. But if they do not consent, they are liable to face severe penalties, including death.

3. Linguistic barriers

The term 'linguistic barriers' does not refer to the process of transmitting and receiving information, nor to the decoding and encoding of messages. It has to do with Islamic claims that the Arabic language is inherently divine and constitutes the living heart of Arabic nationalism. The Arabic language of the Quran is believed to be inseparable from the character of Allah. It is an extension of Allah's attributes. Therefore, the language itself is considered to be intrinsically celestial and holy. It is known as the sole language of the Quran. *Surah* 16:105 speaks of the Quran as an Arabic revelation that demands total obedience by all people.

Thus this alleged superiority is based first of all on the claim of a divine, literal and mechanical transmission of each word of the Quran. Any criticism of the Quran is an unforgivable crime, according to Islamic fundamentalist belief.

The fact that the Bible was written in more than one language (Hebrew, Aramaic and Greek) is considered a sign of weakness. Some Muslims go further and claim that the multiplicity of the biblical languages is proof that Christians have altered its original format and content.

4. Theological barriers

Perhaps the greatest stumbling block to the evangelism of Muslims is found in their theological objections to the most fundamental truths of Scripture. The doctrines of the Trinity, the nature of man, the means of atonement and the authority of the Bible all come into direct conflict with traditional Islamic theology. This has been a cause of great concern among missionaries and has caused them to seek divine guidance as to how to answer Muslim objections.

The following tables set out the major Islamic beliefs in a number of important doctrinal areas and contrast these with the biblical affirmations. We start with a brief contrast followed by an expanded discussion, leading to a closer look at the person of Christ as seen in the Bible.

Christianity	Islam
The Trinity	No Trinity
There is only one true and living God, Father, Son and Holy Spirit — three persons in the unity of the Godhead, equal in power and glory.	There is a definite emphasis on the oneness, or Tawheed (توحيد), of Allah, who has no partners.
Man is fallen	No fall of man
By the sin of our first parents, they fell from their original righteousness and fellowship with God. All humanity is guilty in Adam, the head of the human race (Rom. 5:12).	The Quran states that Adam was created weak; his moral disposition remained the same as it was prior to the Fall (4:28). Thus, sin did not affect human nature.

Christianity	Islam
The cross	**No cross**
Sin necessitates salvation, including the entire plan of redemption — the incarnation, the death and the resurrection of Christ.	According to Islamic argumentation, since sin did not affect human nature, there is no need for a divine act of reconciliation (i.e., the cross).
Scripture	**Scripture**
God revealed his will in the Bible, which is the very Word of God given by inspiration of God the Holy Spirit to be the rule of faith and life for all believers: 'All Scripture is God-breathed and is useful for teaching, rebuking, correcting and training in righteousness, so that the man of God may be thoroughly equipped for every good work' (2 Tim. 3:16-17).	The Quran is considered the final revelation from Allah. However, it testifies to the validity and authority of both the Torah, Zabour (Psalms) and the Gospel, while at the same time it charges both the Jews and the Christians with corrupting their Scriptures (Quran 2:75,101; 3:70,78,187; 4:46). It suffices to say here that Muslim scholars have not provided cogent proof to justify this claim.
The Day of Judgement	**The Day of Judgement**
The salvation of sinners is wholly of God's grace through Jesus Christ. When Jesus returns in power and glory, he will raise the dead to judge them. Those who have not repented of their sinfulness and trusted him, he will consign to hell for ever; those who are his own, he will take to be with him in eternal joy in heaven.	The Arabic term *Akhirah* (أخيرة), meaning 'Last Day', refers to the appointed day on which Allah will judge people according to their deeds. Two main conditions must be met: belief in the creeds and performance of good works (2:25; 29:58; 4:57). Thus, if more than 50% of a person's actions are good, he or she is considered righteous and sent to Paradise, while the wicked are sent to hell.
Heaven — fellowship with God	**Paradise — no fellowship with God**
The Bible speaks of heaven as the eternal abode of the triune God. It is a holy place, full of the perfect	The Muslim concept of Paradise, *Fardous* (فردوس), is described in sensual and physical terms. The

Christianity	Islam
experience of God's people enjoying full fellowship with him. It is a place of utter beauty prepared for those who love God, (I Cor. 2:9); it is a place of holiness, love, joy and eternal praises and service to God the Father, God the Son and God the Holy Spirit (Isa. 35:8; I Cor. 3:13; Rev. 21:3).	Quran is replete with details about the pleasures that await believers. These include beautiful virgins, fruit, food and drink, wine, dishes and goblets made of gold and everything the heart could desire (37; 56; 74; 83).

Christianity and Islam — an expanded contrast

The following tables are intended to further clarify the theological barriers to evangelism of Muslims and provide a basic answer to Muslim objections.

The Trinity	No Trinity
The following are brief propositions designed to explain and clarify the biblical doctrine of the Trinity to our Muslim friends:	The majority of Muslims believe that the concept of the Trinity is incompatible with monotheism. The Arabic word for the Trinity is *Tathlith* (تثليث), meaning 'three'.
1.The oneness of God is a biblical characteristic (Gen. 1:1; Exod. 6:3; Deut. 6:4; Isa. 45:5; John 5:44; Eph. 4:5; I Tim. 1:17).	Prior to his death Muhammad gave this command: 'Believe, therefore, in God and his apostles and say not three.'
For Muslims, believing in other gods is blasphemous. Those who commit such a sin will die in a state of unbelief (Quran 47:34). This has very serious missiological implications for Christian workers among Muslims. Since Muslims mistakenly equate the Christian concept of the Trinity with the idea of 'Shirk' (the	It is important to note that Muhammad and his followers never had a true conception of the biblical doctrine of the Trinity. Muhammad, as we saw in chapter 1, gained much of his understanding of Christianity from heretical Christian and Jewish sects, in addition to other pagan religions.

The Trinity	No Trinity
association of other gods with Allah) it is of the utmost importance for the missionary to emphasize and clarify the biblical teaching about the one-ness of God.	Consequently, the authentic biblical concept of the Trinity was misconstrued. Muhammad's reactionary attitude is reflected in the Quran: 'Allah pardoneth not that partners should be ascribed unto him' (4:116). Associating other deities with God, or *Ishrak* (اشراك), is the most heinous of all sins in Islam.
2. Trinity does not mean 'tri-theism' (three gods), such as the Egyptian Triad Osiris, Isis and Horus; or the Hindu Triad of Brahma, Vishnu and Shiva; or the pre-Islamic Triad, the Manat, al-Lat and al-Uzza. Nor does it refer, as Muslims wrongly assume, to Jesus being the son of Mary and to Allah being his father in a physical sense. Contrary to the Islamic Unitarian view of Allah, who not only transcends, but is totally detached from his creation, the God of the Bible is personal in nature — one God who reveals himself as Father, Son and Holy Spirit, three eternal persons equal in essence and glory: one God the Father (I Cor. 8:6), one God the Son (Col. 2:9) and one God the Holy Spirit (Act. 5:3-4).	Here are a few representative questions Muslims ask, including Christ's relationship with the Trinity. All will be answered in later discussion:
	1. Since Christians say that Jesus is fully God and fully man, how can the infinite be finite?
	2. How could Jesus be God and the Son of God at the same time?
	3. How could Jesus be God if he was called 'Son of Man'?
3.As finite beings dealing with the infinite, we need not presume that we can give a full explanation of the Trinity by mere natural human reason. As someone said, 'We must distinguish between apprehension and comprehension. We can know what God is, without knowing all he is. We can touch the earth while not being able to embrace it in our arms.' We can know the facts of	4. How could God be three in one and one in three at the same time?
	5. Some Muslims today borrow an argument against the Trinity from some of the cults, such as the Jehovah's Witnesses. It goes something like this: 'John 1:1 says "In the beginning was the Word, and the Word was with God, and the Word was God." The Greek word

The Trinity	No Trinity
electricity, life and human biological growth without being able to comprehend the functional dynamic of the exact process. Muslims often demand an objective and scientific evidence for the Trinity. Yet, this demand places Muslim theologians in a self-contradictory situation. Muslim statements about Allah, creation, miracles and the Day of Judgement are to be taken by faith; there is no one scientific objective formula to provide proof of these. Moreover, as we mentioned earlier, Muslims believe that both the Quran and Allah are eternal (see pp. 101-3). To that we ask the questions: 'How can we allege that two distinct eternal entities exist together? How can we account for such dualism?'	for the first occurrence of God is "ho-theos", which means "the God" or "God" with a capital "G", while the Greek word for its second occurrence is "theos", which means "a god" or "god" with a small "g". Is this an inconsistency?' Accordingly, it is crucially important for the missionary to Muslims to refrain from avoiding this subject and to engage in clarification. A few suggestions for explaining the Christian view of the Trinity are listed in the left column.
4. Some Muslims allege that the Trinity is not taught in the Scripture. But the tri-personality of God is clearly taught and revealed in the Bible. Over fifty biblical references refer to the Trinity. Here are a few examples: Gen. 1:26; 2 Sam. 23:2; Matt. 3:16; 28:19; Luke 1:35; John 1:33; Acts 10:36; Rom. 8:9; Eph.1:13; 1 Peter 1:2; 1 John 5;7 (NKJV); Jude 20-21. 5. The church, for two thousand years, has articulated the doctrine of the Trinity in unambiguous terms through the creeds and confessions. The Nicene Creed, the Apostles' Creed,	Do you know that there is actually an allusion to the Trinity in the Quran? Consider this verse which mentions God, Jesus the Messiah and the Holy Spirit: 'O people of the Scripture! Do not exaggerate in your religion nor utter aught concerning Allah save the truth. The Messiah, Jesus son of Mary, was messenger of Allah, and His Word which He conveyed unto Mary, and a Spirit from Him' (4: 171). Now, compare the verse quoted with the Word of God, which was written 600 years before the Quran, as the angel foretells the

The Trinity	No Trinity
the Geneva, Heidelberg and Westminster Confessions all acknowledge the unity of the Godhead in three persons, of one substance, power and glory. These creedal statements are merely a reflection of what is found in the Scriptures. 6. The doctrine of the Trinity is much more than a sublime metaphysical reality. It is an important practical doctrine relating directly to the nature of God and his plans of redemption and salvation. The Father is the source of salvation, the Son achieves redemption and the Holy Spirit applies it. B. B. Warfield maintains that the practical aspect of the Trinity leads to the only cogent understanding of true theism: 'The Trinity does not come to us as an added burden upon our intelligence [as liberals and Muslims claim]; it brings us rather the solution of the deepest and most persistent difficulties in our conception of God as infinite moral being, and illuminates, enriches and elevates all our thoughts of God. It has accordingly become a commonplace to say that Christian theism is the only stable theism. The mind finds it difficult to rest on the idea of an abstract unity for its God; and that the human heart cries out for the living God in whose being there is that fulness of life for which the conception of the Trinity alone provides. By means of this doctrine he [the	birth of Jesus and in so doing speaks of the triunity of God: 'The angel answered, "The Holy Spirit will come upon you, and the power of the Most High will overshadow you. So the holy one to be born will be called the Son of God"' (Luke 1:35). Do you know that pre-Islamic religious cults contributed to Muhammad's misconception of the Christian idea of the Trinity and of what was meant by Christ's being called the Son of God? In fact Muhammad's charge was not directed against orthodox Christianity, since he never read the Bible in his own Arabic language, but against some heretical groups existing in Arabia prior to Islam. Muhammad had to deal with the Jews and various Christian sects including the Nestorians, the Jacobites, the Copts, the Melkites and others. (For more details see the question, 'Where did the confusion in Islam about the Trinity come from?', pp. 19-21). Do you know that, while the Quran includes a number of verses describing Christians as polytheists, it also confirms that Christians are monotheists? Consider this verse: 'And argue not with the people of the Scripture [Christians and Jews] unless it be in a way that

The Trinity	No Trinity
believer] is able to think clearly and consequently of his threefold relation to the saving God, experienced by Him as Fatherly love sending a redeemer, as redeeming love executing redemption, as saving love applying redemption: all manifestations in distinct methods and by distinct agencies of the one seeking and saving love of God.'[2]	is better, save with such of them as do wrong; and say: We believe in that which hath been revealed unto you; our God and your God is one, and unto Him we surrender' (29:46).
7. Some anthropomorphic and natural analogies of the Trinity might be helpful, though they have their limitations. For example, man is often described in terms of a triad: functionally, he has body, soul and spirit. In addition, being created in the image of God, he is capable of relationships. From the beginning, Adam and Eve became one flesh. This unity, likewise, is found in a triad construct in society, consisting of father, mother and child. Additionally, the substance of water, though one element, can be manifested in three forms — liquid, gas and solid. Time is divided into three aspects — past, present and future.	Do you know that Muslims hold that the Arabic Quran is the exact replica of a prototype consisting of tablets which are eternally preserved in heaven, communicated verbatim to the prophet Muhammad? (Quran 43:3; 85:21-22; 56:76-77). This raises a number of questions which are much harder to explain than the biblical teaching about the Trinity. (Find these questions on pages 101-5.)
These are only analogies and are not meant to serve as simple explanations of the Trinity, but are intended to show that when we talk about three persons in the Godhead we mean, not three different gods, but three persons in one, one God in three persons, who are equal in substance and glory.	Do you know that adoration of Mary was practised constantly prior to and during Muhammad's time? The Quran wrongly impugns Christians for believing in three gods. It connects the Trinity with God, Mary and Jesus. It is obvious that this disputation is about tritheism, not the Trinity, and is far removed from the biblical teaching and from historic Christian beliefs as found in the creeds.

The Trinity	No Trinity
John of Damascus (675–749), who was appointed by the Muslim caliph Abdul-Malik as the Chief Minister of Finance following the death of his father, shortly after the spread of Islam into Syria, wrote at some length to defend the Christian faith against Islam. In his treaty *On Heresies*, he confronted Muslim objections to a number of Christian theological issues, including the Trinity. He wrote, 'Do not ask how the Trinity is Trinity, for the Trinity is inscrutable. But, if you are curious about God, first tell me of yourself and the things that pertain to you. How does your soul have existence? How is your mind set in motion? How do you produce your mental concepts? How is it that you are both mortal and immortal? But, if you are ignorant of these things, which are within you, then why do you not shudder at the thought of investigating the sublime things of heaven? Think of the Father as a spring of life begetting the Son like a river and the Holy Ghost like a sea, for the spring and the river and the sea are all one nature. Think of the Father as a root, and of the Son as a branch, and of the Spirit as a fruit, for the substance in these three is one. The Father is a sun with the Son as rays and the Holy Ghost as heat. The Holy Trinity transcends by far every similitude and figure. So, when you hear of an offspring of the Father, do not think of a corporeal	

The Trinity	No Trinity
offspring. And when you hear that there is a Word, do not suppose him to be a corporeal word. And when you hear of the Spirit of God, do not think of wind and breath. Rather, hold your persuasion with a simple faith alone. For the concept of the Creator is arrived at by analogy from his creatures. Be persuaded, moreover, that the incarnate dispensation of the Son of God was begotten ineffably and without seed of the blessed Virgin, believing him to be without confusion and without change both God and man, who for your sake worked all the dispensation. And to him ... give worship and adoration. Doing thus, you will be a right worshipper of the holy and undivided Trinity, Father and Son and Holy Ghost, of the one Godhead, to whom be glory and honour and adoration for ever and ever. Amen.[3] More profoundly, in Matthew 3:13-17 we find ourselves in the historical presence of the Holy Trinity at the baptism of Jesus. God the Holy Spirit was visibly descending like a dove and lighting on Jesus; the audible voice of God the Father was heard saying, 'This is my Son whom I love.' Hence, the Bible reveals unquestionably that God exists as Father, Son and Holy Spirit. No wonder that Saint Augustine said to the heretic Marcion, 'Go to Jordan, and then you shall see the Trinity.'	

The fallen nature of man	No fall of man
A number of references have already been made to the fallen nature of man. It will suffice here, however, to summarize the main biblical concept.	The Quran states that Adam, considered in Islam to be the first prophet, was created weak. His moral disposition remained the same as it was prior to the Fall (4:28). Thus, according to Islamic argumentation, since sin did not affect the human nature, there is no need for a divine act of reconciliation (i.e., the cross).
Adam and Eve were given freedom to live for ever in the presence of God, subject to only one stipulation. They were forbidden access to the tree of the knowledge of good and evil (Gen.2). God was gracious in revealing to them what the ramifications would be if they disobeyed the single restriction he had instituted. However, they rebelled against God. They sided with the devil and defied God to his face, violating his command and committing evil against his holiness.	Moreover, the Quran says that Adam was created essentially good and his goodness was not affected after the Fall. It is interesting, however, that Islam asserts that when a group of angels led by Iblis (ابليس), i.e., Satan, refused the command of Allah to bow down to Adam and worship him, Satan was expelled from Paradise, severely punished by Allah and condemned to eternal damnation (18:50), while Adam and Eve, who defied God, remained unaffected by their sin, except for being banished from Paradise.
Because God is holy and just, he must punish evil. Consequently they were driven out of Eden and from the presence of God. Guilt, shame and fear entered their lives. Far-reaching and cataclysmic consequences ensued. Sin entered the world and brought physical and spiritual death with it: 'Therefore, just as sin entered the world through one man, and death through sin, and in this way death came to all men, because all sinned — for before the law was given, sin was in the world. But sin is not taken into account when there is no law. Nevertheless, death reigned from the time of Adam to the time of Moses, even over those who did not sin by	

The fallen nature of man	No fall of man
breaking a command, as did Adam, who was a pattern of the one to come' (Rom. 5:12-14).	

The cross	No cross
The centrality of the atonement and the cross in the Bible is unmistakable. It deals directly — as we have already said, with the real, objective guilt of man's sin which offended the holiness of God. The New Testament speaks both of the historicity and the crucial significance of the event. Paul says, 'For what I received I passed on to you as of first importance: that Christ died for our sins according to the Scriptures, that he was buried, that he was raised on the third day according to the Scriptures, and that he appeared to Peter...' (I Cor. 15:3-5).	Since Islam rejects the whole concept of a fallen human nature and the principle of vicarious atonement for sin, it follows naturally that denial of the meaning of the cross becomes a condition of their theology.
Moreover, Paul says that righteousness and salvation come only through faith in Jesus Christ's finished work on the cross: 'But now a righteousness from God, apart from law, has been made known... This righteousness from God comes through faith in Jesus Christ to all who believe ... for all have sinned and fall short of the glory of God, and are justified freely by his grace through the redemption that came by Christ Jesus. God presented him as a sacrifice of atonement, through faith in his blood' (Rom. 3:21-25).	One of the peculiarities of Islam is the close correlation between its theological and cultural themes. For example, the cross, which is the dominant symbol of redemption and victory in Christianity, is seen in Islam in relation to their cultural themes. For a Muslim the cross is a symbol of shame and ignominy. Thus it is no surprise that among the reasons for the rejection of the cross in Islam is that it violates the honour of Allah.

Islam does not deny the event of the crucifixion, but the identity of the one who was crucified. The following verse from the Quran is often quoted by Muslims to support their denial of the cross: 'That they said, "we killed Christ Jesus the son of Mary, the apostle of God"; but they killed him not, nor crucified him, but so it was made to appear to them ... for of surety they killed |

The cross	No cross
Now the question is: how should we explain the cross to our Muslim friends? If you read the verses quoted above to a Muslim, there is a good chance that he will ask several questions, and do so with feeling:	him not, but God raised him up to Himself' (4:157-158).
	As for the identity of the person who was crucified, Muslims traditionally believe it was Judas. This idea of substitution is based mostly on the phrase, 'Shupeha Lahum' ('It appeared to them').
1. Why does the Bible say that Jesus must die on the cross to save people?	Muslim theologians still need to answer some questions regarding this crucial issue:
2. If God had wanted to save us, couldn't he have done that without sacrificing Jesus? Why did the great prophet of Allah have to be condemned in such a heinous and shameful manner?	1. As for the words, 'but it was made to appear to them [that he was crucified] for of surety they killed him not' — to whom does this refer?
3. Nobody should be punished for the sins of others. Why was Jesus punished for something he did not do?	2. Why does Allah have to resort to some kind of deception by crucifying another man who was supposed to look exactly like Christ?
4. If salvation comes about as a result of trusting in the finished work of Jesus, then no matter how we live, we still go to heaven; what difference does it make?	3. How can we harmonize the inconsistency in the Quran itself when it says of Christ on one hand that he was taken unto heaven, and on the other that he died? For in Surah 19:33-34 we read the following: 'Peace on me the day I was born, and the day I die, and the day I shall be raised alive, such was Jesus, son of Mary, this is a statement of truth.'
Certainly these are good questions by which our Muslim friend is in fact giving us an opening to enter into a discussion concerning the very heart of the Christian faith. Accordingly, we must obey the biblical injunction: 'But in your hearts set apart Christ as Lord. Always be prepared to give an answer to	

The cross	No cross
everyone who asks you to give the reason for the hope that you have. But do this with gentleness and respect, keeping a clear conscience, so that those who speak maliciously against your good behaviour in Christ may be ashamed of their slander' (1 Peter 3:15-16). I hope the following related themes will help to stimulate our minds as we tackle these questions when sharing the gospel with our Muslim friends.	

1. The holiness of God

Our concept of God is the single most crucial element in all the Bible. At the centre of his perfections, as revealed in the Bible, is his holiness, which is the essence of God's character. He alone is holy, and all righteousness and morality finds its origin in him: 'A faithful God who does no wrong, upright and just is he' (Deut. 32:4). 'He is a holy God; he is a jealous God' (Josh. 24:19). 'His way is perfect' (Ps. 18:30). Therefore, sin and evil provoke God's holy wrath: 'O LORD ... your eyes are too pure to look on evil; you cannot tolerate wrong' (Hab. 1:13).

When we sin we serve the devil and abandon God. What is at stake is the honour and the holiness of the Almighty. The Bible says, 'He who does what is sinful is of the devil (1 John 3:8). When man sins and

The cross	No cross
does evil, he in fact sins against God. For this reason, the Bible says, 'The wages of sin is death' (Rom. 6:23).	

2. The fall of man

A proper understanding of the Fall is a prerequisite to the understanding of human behaviour and value systems, while at the same time it demonstrates the necessity of the atonement. The fall of man must be seen in the light of the holiness of God, as mentioned above. The Fall was more than a circumstantial event. It was a plunge from a state of purity into a life of sinfulness, from fellowship with God into alienation from him.

Adam and Eve's guilt compelled them to hide behind fig leaves — an act that was not necessary before the Fall. From that moment, man has continued to mask his guilt by inventing new brands of fig leaves, including the invention of religious rituals as a means for trying to atone for one's own sins. As we have seen on several occasions, the book of Hebrews gives concrete teaching that we can never satisfy the demands of conscience through our own efforts at expiation (see also ch. 6). In the strict sense, all religions are reflections of this yearning, which was greatly affected by the Fall.

The cross	No cross
### 3. The promise	

The God of the Bible is the God of grace, mercy and love. He abhors sin and must judge it; as we have seen above. Yet, now we discover the precious first gospel promise of redemption:

And I will put enmity
between you and the woman,
and between your offspring
and hers;
he will crush your head,
and you will strike his heel
(Gen. 3:15).

The punishment of sin would involve enmity between two seeds, the seed of the devil (the serpent) and the seed of the woman (the Messiah, Jesus Christ), who would ultimately crush Satan's head (cf. Rom. 16:20). Satan and evil are not destined to triumph over righteousness; God had in mind a Messiah, a victor for us. The promise of the Redeemer came to Abraham (Gen. 12), a most notable figure in Judaism, Islam and Christianity. The promise was given that through Isaac — Abraham's child of the promise, the beneficiary of God's covenant with his father, Abraham (Gen.17:19; Gal. 4:22-23) — the Messiah would come, and all the nations of the earth would be blessed.

The Old Testament Scriptures progressively foreshadow the coming of

The cross	No cross
the promised Messiah. Over one hundred prophecies were fulfilled in Jesus Christ. For example, the prophet Isaiah foretold: 'Therefore the Lord himself will give you a sign: The virgin will be with child and will give birth to a son, and will call him Immanuel' (Isa. 7:14). This prophecy comes to fulfilment in the Word of God: 'Today in the town of David a Saviour has been born to you; he is Christ the Lord' (Luke 2:11).	

4. The necessity of atonement

The Word of God expressly declares that 'Without the shedding of blood there is no forgiveness' (Heb 9:22). This is the very heart of the Christian gospel. The word 'atonement' is recorded more than eighty times in the Bible, reflecting its vital theological importance. Without the atonement of Christ, the message of the Bible would be lost and the Christian faith would be no different from other religions. The advent of Christ would be meaningless, and humanity would have lost all hope. However, by demanding the shedding of blood, God emphasizes the awfulness of sin, while displaying his grace when he provided the 'Lamb ... who takes away the sin of the world' (John 1:29).

In trying to convey this wonderful truth to Muslims, we need to remember certain facts:

The cross	No cross
Firstly, the rituals of sacrifice are known throughout the millennia of history and became one of the principal features of most religions, including Islam. Though such sacrifices are in themselves utterly worthless and powerless to atone for sin, the widespread nature of the practice is evidence of the biblical assertion that man, being created in the image of God and endowed with a God-given conscience, will always be religious (cf. Rom. 1:18-32; 2:14-18). Augustine's well-known words are a good description of man's persistent inner religious restlessness: 'O God, our hearts are restless until we find our rest in thee.' However, attempting to enter into communion with the divine without acknowledging the cardinal fact that human nature is marred by sin makes religion an exercise in futility. Secondly, the doctrine of atonement and sacrifice in the Bible is always connected with the idea of thanksgiving, forgiveness of sin and reconciliation with God. The following are some of its manifestations: 1. *Abel's sacrifice to God* was the first recorded sacrifice in the Bible (Gen. 4:4). This sacrifice was an act of worship that he brought to God, and it gained God's approval. The book of Hebrews uses the example of Abel's sacrifice to set forth the principle that we are accepted	

The cross	No cross
by God only by faith in Jesus Christ, the perfect sacrifice for the sins of the world (Heb. 11:4).	

2. *God commands Abraham to sacrifice his son Isaac.* However, Isaac was spared when God provided a substitute, a ram offered in his place on Mount Moriah (Gen, 22:13). This is a powerful anticipation of the Lord Jesus Christ being sacrificed in our place on Mount Calvary. Forgiveness of sins is no longer achieved by animal sacrifices, but by the ultimate sacrifice of Christ (Heb. 10 1-18). The theme of sin and guilt offerings continues in the Old Testament (Lev. 4:1-35; 5;14 - 6:7), temporarily and symbolically as the preparatory stage for approaching God, until the advent of the perfect sacrifice.

3. *The prophet Isaiah* reinforced the idea that there must be a perfect sacrifice which is much more effectual than all other sacrifices. He foretold the coming of the sinless, suffering Messiah. From the New Testament affirmation (Matt. 8:17; 1:22), this Messiah is none other than Jesus Christ. In a precise and descriptive manner, he said:

He took up our infirmities
    and carried our sorrows...
He was pierced for our trans-
    gressions,

The Quran speaks of atonement in connection with Abraham's sacrifice. Allah's covenant with Abraham and the sacrifice of his son are recorded in the Quran. However, it is silent about the identity of the son intended for sacrifice to God, Muslims insist that Ishmael was the beneficiary of Allah's promises. He is considered to have been the father of the Arab race and the first to build the Kaaba along with his father Abraham (*surah* 2:124-127). The title given to Ishmael is 'Abu-al-fida', meaning, 'Father of the ransom' (see p. 25).

We read, 'Then, when [the son] reached [the age of serious] work with him, he said: "O my son! I see in vision that I offer thee in sacrifice: Now see what is thy view!" [The son] said: "O my father! Do as thou art commanded: thou wilt find me, if Allah so wills one practising patience and constancy!" We called out to him "O Abraham! Thou hast already fulfilled the vision!" — thus indeed do We reward those who do right. And We ransomed him with a momentous sacrifice' (Quran 37:102-107).

The ritual sacrificing of animals during the month of Ramadan commemorates Abraham's sacrifice

The cross	No cross
he was crushed for our iniquities; the punishment that brought us peace was upon him, and by his wounds we are healed. We all like sheep, have gone astray ... and the LORD has laid on him the iniquity of us all... He was led like a lamb to a slaughter... For he bore the sin of many, and made intercession for the transgressors (Isa. 53:4-7,12). 4. The sinlessness and moral perfection of Christ make him the only candidate to atone for our sins (see the discussion below on the sinlessness of Christ). Moreover, no mere human being can effectively deal with evil and destroy the devil's work: 'He who does what is sinful is of the devil, because the devil has been sinning from the beginning. The reason the Son of God appeared was to destroy the devil's work' (I John 3:8). 5. Consequently, God's absolute righteousness and justice demand nothing less than perfect restitution in order to justify those who have faith in Jesus Christ (Rom. 3:21-26).	of a ram to Allah instead of his son. All pilgrims to Mecca are required to offer an animal sacrifice. The acts of sacrifice and the subsequent feast both last for three days and coincide with the same celebration by Muslims worldwide. This feast is called the 'Greater Feast' while the other feast at the end of the fasting of Ramadan is called 'the Lesser Feast'. The Quran speaks of Christ as the advocate before God: 'Behold! the angels said: "O Mary! Allah giveth thee glad tidings of a Word from Him: his name will be Christ Jesus, the son of Mary, held in honour [the Arabic word, *wajihon*, translated 'held in honour', conveys the sense of advocacy] in this world and the Hereafter and of (the company of) those nearest to Allah..."' (3:45). It is widely held among Muslims, on the basis of the teaching of the Quran and the *Hadith* that Christ is morally perfect. We read in the Quran: 'And He hath made me blessed wheresoever I be, and hath enjoined on me Prayer and Charity as long as I live... Such [was] Jesus the son of Mary: [it is] a statement of truth, about which they dispute' (Quran 19:31-34). The *Hadith* confirms that all the prophets were subject to sins and only Christ was never charged with any sin (*Mishkat*, book 23, chapter 12).

The cross	No cross
6. According to Hebrews 9:9, no human effort, rituals, or sacrifices are able to make the conscience free from guilt. The true guilt is the real and objective moral offence against the holy God, which implies responsibility for sin and liability to judgement. It is the recognition of our guilt before God as fallen beings who are impoverished, and needing forgiveness. An informed conscience vouches for the gospel message and continues to contribute to man's awareness of his fallenness, restlessness and desire for freedom from the guilt and bondage of sin. This guilt, however, can be removed only by God's gracious act in the atonement accomplished by Jesus Christ (Rom. 5:1,8-10).	
7. Christ's ultimate sacrifice on the cross marks the fulfilment of all that was prefigured by the Old Testament sacrificial system. The atonement was accomplished once and for all through his death and resurrection. He was the very embodiment of the grace of God. God made a promise to send the perfect Messiah who would crush the head of Satan (Gen. 3:15), and he fulfilled it in the coming of his sinless, beloved Son, culminating on the cross (Phil. 2:5-11). The gospel makes it unmistakably clear that through Christ, God spoke and acted once and for all (Heb. 1:1-4; 10:10), in order 'to reconcile to	

The cross	No cross
himself all things ... by making peace through his [Christ's] blood' (Col. 1:20). Christ did not die for his own sins. He took our place, and by his perfect obedience to the will of the Father, he satisfied the righteous and just demands of God while securing reconciliation and salvation for all who embrace and trust in him.	

Scripture	Scripture
The Bible is clear on its inspiration and authority. Throughout the Old Testament, we come across phrases such as: 'Thus says the LORD ...'; 'These are the commands of the LORD ...'; 'The Word of the LORD came to me'. Such phrases indicate that God is the source of the Scriptures. 2 Timothy 3:16 leaves no doubt concerning the inspiration of the Scriptures: 'All Scripture is God-breathed and is useful for teaching rebuking, correcting and training in righteousness.' God the Holy Spirit inspired the writers by using their own gifts, talents and personal characteristics. As the Holy Spirit illuminated their minds, they expressed in their own words the revelation of God without hindering the clarity of the divine message (2 Peter 1:20-21).	While Muslims believe that the Quran is the final revelation from Allah, they also accept the previous revelations of both Jews and Christians: the books of Moses (Ar. Tawrat); the book of Psalms (Ar. Zabur); the Gospels (Ar. Injil). However, they have charged both Jews and Christians with corrupting their Scriptures (see pp. 21-22). Thus they regard the Quran as replacing them.
Moreover, the Scripture is complete and final. Hebrews 1:1-4 teaches that Christ is the final	The Quran is the sacred book of Islam. 'Quran' is an Arabic name which means 'reading' or 'recitation'. It contains what Muhammad claimed to be Allah's revelation given to him verbally in the Arabic language by Gabriel at a cave on Mount Hira near Mecca. Muslims believe that the Quran is inscribed in heaven on tablets which are eternally preserved. Other names are given to the Quran, including, 'Ar. Al-Furkan' (demarcation), 'Ar. Al-Huda' (guidance).

Scripture	Scripture
Word. He is the culmination of the revelation of God, who spoke to us in these last days by his Son, the one who 'is the radiance of God's glory and the exact representation of his being'. The Bible gives a warning in Revelation 22:18-19 to any who add to the finished revelation of God. Thus there is no need of any new revelation to complement the perfect revelation of God in Jesus Christ, who is the fulness of God (Col. 2:9) and the only way and the truth (John 14:6).	The Quran is slightly smaller than the New Testament. It contains 114 'Ar. Sura' (chapters). The surahs are not arranged logically, chronologically, or by theme or by genre, but according to their length. They deal with a variety of subjects, such as the oneness of Allah, his wrath if he is not heeded, stories analogous to the Old and New Testament narratives, and laws and regulations about religious and social life.

The Day of Judgement	The Day of Judgement
While the concept of the Day of Judgement in Islam to some degree overlaps with certain aspects of the Bible teaching, there are a number of discrepancies. The major difference, however, relates to the person of Jesus Christ, who is the central figure in the Day of Judgement. *The Westminster Confession of Faith* says it well: 'God hath appointed a day wherein he will judge the world in righteousness by Jesus Christ. In which day, not only the apostate angels shall be judged, but likewise all persons that have lived upon earth shall appear before the tribunal of Christ...' The following are a few examples of how the Day of Judgement is inseparably connected with the Lord Jesus Christ:	The Day of Judgement *(Ar. Youm Al-din)* is also named a Day of Reckoning *(Ar. Youm Al-Hisab)* and the Last Day *(Youm al-Akherah)*. The Day of Judgement is the appointed day on which Allah will judge people according to their deeds (Quran 2:25, 29:58; 4:57). The good and evil deeds of everyone are recorded on a daily basis by two angels who keep a record of them. This belief is based on verses in the Quran such as: 'Say: Lo! The death from which ye shrink will surely meet you. And afterward you will be returned unto the Knower of the invisible and the visible, and He will tell you what you used to do' (62:8). Moreover, the Quran makes the following declaration in the *surah*

The Day of Judgement	*The Day of Judgement*
1. The Second Coming of Jesus Christ is a central fact in Scripture. Christ spoke of his return in a number of passages in the Gospels. We speak of the glorious 'Second' Coming because we know he came the first time. When Muslims are asked, 'How can you identify Christ when he descends from heaven, since you maintain that he will appear as a typical man?' no convincing answer is given. On the contrary, the Bible says that Christ will appear in glory:	entitled 'The Israelite': 'And every man's augury [fate] have we fastened to his own neck, and we shall bring forth for him on the Day of Resurrection a book which he will find wide open' (62:13). 'But those who believe and work righteousness will be admitted to gardens beneath which rivers flow, To dwell therein for aye with the permission of their Lord' (14:23).

Look, he is coming with the
    clouds,
and every eye will see him,
even those who pierced him;
  and all the peoples of the
    earth will mourn because of
    him.
        So, shall it be! Amen
            (Rev. 1:7).
	It is reasonably accurate to say that since Islam provides no assurance of salvation in the Day of Judgement, the need to perform more good than evil deeds (in an attempt to build up a righteousness based on one's own works) becomes the dominant obsession of the believer, for fear of divine wrath.
	
	Thus such conformity can actually be a source of debilitating guilt. When the individual fails to be motivated by love and structures his life according to a series of dos and don'ts, by a rigid observance of laws and regulations, he eventually works at cross-purposes with his own conscience.

2. The Day of Judgement will include the judgement of Satan, who incited man to rebel against God. Moreover, Satan seeks to blind the eyes of men to the gospel (2 Cor. 4:3-4), to snatch the Word of God from people's hearts before it can take root (Matt. 13:19), to incite disobedience against God (Eph. 2;2) and to destroy God's people and God's kingdom (Eph. 6:11-13). His judgement by Christ was promised in	When performance becomes the goal of life, it eventually stands between the worshipper and his God. There is an innate tendency to perform works in order to avoid guilt feelings by placating God and meriting his favour.

The Day of Judgement	The Day of Judgement
the opening pages of the Bible (Gen. 3:15). His final doom will take place when he will be cast into hellfire for ever (Rev. 20:10). 3. The final salvation of men and the punishment of sinners is not based on our meritorious work, as Islam teaches, but upon the acceptance or rejection of the gospel of Jesus Christ. Those who believe in, receive and rest on Christ alone are saved to eternal life (John 11:25-26). Those who have not repented of their sinfulness and trusted him, he will consign to hell for ever; those who are his own, he will take to be with him in eternal joy in heaven (John 5:28-29; Matt. 25:34,41,46; John 14:3; 17:24; Rev. 21:1 - 22:16). 4. Eventually, as we shall see below, in a sharp contrast with the Islamic belief, after the judgement of Christ, a new order is ushered in where 'God is with men and he will live with them... He will wipe every tear from their eyes' (Rev. 21:3,4).	Muslims believe that Jesus Christ will descend from heaven to destroy the 'Antichrist' *(Ar. Dajjal)*. Traditions and some references in the Quran maintain that Christ will descend on the Middle East. Some say it will be in Jerusalem; others in Damascus; still others say he will land in Mecca. The goal of his coming, however, is to declare a *jihad* on the infidel and call the world to embrace Islam. In one of the most trusted Islamic traditions we read, 'Abu Huraira reported that the Messenger of Allah ... said: "By Him in Whose hand is my life, the son of Mary ... will soon descend among you as a just judge. He will break crosses, kill swine and abolish *Jizya*, and the wealth will pour forth to such an extent that no one will accept it' *(Sahih Muslim,* vol.1, p.92). At the end of his mission Christ will remain on earth where he will die and buried.

Heaven — fellowship with God	Paradise — no fellowship with God
We have seen earlier that although both Christianity and Islam have a concept of heaven these are dissimilar. The Bible speaks of heaven as the eternal abode of the triune God. Moreover, it is the ultimate abode of	The Muslim concept of Paradise, *Fardous* (فردوس), is very different. It is referred to as 'the gardens'. These gardens are believed to be the original abode of Adam and Eve. Muslims believe that they are composed of

Heaven — fellowship with God	Paradise — no fellowship with God
the redeemed. It is a holy place, full of the perfect experience of God's people enjoying full fellowship with him. In this connection, I have found what Jesus said to his disciples about heaven to be very helpful in communicating the gospel to Muslims: 'Let not your heart be troubled; you believe in God, believe also in me. In my Father's house are many mansions.... I go to prepare a place for you. And if I go and prepare a place for you, I will come again and receive you to myself; that where I am, there you may be also. And where I go you know, and the way you know' (John 14:1-4, NKJV). Note the following:	seven levels (Quran 23:17). At the highest level is the throne of Allah, separate from the other levels in which the believers abide. In order for the believer to enter Paradise he / she needs to live a virtuous life by performing more good deeds (Ar. Salehat) than 'evil deeds' (Ar. Sayeatt). Paradise is described in sensual and physical terms. The Quran is replete with details about the pleasures that await believers (surahs 37; 56; 74; 83). Compare with points from John 14:1-4 in the left column:
1. A promise and assurance: 'Do not let your hearts be troubled.'	No assurance.
2. To believe in God is equal to believing in Jesus: 'You believe in God, believe also in me.'	Believe in God. Christ is not Saviour.
3. Christ ascended to heaven that we may follow him: 'I go to prepare a place for you. And if I go and prepare a place for you, I will come again and receive you to myself...'	Christ was taken up to heaven.
4. Christ is coming again: 'I will come again.'	Christ is coming back.
5. Heaven is a place of fellowship with God: 'Where I am, there you may be also.'	Heaven is a place of sensual pleasure.
6. There is one way to heaven: 'And where I go you know, and the way you know.'	Paradise is gained through good works.

Christ in Islam

There is no doubt that Christ is honoured in Islam. Although the titles given to him are lofty, and some argue that they are evidence of his divinity, nevertheless, Christ, 'the bright Morning Star' (Rev. 22:16), is very much eclipsed in Islamic teaching.

Christ in the Quran	Reference
Born of a virgin	3:47 (*Surah Al-Imran*)
Performed many miracles	3:49 (*Surah Al-Imran*)
Righteous	6:85 (*Surah Al-An'Am*)
Word of God	4:171 (*Surah* 'Women')
Spirit from God	4:171 (*Surah* 'Women')
United with the Holy Spirit	2:87 (*Surah* 'The cow')
Most honoured in this life and in the hereafter	3:45 (*Surah Al-Imran*)
Pure	19:19 (*Surah* 'Mary')
Messiah	4:157 (*Surah* 'Women')
Taken up to heaven	4:158 (*Surah* 'Women')
Only a man	3:59 (*Surah Al-Imran*)

In his well-known book, *The Call of the Minaret*, Kenneth Cragg makes an eloquent and moving statement comparing the Christ of the Bible with Christ of Islam: 'If one sought a single justification for the Christian mission to Islam one might well be content to find it in the Quranic picture of Jesus of Nazareth. It is not simply what the picture fails to tell, vast as that is, but also what. Consider the Quranic Jesus alongside the New Testament. How sadly attenuated is this Christian prophet as Islam knows Him! Where are the stirring words, the deep insights, the gracious deeds, the compelling qualities of Him Who was called the Master? The mystery of His self-consciousness as the Messiah is unsuspected: the tender, searching intimacy of His relation to the disciples undiscovered. Where is "the Way, the Truth and the Life" in this abridgement? Where are the words from the Cross in a Jesus for whom Judas suffered? Where the triumph of the Resurrection from the grave which was not occupied? We have in the Quran neither Galilee, nor Gethsemane; neither Nazareth nor Olivet... Is the Sermon on the Mount to be left to silence in the Muslim's world? Must the Story of the Good Samaritan never be told there? Is "Come unto Me all ye that are weary ... and I will give you rest" an invitation that need not be heard...? In Sum, must not the emasculated Jesus of the Quran be rescued from misconception and disclosed in all His relevance, in words, deeds, and sorrows, to the whole plight and aspiration of men? To do this is what is meant here by retrieval. Our concern about saying it will surely measure our own estimate of who and what He is — the Christ who questioned His disciples on one crucial occasion: "Whom do men say that I am?" The answer matters, to Christ and to all the world. We have no right either to suppress the question or to neglect the response. Rather, inseparable from our Christianity, is the duty so to bring men to Him Who asks that they may answer for themselves.'[4]

Christ in the Bible

The misconceptions concerning orthodox Christianity in general, and the person of Christ in particular, on the part of Muhammad and his followers have from the very beginning been detrimental to the relationship between Islam and Christianity and this has continued right up to our own day.

Muhammad rejected Christ as he was presented by early Christian heresies and replaced him with an intensely legalistic system that is based on the teachings of both the Quran and the *Sunnah* — the regulative standard for morals and ethics in the Islamic tradition. Experts on cults tell us that they have certain distinguishing characteristics, and certainly Islam is no exception in this respect:

> 1. Claim of another revelation besides the Bible.
> 2. Denial of salvation by faith in Christ and by grace alone.
> 3. Devaluation of Jesus Christ.
> 4. An exclusive community.
> 5. Belief in some truths from the Bible.

It is true that the final goal of every genuine evangelist is to preach Christ crucified. The problem comes when we attempt to articulate this sublime truth to folk with minds and consciences that are inhibited by religious and cultural teaching to which they have been subjected from early childhood, and which is opposed to the deity of Christ. However, witness to Muslims must be centred on Jesus Christ, the Son of the living God; otherwise, we follow on the path the Galatian Christians were taking when the apostle Paul accused them of deserting Christ for a different gospel (Gal. 1:1-9).

Thus it is incumbent upon us to communicate to our Muslim friends what the Bible says about the person of Jesus Christ, 'in whom are hidden all the treasures of wisdom and knowledge' (Col. 2:3). An understanding of these truths is also essential for the strengthening of our own faith and deepening our relationship with him. To the Christ of the Scripture we now, therefore, turn.

Jesus asked the question: 'Who do people say the Son of Man is?' (Matt. 16:13). Both Jews and Muslims recognize the coming of the Messiah. Jews still await his advent, which they identify primarily with politico-nationalistic themes. Muslims, on the other hand, speak of Jesus Christ in religious terms such as *'Al-Masih'* ('the Messiah' — Quran 3:45). However, both Jews and Muslims identify the Messiah in merely human terms. The Jews rejected Christ's claim of being the divine Messiah, and they condemned him to death. Then, later, they rejected the core teaching of the gospel by denying Christ's claim to deity.

In answering the question, 'Who do people say the Son of Man is?', Peter voiced not only his own personal conviction, but also the belief of all faithful Christians throughout history, when he said, 'You are the Christ, the Son of the living God' (Matt. 16:16). Peter's answer, which secured Christ's commendation, was remarkable not for the fact that Peter recognized the Messiah, but for his recognition of the divine nature of Christ.

Since Muslims deny the deity of Christ, how can we establish this cardinal doctrine and explain it to our Muslim friends?

The doctrine of the person of Christ is the most fundamental in the Word of God. Loraine Boettner, to whom I am grateful for permission to incorporate much of his discussion on this subject, says, 'We would define Christianity as follows: Christianity is that redemptive religion that offers salvation from the guilt and corruption of sin through the atoning death of Christ. Consequently, we hold that to admit the Deity of Christ and to trust Him for salvation constitutes one a Christian, and that to reject His Deity marks one a non-Christian.'

The evidence is abundantly sufficient to prove that Christ was indeed the incarnate Deity, the eternal Son of God, who came to this earth in order that he might provide a way of redemption for sinful men. In both theological and missiological terms, the mastery of the following discussion is of the utmost importance as we endeavour to defend the deity of Christ while communicating the gospel to Muslims. With our eyes on the Bible, let us consider the following questions.

What did Christ say concerning his deity?

The most important witness to the deity of Christ is, of course, Christ himself. The New Testament records make it abundantly clear that he possessed not only a sense of unbroken fellowship with God, but also a distinct consciousness that he himself was God. From the age of twelve at least, when in reply to his mother's question he said, 'Why were you searching for me? ... Didn't you know I had to be in my Father's house?' (Luke 2:49), this consciousness appears, and it later becomes one of the dominant notes of his doctrine. He expressly claims equality with God the Father: 'I and the Father are one' (John 10:30). 'Anyone who has seen me has seen the Father' (John 14:9). 'When a man believes in me, he does not believe in me only, but in the one who sent me' (John 12:44). Wherefore, Christ alone is the true Revealer of God to men: 'All things have been committed to me by my Father. No one knows the Son except the Father, and no one knows the Father except the Son and those to whom the Son chooses to reveal him' (Matt.11:27). His activity is co-extensive with that of the Father: 'Whatever the Father does the Son also does' (John 5:19).

That Jesus' claim to sonship and to oneness with the Father was understood by the Jews to imply deity is quite clear. When on one occasion they took up stones to stone him, he said, ' "I have shown you many great miracles from the Father. For which of these do you stone me?" "We are not stoning you for any of these," replied the Jews, "but for blasphemy, because you, a mere man, claim to be God" ' (John 10:32,33). And when they accused him before Pilate they said, 'We have a law, and according to that law he must die, because he claimed to be the Son of God' (John 19:7).

In the intercessory prayer in John 17 he prays that the Father may glorify the Son in order that the Son may glorify the Father. He claims authority to give eternal life to all those whom the Father has given him, and that life consists in knowing God and himself. He prays that the Father may glorify him with the Father's own glory, the glory which he had with the Father before the world was.

During the trial before the Sanhedrin Jesus publicly and explicitly claimed deity and was condemned to death on the charge that he had spoken 'blasphemy'. In answer to the high priest's question, 'Are you the Christ, the Son of the Blessed One?' (or as Matthew says, 'the Son of God'), Jesus replied, 'I am... And you will see the Son of Man sitting at the right hand of the Mighty One and coming on the clouds of heaven.' And then we are told, 'The high priest tore his clothes. "Why do we need any more witnesses?" he asked. "You have heard the blasphemy. What do you think?" They all condemned him as worthy of death' (Mark 14:61-64).

In giving the Great Commission to his disciples Jesus said, 'All authority in heaven and on earth has been given to me. Therefore go and make disciples of all nations, baptizing them in the name of the Father and of the Son and of the Holy Spirit, and teaching them to obey everything I have commanded you. And surely I am with you always, to the very end of the age' (Matt. 28:18-20). There he placed his own name at the centre of the triune name of God, commanded that those who believe on him should he baptized in that name and promised to be with them always, even unto the end of the world.

What does the Word of God say concerning the deity of Christ?

In full harmony with the claims and testimony of Jesus concerning his deity are those of all the others who speak of him in the New Testament.

Heaven announces Christ's deity

In announcing to Mary that she was to be the mother of a son who, without any human father, was to be conceived through the power of the Holy Spirit, the angel Gabriel said, 'He will be great and will be called the Son of the Most High. The Lord God will give him the throne of his father David, and he will reign over the house of Jacob for ever; his kingdom will never end' (Luke 1:32-33). No one who is less than deity can meet these qualifications.

The angel told Joseph that his name was to be called Jesus: 'She will give birth to a son, and you are to give him the name Jesus, because he will save his people from their sins' (Matt. 1:21). Again this is a work which can be performed by no one who is less than deity.

Old Testament prophecies

Matthew, citing one of the Messianic prophecies in the Old Testament, says, 'All this took place to fulfil what the Lord had said through the prophet: "The virgin will be with child and will give birth to a son, and they will call him Immanuel" — which means, "God with us"' (Matt. 1:22-23).

The Wise Men

The Wise Men, finding the newborn baby after their long journey from the East and possessing a spiritual insight above that commonly given to men, 'bowed down and worshipped him' (Matt. 2:11). In doing so they rendered to him the homage which it is idolatrous and sinful to render to anyone other than deity.

John the Baptist

John the Baptist, stern preacher of righteousness that he was, acknowledged himself to be only the forerunner of one who was coming later and declared that this one was so much greater than he himself was that John was not worthy even to unloose the thongs of his sandals. When Jesus did appear and was baptized, John saw the heavens opened and the Spirit of God descending upon him, and the Father's voice spoke from heaven, saying, 'This is my Son, whom I love; with him I am well pleased' (Matt. 3:17). The following day John pointed out Jesus with the words: 'Look, the Lamb of God, who takes away the sin of the world!' and went on to describe him as the one 'who will baptize with the Holy Spirit' and as 'the Son of God' (John 1:29-34).

The prologue to the Gospel of John

In the prologue to John's Gospel we have a clear and unmistakable assertion of the deity of Christ: 'In the beginning was the Word, and the Word was with God, and the Word was God' (John 1:1). John applies to Christ a term that is not found anywhere else in the New Testament, and the functions which he ascribes to him can be ascribed to none other than full Deity. It is his office to make God known to his creatures: 'No one has ever seen God, but God the One and Only, who is at the Father's side, has made him known' (John 1:18). His eternality is set forth by the statement that 'in the beginning', when things began to come into existence, he already 'was'.

The testimony of Peter and the other apostles

Peter doubtless spoke for most of the disciples when, in his great confession, he said, 'You are the Christ, the Son of the living God' (Matt. 16:16). And as the revelation proceeded towards its climax even the disciple who entertained the most doubts, Thomas, came, like Peter, to the point where he fell down at Jesus' feet with the acknowledgment: 'My Lord and my God!' (John 20:28). The fact that Jesus allowed those words to pass without any rebuke amounted to an assertion on his own part of his claim to deity.

The testimony of the apostles as they wrought miracles in his name is further proof of his deity. 'In the name of Jesus Christ of Nazareth, walk,' said Peter to the lame man at the door of the temple (Acts 3:6). 'If we are being called to account today for an act of kindness shown to a cripple and are asked how he was healed, then know this, you and all the people of Israel: It is by the name of Jesus Christ of Nazareth, whom you crucified but whom God raised from the dead, that this man stands before you healed' (Acts 4:9-10).

Paul's testimony

Paul repeatedly and consistently teaches the deity of Christ. Immediately after his conversion he went into the synagogues in Damascus and 'began to preach ... that Jesus is the Son of God' (Acts 9:20). Writing to the Colossians, he set forth Christ as 'the image of the invisible God' (Col. 1:15), and declared that 'In him dwells all the fulness of the Godhead bodily' (Col. 2:9, NKJV) — in other words, that Christ is an incarnation of the Godhead in all its fulness, a form of statement that cannot be harmonized with any view that makes him anything less than God.

The testimony of the Epistle to the Hebrews

The writer of the Epistle to the Hebrews ascribes deity to Christ when he says that God, having spoken in earlier times through the prophets and in other ways, in these later days has spoken unto us 'by his Son, whom he appointed heir of all things, and through whom he made the universe. The Son is the radiance of God's glory and the exact representation of his being, sustaining all things by his powerful word. After he had provided purification for sins, he sat down at the right hand of the Majesty in heaven' (Heb. 1:1-3).

The testimony of non-Christians

Furthermore, the Roman centurion who witnessed the crucifixion adds his testimony: 'Truly this man was the Son of God!' (Mark 15:39, NKJV). And even the demons — fallen beings who had known him in a former state of existence — came out of possessed persons at his command shouting, 'What do you want with us, Son of God? ... Have you come here to torture us before the appointed time?' (Matt. 8: 29).

The evidence of the resurrection

Christ's resurrection from the dead is also an inescapable proof of his deity. Both his death and his resurrection were within his own power. Concerning his life he said, 'No one takes it from me, but I lay it down of my own accord. I have authority to lay it down and authority to take it up again' (John 10:18). Repeatedly he predicted his resurrection from the dead: '... the Son of Man will be betrayed to the chief priests and teachers of the law. They will condemn him to death and ... kill him. Three days later he will rise' (Mark 10:33-34; cf. 8:31; 9:31; Luke 18:33; 24:7; Matt. 20:19; 27:63). Paul points to the resurrection as a proof of his deity, saying that by it 'through the Spirit of holiness [he] was declared with power to be the Son of God' (Rom. 1:4). It was this which convinced Thomas, the most unconvinced of the disciples, so that at the mere sight of the risen Jesus he acknowledged him as his Lord and his God (John 20:26-29).

Divine titles ascribed to Jesus Christ

Title	Reference
The Son of God	John 1:34
[God's] only begotten Son	John 3:16 (NKJV)
Lord and God	John 20:28
The Lord of glory	1 Cor. 2:8
The image of God	2 Cor. 4:4
The radiance of God's glory	Heb. 1:3
The exact representation of his being	Heb. 1:3
The Messiah	John 1:41
The Word	John 1:1
Saviour	2 Peter 1:1; John 4:42
The author of salvation	Heb. 2:10
The Redeemer	Gal. 3:13
The mediator of a new covenant	Heb. 12:24
The Lamb of God	John 1:29
The Holy and Righteous One	Acts 3:14
The Holy One of God	John 6:69
The power of God	1 Cor. 1:24
The wisdom of God	1 Cor. 1:24
The creator of all things	John 1:3
Heir of all things	Heb. 1:2
The Beginning and the End	Rev. 21:6
The author of life	Acts 3:15
The bread of life	John 6:35
The door	John 10:7 (NKJV)
Master	Matt. 23:10 (AV)

What does the title 'Son of God' mean?

Scripture clearly answers Muslims' objection to Christ's being called 'the Son of God'. One of the most exalted titles applied to Jesus is that of 'the Son of God'. It is a divine title or name, which calls attention to the dignity of his person, particularly to his deity, and indicates that he is fully qualified to speak to men concerning the things of God. It was this aspect of his nature that impressed Nathaniel when, amazed at Jesus' familiarity with his past life, he exclaimed, 'Rabbi, you are the Son of God; you are the King of Israel' (John 1:49). It was in an attempt to cast doubt on this side of his nature that the devil issued the challenge: 'If you are the Son of God, tell these stones to become bread' (Matt. 4:3). It was also in a reluctant acknowledgement of his divine nature that the demons cried out, 'What do you want with us, Son of God? … Have you come here to torture us before the appointed time?' (Matt. 8:29). Peter's great confession, 'You are the Christ, the Son of the living God' (Matt. 16:16), was prompted by his perception of Christ's essential deity. And John declared specifically that his purpose in writing his Gospel was: '… that you may believe that Jesus is the Christ, the Son of God, and that by believing you may have life in his name' (John 20:31).

Wherever the Scriptures call Christ the 'Son of God', they assert his true and proper deity. This title signifies a unique relationship that cannot be ascribed to, nor shared with, any creature.

As any human son is like his father in his essential nature — that is, possessed of humanity — so Christ, the Son of God, was like his Father in his essential nature — that is, possessed of deity. The Father and the Son, together with the Holy Spirit, are coeternal and coequal in power and glory, and partake of the same nature or substance.

Christ is the Son of God by nature; we become the sons of God by grace. He is the Son of God in his own right; we become sons of God by adoption. He has existed thus from eternity; we become sons in time as we are regenerated to a new life and have his righteousness imparted to us. This, of course, does not mean that we ever come to partake of the nature of deity. But it does mean that we have restored to us and perfected in us that moral and spiritual likeness of God with which we were created, but which became lost through sin.

It is thus abundantly clear that the name 'Son of God' was designed to set forth Christ in his essential nature as deity. He who was 'born of the seed of David according to the flesh' is also 'declared to be the Son of God with power,' (Rom. 1:3,4, NKJV); and he who 'according to the flesh' came of the Jews is also declared to be 'over all, the eternally blessed God' (Rom. 9: 5, NKJV). We are, therefore, to believe in the Son as we do in the Father, and to honour the one as we do the other.

What does the title 'Son of Man' mean?

It is habitual practice among Muslims to question the deity of Christ by referring to his title 'Son of Man'. This misconception needs to be put right. The title which Jesus used most often when speaking of himself, and which therefore appears to have been his favourite title, was 'Son of Man'. This much-discussed title certainly was designed to call attention to the fact that he possessed real humanity, being perfect God and perfect man. In him human nature is seen in its perfection, functioning as it was intended to do when it left the hands of the Creator. He is the ideal whom all others should take as the pattern for their lives. And, since he thus possessed human nature in his own person, he is vitally related to all other members of the human race and, by divine appointment, is capable of acting as their representative before God.

In the Eighth Psalm this title is used with reference to mankind in general: 'What is man that you are mindful of him, the son of man that you care for him?' (Ps. 8:4). But as applied to Jesus in the New Testament it had more than merely human connotations. It looked back to the heavenly figure in Daniel chapter 7, where it is prophetic of the return of Christ to heaven after the completion of his work of redemption: 'In my vision at night I looked, and there before me was one like a son of man, coming with the clouds of heaven. He approached the Ancient of Days and was led into his presence. He was given authority, glory and sovereign power; all peoples, nations and men of every language worshipped him. His dominion is an everlasting dominion that will not pass away, and his kingdom is one that will never be destroyed' (Dan. 7:13-14).

To Jewish ears, therefore, it was a clear assertion of Messiahship. And it is evident that Jesus used it with full consciousness of its significance, for he himself said, 'At that time the sign of the Son of Man will appear in the sky, and all the nations of the earth will mourn. They will see the Son of Man coming on the clouds of the sky, with power and great glory' (Matt. 24:30).

What does Christ mean when he says, 'Before Abraham was born, I am!'?

In a rather remarkable series of statements, including these words in John 8:58, Jesus conveys to our minds the idea that his existence did not merely begin when he was born in Bethlehem, but that he 'came', or 'descended', from heaven to earth, and that he was 'sent' by the Father. Very evidently if he came, or descended, or was sent, he must have existed before he came, or descended, or was sent. These verses afford not only a unique testimony to his divine mission, but also to his heavenly origin, and set him forth not only as the greatest of the sons of men, but as a pre-existent person, in some instances as an eternal being.

Furthermore, Jesus teaches not only that he existed before coming into the world, but that he has existed from eternity: 'And now, Father, glorify me in your presence with the glory I had with you before the world began' (John 17:5).

Writing to the Colossians Paul says of him, 'For by him all things were created: things in heaven and on earth, visible and invisible, whether thrones or powers or rulers or authorities; all things were created by him and for him. He is before all things, and in him all things hold together' (Col. 1:16-17).

Moreover, even the Old Testament predictions in regard to the Messiah who was to come set him forth not merely as one who would be 'born' like other men, but as one who existed before he came to earth — in fact, as one whose existence extends back into eternity. The prophet Micah wrote:

But you, Bethlehem Ephrathah,
    though you are small among the clans of Judah,
out of you will come for me
    one who will be ruler over Israel,
whose origins are from of old,
    from ancient times

(Micah 5:2).

And Isaiah described the promised Messiah not only as the 'Wonderful Counsellor' and 'Prince of Peace', but also as the 'Mighty God' and as the 'Everlasting Father' (Isa. 9:6).

In all the history of the world Jesus emerges as the only 'expected' person. No one was looking in this way for persons such as kings, emperors and founders of other religions to appear at the time and place that they did. No other person has had his course foretold, or his work laid out for him, centuries before he was born. Yet the coming of the Messiah had been predicted for centuries. In fact, the first promise of his coming was given to Adam and Eve soon after their fall into sin. As time went on, various details concerning his person and work were revealed through the prophets; and at the time Jesus was born there was a general expectation throughout the Jewish world that the Messiah was soon to appear. Even the manner of his birth and the town in which it would occur had been clearly indicated.

What are the attributes of deity ascribed to Christ?

Throughout the New Testament we find that the attributes of Deity are repeatedly ascribed to Christ, not merely in a secondary sense, such as might be predicated of a creature, but in a way that is applicable to God alone. The following attributes are ascribed to him:

Holiness

Holiness is intrinsic to the nature of God. Peter said to Jesus, 'We believe and know that you are the Holy One of God' (John 6:69). Peter also affirms that Jesus 'committed no sin, and no deceit was found in his mouth' (1 Peter 2:22). Paul refers to him as 'him who had no sin' (2 Cor. 5:21). Speaking of Christ, the writer of the Epistle to the Hebrews says, 'Such a high priest meets our need — one who is holy, blameless, pure, set apart from sinners, exalted above the heavens' (Heb. 7:26). 'Can any of you prove me guilty of sin?' was his challenge to his enemies (John 8:46). Even the demons bore witness that he was 'the Holy One of God' (Luke 4:34).

Eternity

'In the beginning was the Word' (John 1:1). He said, 'Before Abraham was born, I am!' (John 8:58). In prayer to God the Father he spoke of 'the glory I had with you before the world began' (John 17:5). 'He is before all things, and in him all things hold together' (Col. 1:17). In the Messianic prophecies he is called the 'Everlasting Father' (Isa. 9:6), and is described as 'one who will be ruler over Israel, whose origins are from of old, from ancient times' (Micah 5:2). He is indeed the King of the Ages.

Life

'In him was life, and that life was the light of men' (John 1:4). 'I am the way and the truth and the life. No one comes to the Father except through me' (John 14:6). 'I am the resurrection and the life. He who believes in me will live, even though he dies' (John 11:25). 'For as the Father has life in himself, so he has granted the Son to have life in himself' (John 5:26).

Immutability (unchangeableness)

'Jesus Christ is the same yesterday and today and for ever' (Heb. 13:8).

> They [the heavens and the earth] will perish, but you
>   remain…
> You will roll them up like a robe;
>   like a garment they will be changed.
> But you remain the same,
>   and your years will never end
>
>   (Heb. 1:11-12).

Omnipotence (unlimited power)

'All authority in heaven and on earth has been given to me' (Matt. 28:18). 'All things have been committed to me by my Father' (Matt. 11:27). 'The Son … sustaining all things by his powerful word' (Heb.1:3). In Messianic prophecy he is fore-told as the 'Mighty God' (Isa. 9:6). He possessed power to restore the dead to life (John 11:43-44; Luke 7:14-15), and he declares that the final resurrection of all men will be accomplished through his power: 'Do not be amazed at this, for a time is coming when all who are in their graves will hear his voice and come out — those who have done good will rise to live, and those who have done evil will rise to be condemned' (John 5:28-29).

Omniscience (knowing everything)

'You know all things' (John 16:30). 'Knowing their thoughts, Jesus said, "Why do you entertain evil thoughts in your hearts?"' (Matt. 9:4). 'For Jesus had known from the beginning which of them did not believe and who would betray him' (John 6:64). 'Christ, in whom are hidden all the treasures of wisdom and knowledge' (Col. 2:3). 'No one knows the Father except the Son and those to whom the Son chooses to reveal him' (Matt. 11:27) — a declaration in which Jesus himself implies that the personality, or being, of the Son is so great that only God can fully comprehend it, and that the Son possesses such unlimited knowledge that he can know God to perfection; in other words, a declaration that his knowledge is infinite.

Omnipresence (presence everywhere at the same time)

Christ himself set forth his omnipresence when he said, 'For where two or three come together in my name, there am I with them' (Matt.18:20); and again, 'And surely I am with you always, to the very end of the age' (Matt. 28:20). Assembled with his disciples on the Mount of Olives after his resurrection, he assured them of his continued presence and power and declared that his influence with them would be, not that of a dead teacher, but of a living presence.

Being thus everywhere present, he is always accessible, able to guard and comfort his people so that no affliction or suffering but such as he sees to be for their own good can come upon them.

Paul teaches the omnipresence of Christ when he says, 'And God placed all things under his feet and appointed him to be head over everything for the church, which is his body, the fulness of him who fills everything in every way' (Eph. 1:22-23).

Creator

'Through him all things were made; without him nothing was made that has been made' (John 1:3). 'For by him all things were created: things in heaven and on earth, visible and invisible, whether thrones or powers or rulers or authorities; all things were created by him and for him. He is before all things, and in him all things hold together' (Col. 1:16-17).

> But about the Son he says, ...
> 'In the beginning, O Lord, you laid the foundations of
>   the earth,
>   and the heavens are the work of your hands'
>   (Heb. 1:8,10).

The writer here applies to Christ words which in the Old Testament are spoken concerning Jehovah, and thereby sets forth his deity in the most absolute sense. 'There is but one Lord, Jesus Christ, through whom all things came and through whom we live' (1 Cor. 8:6).

Authority to forgive sins

Mark tells us in the second chapter of his inspired Gospel about the increasing opposition and antagonism to Christ on the part of the religious establishment, who questioned the divine authority of Christ. He tells the story of the paralysed man, illustrating the deity of Christ, who is equal to God in being able to forgive sins (Mark 2:5-12).

No human being, not even a priest or prophet, can forgive sins. The scribes were right in saying that only God can forgive sins. Only God can pardon a man and declare him innocent. Consequently, when Jesus forgave sin he was in essence declaring himself to be God.

Moreover, in instituting the Lord's Supper Jesus made it plain that the remission of sins was to be accomplished through his shed blood (Matt. 26:28). Not only did he calmly assume the authority to forgive sin in others, but also asserted that in his own person, and as their substitute, he bore the penalty of sin for them. After his resurrection he taught the disciples that 'repentance and forgiveness of sins will be preached in his name to all nations' (Luke 24:47). Peter declares, 'All the prophets testify about him that everyone who believes in him receives forgiveness of sins through his name' (Acts 10:43). Paul refers to him as the one who 'has rescued us from the dominion of darkness and brought us into the kingdom of the Son he loves, in whom we have redemption, the forgiveness of sins' (Col. 1:13-14). To assume the authority to forgive sins is to assume one of the prerogatives of God. Christ claims this authority, and in doing so very definitely sets himself forth as God.

Christ — the author of salvation and the object of faith

The Bible says, 'Whoever believes in the Son has eternal life, but whoever rejects the Son will not see life, for God's wrath remains on him' (John 3:36). 'Believe in the Lord Jesus, and you will be saved — you and your household (Acts 16:31). 'Jesus said..., "I am the resurrection and the life. He who believes in me will live, even though he dies; and whoever lives and believes in me will never die. Do you believe this?"' (John 11:25-26).

Faith in Christ is involved in, and in fact is declared to be identical with, faith in God: 'When a man believes in me, he does not believe in me only, but in the one who sent me. When he looks at me, he sees the one who sent me' (John 12:44-45).

Even the name 'Jesus' is not of human but of divine origin, and is the equivalent of the Hebrew 'Joshua', meaning 'Saviour'. Even before he came into the world the purpose of his mission was designated by the choice of this name: '... and you are to give him the name Jesus, because he will save his people from their sins' (Matt. 1:21).

These are indeed exceedingly great and precious promises. Certainly they make clear that faith in Christ is necessary for salvation, and that apart from him there is no salvation. It is impossible for anyone to make more stupendous claims than Jesus makes concerning his own person and his influence over the lives of others.

Prayer and worship are ascribed to Jesus

It is universally acknowledged that God alone can hear and answer prayer, and that the worship of anything less than Deity is idolatry. Yet Jesus repeatedly sets himself forth not only as the one who reveals God, but also as the object of worship: 'In that day you will no longer ask me anything. I tell you the truth, my Father will give you whatever you ask in my name. Until now you have not asked for anything in my name. Ask and you will receive, and your joy will be complete' (John 16:23- 24).

We read that on numerous occasions Jesus did receive worship while on earth. The Wise Men, having been divinely guided to the Christ-child, when they saw him, 'bowed down and worshipped him' (Matt. 2:11). After Jesus had come to the disciples walking on the water, '... those who were in the boat worshipped him, saying, "Truly you are the Son of God"' (Matt. 14:33). Concerning the blind man whose sight was restored when he washed in the pool of Siloam we read, '... and he worshipped him [Jesus]' (John 9:38). When confronted with the visible proof of Christ's resurrection, Thomas said to him, 'My Lord and my God!' (John 20:28), a direct ascription of deity to Christ. Since it went unrebuked, it was the equivalent of an assertion of deity on Jesus' part. After the resurrection, the disciples went into Galilee, to the place where Jesus had appointed them and 'When they saw him, they worshipped him' (Matt. 28:17).

6.
Conscience — a forgotten factor in Muslim evangelism?

Implications of the relationship between culture, conscience and the gospel in relation to the evangelism of Muslims

In addition to the considerations discussed in the previous chapter in connection with Muslim objections to the gospel, we need to consider an internal factor, that of conscience. Culture plays a crucial role in the formation of each individual conscience, including that of the person bringing the message as well as that of the one to whom the message is addressed. When the recipient's conscience is conditioned by cultural values that are incompatible with the gospel (as is the case for Muslims), conscience works adversely to the gospel message.

The concept of conscience in the Bible is distinctive and is not found in other religions, such as Islam. It is a God-given, universal and innate faculty of the human psyche reflecting God's moral image; it monitors right and wrong. It is the voice of conscience providing a universal standard that makes all men accountable to God, but though it convicts man of his sin, it cannot save him from it. Only God's special revelation — his Word and the incarnate Word, Jesus Christ — is able to save. Nevertheless it is lamentable that conscience can be misinformed, conditioned, dulled and ultimately seared.

One finds a close parallelism between Islam and Judaistic legalism. Any attempt to avoid a sense of guilt by adherence to the law ultimately works at cross purposes with conscience (cf. Heb. 9:9). Conscience is intended to work with the missionary to authenticate the gospel. None the less, a wrongly educated conscience can work counter to the gospel's message. A Muslim, with a conscience that has been conditioned in this way, is not likely to respond to the message — or at least not at first. We have seen in earlier chapters that the message of Islam is embodied in the Quran and the *Sunnah*, and both have the potential to exert enormous religious indoctrination and instil social conditioning into the consciences of individuals and, indeed, of society as a whole.

In our effort to reach Muslims, we need, ultimately, to appeal to the troubled conscience and aim for the heart. Effective cross-cultural mission work demands a proper study of the relationship between culture, conscience and gospel. This becomes of even greater importance in the context of Islam. Islam is a way of life that controls all facets of the lives of its adherents and exerts a commanding influence in shaping the conscience and eclipsing its proper testimony. The book of Hebrews puts its finger on the very heart of the Muslim's predicament, as represented by his relentless acts of repeating prayers, ceremonial washing, sacrifices and other rituals of worship, when it states that all such practices are 'not able to clear the conscience of the worshipper'. Consequently, a Muslim, though sincere, is a troubled worshipper with a troubled and guilty conscience.

We should keep in mind that the Christian view of the origin of guilt is radically different from that of Islam, and this has important implications with regard to man's nature (i.e., moral disposition) and his relationship to God and his environment. The Bible maintains that guilt, seen in the light of the Fall, cannot be expunged by the performance of good works, obedience to the law, or external acts of religious practice, as is the case in Islam (see Rom. 3:10-20; Titus 3:5-7). The Bible asserts that man's objective guilt results from moral offences committed as a consequence of his fallen condition and that this is the root of a disquieted conscience. Thus, addressing a Muslim at this pivotal felt need can be an effective starting point. Perhaps it will lead to a better understanding of the nature of sin and guilt, and in turn to a greater appreciation of the good news of the gospel, the only force that can satisfy the conscience and regenerate the heart.

Abraham Kuyper expressed it well: 'As soon as you, as a man, encounter a person as a man, whether he be a pagan or [a Muslim], you possess with him a common starting point, and this is first of all, the sin you both have committed, and, secondly, the grace which saves you and which alone can save him when the light from Christ penetrates into the darkness, and a sinner is gripped by the mercy of God. Thus there arises on the one hand a feeling of a common tie with the pagan, a common human heart, and in that heart, there is the same *sensus divinitatis*; that heart is disturbed by the same sin; you are as heathen as he, the sole difference is the grace which has been given to you, and he too can share in.'[1]

Conscience and cross-cultural ministry[2]

The Bible is a book mainly about God and man. Its theology and anthropology (or study of humankind) go hand in hand. Therefore, without a proper understanding of the human race, there is no proper doctrine of salvation, and no proper theory of missions. An essential and wonderful truth about man is the fact that he is created in the image of God. At the deepest aspect of man's soul, God endowed him with many faculties, among which is the conscience, which constitutes an essential part of his moral nature.

In seeking to understand the place, the role and the importance of conscience, two points need to be emphasized. First, the idea of conscience is universal, found in most — if not all — ancient and modern cultures, as can be seen in the review of literature. Anthropologists tell us that there has never been a people without religion, and religions always include teaching on ethics and morality. Scripture teaches that man, being created in the image of God and endowed with a moral faculty (i.e., conscience), testifies to the fact that God's law is written in his heart, encouraging him to do good and forbidding what is evil.

However, the second point is that conscience is not totally reliable, since it is culturally adaptable and functions either correctly or incorrectly according to the moral standards learned in a particular culture. For example, Muslims reared in families with unbiblical values may feel a heavy burden of guilt when applying biblical values that violate their cultural standards.

Thus understanding the role of conscience is vitally important in mission work, particularly in a Muslim context. There is a need to consider the close connection between sin, guilt and conscience if we are to communicate effectively God's message of salvation, as revealed in Scripture. The Bible does define conscience and its vital role in the life of believers and non-believers.

The following section discusses some basic principles in connection with the operation of conscience in the life and culture both of the missionary who brings the message and of the recipient of the message, the person he is seeking to evangelize. Particular applications to Muslim culture will be made briefly throughout the discussion.

Conscience, the universal link

This principle, already referred to in the previous discussion, has certain implications. In Romans 2:14-16, conscience is introduced as a major witness implanted by God, monitoring whether the requirements of the law of God, written on the tablets of human hearts, are being obeyed or not. Missionaries ought to rejoice that this co-worker is operating in people's lives even prior to their arrival with the gospel message. The passage implies that conscience has value in the fields of both mission and apologetics. Paul asserts that all people are morally aware of God's requirements, though they may lack access to God's special revelation in Christ and his Word. In this sense, there is no such thing as objective atheism. Atheism is nothing more than man's attempt to suppress the witness of his conscience. Therefore, the testimony of conscience does not rest merely on psychological or cultural factors — although it is greatly influenced by them — but on a divine foundation. The awareness of this should provide an even greater incentive for missionaries who labour among Muslims, who are not only endowed with conscience but are also devoutly religious people.

This knowledge that God's law is engraved in the hearts of men of all cultures is not to be overlooked as a pre-evangelistic tool. Because of the Fall and the existence of sin, however, conscience is not totally reliable. It no longer perfectly reflects the law of God. Yet conscience, though affected by the Fall, cannot be eradicated and can play a crucial role in conversion.

Augustine's well-known words are a good description of man's persistent inner turmoil: 'O God, our hearts are restless until we find our rest in thee.' Conscience continues to contribute to man's awareness of his fallen condition, restlessness and desire for freedom from the guilt and bondage of sin. As we have already seen, conscience is intended to work with the missionary to endorse the message he brings as he communicates the gospel, but a wrongly educated conscience can work at cross-purposes to it.

Masood was a dedicated Muslim prior to his conversion to Christianity. He gives an insight into some of the barriers that kept him from accepting Christ, including his troubled conscience:

> From the beginning my education had been grounded in the Quran. We were people of the book and took pride in learning the Holy Book of the Muslims by heart. By the time I was ten, I had learned long portions of the Quran by heart. I spent more time in the mosque as I grew up listening to the elders. On a visit to a friend I saw the Gospel of John; I took it and read it with great interest, but I was restless and deep in thought as I made my way to the central mosque for Friday prayer. I noticed Muhammad Ismail, my old teacher, among the worshippers. I approached him and explained the situation. My teacher told me that the Injil [Gospel] is incomplete without the Quran. He answered my questions. He walked me home and I promised to give him the Gospel of John I had, and never to think about false things again. Later I was resolved to carefully study the lives of Jesus and Muhammad and to compare them. The next evening I opened my Bible and read: 'And many other signs truly did Jesus in the presence of his disciples, which are not written in this book: But these are written that ye may believe that Jesus is the Christ, the Son of God; and that believing ye might have life through his name' (John 20:30-31). These words seemed to have been written specifically for my need, but again the deity of Jesus stuck in my throat and I could not easily accept it. Miracles! Faith! Eternal life! What sort of man was Jesus Christ? I wondered. More than ever, I knew that the Quran mentioned the miracles of Jesus, though they were not

always the ones that the Bible mentioned. The *Hadith* speaks of Muhammad turning the moon into two pieces, though it also speaks of his healing the sick, etc. Were the miracles of Jesus any different from those that Muhammad was supposed to have done, I wondered? But the Quran definitely stated that Muhammad did not perform miracles! Did Muslims feel bound to say that he did in order to counter the claims of Jesus? Only God could do miracles. Christ did miracles. Did I dare to draw the logical conclusion — that Christ was God? My heart trembled in prayer: O Creator Allah, show me the straight path, the path of those whom thou hast favoured, not the path of those who earn thine anger nor of those who go astray. I wept as I prayed.[3]

There is no doubt that Masood was sincere in seeking the truth. The paradox is that he was troubled by the very thing that should have eased his burdened conscience. He writes, 'Did I dare to draw the logical conclusion — that Christ was God? My heart trembled...' What was the source of his guilt? Was it derived from divine conviction, or was it a psychological feeling? We don't know the answer to that for certain. However, Masood gives us a clue when he affirms that, from his early childhood, he was trained systematically and fervently in the religious matters of Islam. These early patterns undoubtedly formed enduring traits that affected not only his behaviour, but also his ethical and moral convictions. When such values and standards are internalized and become part of one's disposition, they become like second nature. Pierce describes such influence upon the conscience: '... habit can take on almost the force of the created limits themselves, so that breach of habit will frequently cause a reaction hardly distinguished from conscience.'[4]

When conscience is cluttered with unreliable, and especially with unscriptural, data, it undoubtedly errs. As was the case with Masood, a misguided conscience can hinder a person from believing in Christ. If a missionary to Muslims hopes to touch his hearers, he must be prepared to go below the surface and see that the failure of Muslims to respond is not necessarily due to external factors, but may be the result of a clash between different consciences shaped by different experiences.

The Bible describes different states of conscience: clear, weak, defiled and seared. The conscience's ability to lapse from being clear to becoming seared is indicative of its variability. This can only be attributed to the amount of light or darkness infused into it. We are born with a conscience witnessing to God's law written in the hearts of men.

The formation and the education of conscience start early in childhood and continue throughout life. Child-rearing, particularly in the moral areas, often reflects the value-system and cultural expectations of the family. The Word of God recognizes this crucial period in the life of a child and gives specific instructions. There are over one hundred passages in Scripture relating directly to the child's physical, emotional, spiritual and moral education and development. The Bible warns that failure to train children according to God's standards resulted in a generation which did not know God (Judg. 2:10). Contrary to secular 'behaviourism', which reduces psychology to concrete observable facts as the only legitimate data for scientific enquiry, the Word of God emphasizes that man is inherently dependent on his Creator. At the heart of this relationship is a conscience inbred in the child by his Creator. However, the content of conscience can be influenced by society, with the result that the law of God, which is written there, is distorted.

Thus, the popular saying, 'Let your conscience be your guide,' can be greatly misleading because it does not take account of the fact that although conscience is innate and indestructible, its contents are largely acquired from society and culture.

Shortly after my arrival in the U.S. in 1977, I developed a close friendship with Bill. Bill was very methodical, schedule-oriented and time-conscious. Being reared in a culture which places greater emphasis on the relationship and spontaneous interactions between people, particularly close friends, it took me a while to adjust to this new lifestyle of punctuality. However, I discovered that things might be even more complicated. On a cold winter day in Colorado, I found that I had locked my car keys inside my car. In the back seat of Bill's nearby truck was an inexpensive metal coat hanger. I borrowed it and unlocked the car. Shortly afterwards, when I told Bill what had happened and thanked him for the use of the hanger, I was shocked by his reaction. With a somewhat emotionally charged attitude, he objected to my having helped myself to his coat hanger. For Bill, my borrowing the hanger implied dishonesty and an invasion of privacy. Bill's understanding of ownership was obviously very different from mine. I took for granted the morally appropriate nature of my behaviour, for in Middle-Eastern culture it is natural and expected for friends to share things and occasionally to use each other's belongings without permission, particularly in a case of urgent need. This is not always the case in the West, where ownership and privacy are highly prized. This demonstrates a clash between values and between understanding of what constitutes right and wrong.

Individuals never act in isolation. Our practices are grounded in our value-orientation and previously held assumptions of our traditions. The values that we learn are internalized in the conscience. Bill's conscience was offended by a matter in which my conscience was at perfect peace. This leads us again to reassert that the values to which conscience is sensitive are to a large extent dictated by culture.

Another example from the recent history of Islam might be helpful. The reaction to Salman Rushdie's book *The Satanic Verses* illustrates how the shared values of one group may come into direct conflict with those of another group.

Rushdie's writings evoked an angry response in the Muslim world, causing Khomeini of Iran to declare a 'fatwa' (a religious and judicial sentence), proclaiming Rushdie to be an apostate deserving death. This action was characterized by Western secular standards as wrong. However, the same action was regarded as justified and did not evoke feelings of guilt in the collective conscience of most Muslims.

Islamic countries, such as Arabia, Iran, Sudan and Libya, often defend themselves against charges of violating human rights by claiming allegiance to the absolute demands of Islamic cultural relativism. International standards cannot be used to judge human rights records in such a context. Said Raja Khorasani, defending his Islamic country against charges of violating human rights, appealed to religious and cultural factors: 'The new political order was ... in full accordance and harmony with the deepest moral and religious convictions of the people and therefore most representative of traditional, cultural, moral and religious beliefs of Iranian society. It recognized no authority ... apart from Islamic law ... conventions, declarations and resolutions or decisions of international organizations, which were contrary to Islam, had no validity in the Islamic Republic.[5]

Cutting off the hand of a thief is not perceived as a cruel punishment that violates the individual's rights in Islam — at least not according to the *Shariah* law. Instead of understanding this kind of punishment as an act of cruelty, Muslims regard it as a righteous duty. In Muslim thought society always takes priority over the individual. According to the Islamic *Shariah*, a crime is ultimately against the *Shariah* and society as a whole. Contrary to Western criminal law, the Islamic laws, particularly those which are based on the *Shariah*, rarely take into account the possible psychological or mental derangement of the criminal. Even an insane person must pay for his crime.

To a Western observer, requiring a Muslim woman to be covered from the top of her head to the soles of her feet is degrading. By Islamic standards, immodest dress is considered suggestive, erotic and shameful. The conscience of each, which has been shaped by different standards, disparages the other morally for behaviour about which the other's conscience does not condemn him.[6]

Conscience holds all people responsible before God Almighty. It reveals our own moral failure and need for God's grace. This principle was advanced by the apostle Paul in chapter 2 of his letter to the Romans. Paul affirms that those who are in possession of God's written law, as well as those who have only general revelation, are held accountable. In the previous chapter, Paul ascertains that one element of the conscience code is universal: the intuitive consciousness of a duty to honour God (Rom. 1:19,21; 2:15). However, Paul shows that the initial content of conscience can be distorted by human sin and tradition: 'For although they knew God, they neither glorified him as God nor gave thanks to him, but their thinking became futile and their foolish hearts were darkened' (Rom. 1:21).

What about those who are sincere in their desire to honour God but go about it the wrong way? Let us listen to a convert from Islam recounting his testimony:

> Sometimes I made a pilgrimage with my family. There I would personally offer my most important prayers, make a vow, and pray constantly toward Mecca. However keeping all the *Shariah* was not an easy task. The fasting, the so many regulations of washing and cleansing, the food restrictions and so on were a heavy burden. How I wanted to please God! But keeping all the laws and commandments of Islam and trying to do good was not enough. I could still feel lack of peace and joy in my heart. There was something missing in my life! Though relatives and friends always admired me as 'the man who is perfect in the law and

doing righteousness before God', deep inside I knew I
was not close to Him.[7]

This testimony is a vivid reminder of Hebrews 9:9: 'The gifts
and sacrifices being offered were not able to clear the conscience of the worshipper.' Such practices are not adequate
to deal with the root of the problem — human sin and the
consequent reaction of the conscience. Conscience, then,
plays a positive role in revealing our moral failures and need
of grace.

How does a missionary relate to the Muslim conscience?

Missionaries ought to rejoice in the fact that man is created in
the image of God and endowed with conscience. When conscience is properly informed, it consents to the message of the
gospel and works as an ally with the missionary. Cornelius
Van Til says, 'Every man has a sense of deity within him. Men
have in their own persons a factory where innumerable oper-
ations of God are carried on. This is revelation within men. It
may be called subjective in the sense that it is mediated
through the constitution of man himself. It is none the less
objective to man as an ethically responsible creature of God.
As ethical reaction to God's revelation, man must reflect upon
himself as made by God in order to own that he comes from
God and owes all of his praise to God.'[8]

But conscience is not always reliable. Apart from the initial
law of God written on the human heart, conscience, as we
have discussed, is primarily formed by cultural determinants.
Because of this cultural infusion of values, conscience cannot
be trusted. Actually, trusting our consciences is sometimes
dangerous. Even the great apostle Paul, prior to his conversion, was not troubled by his conscience when he partici-
pated in the stoning of Stephen and persecuted the church of
Jesus Christ. Paul had been a vivid example of a Pharisee.

Pharisees were convinced in their hearts and consciences that the ceremonial law and the tradition of the elders were meritorious and the only way to righteousness. Jesus called them blind (Matt. 23:16,17,19). As a result of this infusion of man-made morality into their hearts and minds, their misinformed consciences were conditioned into excusing their actions even when they were harassing and plotting to kill the Lord. If they were sincere, they were sincerely wrong. Their moral dilemma, which they did not recognize, was that instead of allowing their guilt to drive them to God, they rebelled against him.

The apostle Paul, after being dramatically delivered from the encumbrance of legalism, recognized that a righteousness based on works is a denial of justification by grace through faith in Jesus Christ alone. His letter to the Galatians warns against the danger of the Judaizers' teaching, which was based on legalism. In responding to such teaching, Paul insisted that a man is only justified through faith on the basis of Christ's finished work (Gal. 2:1-10). His message aroused vehement opposition. Paul called his opponents' teaching (which they claimed to be superior to the gospel of Jesus that he proclaimed) a '… different gospel — which is no gospel at all' (Gal. 1:6-7).

A cursory look at Islam, which is resistant to the gospel and where law is 'the epitome of Islamic thought, the most typical manifestation of the Islamic way of life, the core and the kernel of Islam itself',[9] reminds us of how applicable Paul's message is to evangelizing Muslims.

Paul realized the power of tradition to influence people, which is frightening, particularly when it can mislead even a Christian like the great apostle Peter (cf. Gal. 2:11-21). In turn, 'even Barnabas was led astray' by Peter's actions (Gal. 2:13). In Acts 10:9-23, we see how God intervened in a vision to correct Peter's biased attitude towards the Gentiles, and at the same time to liberate his conscience from his 'deeply ingrained … observance of the laws of clean and unclean'.[10] His scruples relating to dietary laws regarding clean and unclean things constricted his conscience to such an extent that he even contested the Lord's command: 'Surely not, Lord! ... I have never eaten anything impure or unclean' (Acts 10:14).

Peter experienced a cross-cultural conversion that freed him to communicate the gospel effectively to the Gentiles. If certain learned cultural values can engender a crisis of conscience within even mature believers, and hinder the efficacy of the gospel's message, how much more can such an influence be exerted over the unenlightened unbeliever, particularly one of the Muslim faith, whose ethics 'bear the character of an outwardly and crudely conceived doctrine of righteousness'.[11]

It is true that understanding the conscience of any target group, particularly Muslims, is not easy, but the missionary regularly finds himself facing challenging tasks of this nature. He will often experience difficulty even in a culture that is in many ways similar to his own and is in the same Christian context. The problem is compounded when he moves to a culture that is unlike his own in almost every way and the consciences of the people are developed and shaped differently (e.g., Arab Muslim *Sunni* culture). This shows that the relation between conscience, culture and gospel is an important consideration for cross-cultural work.

It is important, first of all, to note that a sense of guilt is universal. People feel guilty when they transgress their internalized values, and this can result in feelings of distress, reproach, self-blame, anxiety, or perhaps remorse. However, it is also possible that an awareness of real, objective guilt which has been incurred can be obscured by focusing the subjective guilt feelings on something quite different from the real cause. Graeme Griffin, in *The Westminster Dictionary of Christian Ethics*, warns against such a displaced sense of guilt: 'Many guilt feelings amount to an obsessive preoccupation with one type of responsibility as a defensive measure to avoid having to come to terms with other, deeper, and even more threatening problems. Since the feelings are painful, the "inner avenging forces" of the personality are satisfied, but at the price of concealing true conflict.'[12]

As we have seen in the cases of Paul and Peter and in the testimonies of Muslim converts, conformity to a legalistic system always fails both to ease the conscience and to remove the objective guilt. In fact, the Word of God warns against the legalism of the Pharisees and the Judaizers, who slavishly sought to conform to the outward requirements of the law but totally missed its true purpose. The results were rigid obedience to commandments, statutes, regulations and the observance of days and seasons. The writer of Hebrews affirms that such activities are '… not able to clear the conscience… They are only a matter of food and drink and various ceremonial washings — external regulations …' (Heb. 9:9-10).

Perhaps the greatest negligence of the church in her endeavour to articulate the gospel to Muslims is the failure to appeal to their consciences. The root of Muslims' misplaced sense of guilt is found in their misplaced trust. When we come before God claiming a righteousness that is of our own making as being adequate to remove our sin and guilt, we are in essence replacing trust in God by trust in our own righteousness. Thus a proper biblical connection between sin, conscience and guilt is essential. By making this connection we are achieving two goals simultaneously. First, we can appeal to the deep and real sense of need felt by Muslims (i.e., guilt, insecurity, lack of assurance of salvation). Second, the plan of redemption and the meaning of the vicarious death of Christ on the cross, which for centuries has been the most potent stumbling block to Muslim evangelism, may make sense as the only remedy for a guilty conscience.

Considerable parallelism exists between the arguments advanced in the Epistle to the Hebrews and Muslims' objections to Christianity (see table on following pages). In his attempt to encourage his readers not to renounce their faith in Christ and revert to the old legal system of Judaism, the writer to the Hebrews makes a compelling case for the superiority of the faith in Christ. He exhorts his readers to exercise their religion not by sight or by works, but by faith in Jesus Christ. He encourages them to lift their eyes above the visible, earthly things to which they are accustomed and rivet them on the glorified Jesus. Donald Guthrie, in his introduction to the epistle, says, 'To appreciate the strong pull of Judaism on Christians who were formerly Jews, it must be remembered that Christianity could offer no parallel to the ritual trappings to which they had been accustomed... He [the writer] was concerned to reassure his readers that the loss of ritual glories was more than compensated by the superiority of Christianity. Another feature, which is clearly brought about here, is that worship is a matter of conscience. It is conscience, which tells a person about himself and makes him aware of his accountability before God. It burdens the person with guilt. Where there is any hardening of conscience or where the conscience is overburdened with guilt, true worship is impossible.'[13]

Parallelism between the Epistle to the Hebrews and Islamic objections

Hebrews	Islamic objections
The Christian gospel is the final revelation from God (1:1-3)	Islam is the final revelation (*Surah* 5:3)
The writer warns against unbelief in the gospel of Jesus Christ (2:5 – 4:13)	The gospel is corrupted (*Surah* 2:105-106)
Christ is the eternal High Priest (4:14 – 7:28)	Christ is merely a human prophet sent by Allah (*Surah* 3:51; 19:34-35).

Hebrews	Islamic objections
The new covenant instituted by Christ is superior to any other covenant (8:1 - 10:18)	Islam is the final covenant between Allah and the world (*Surah* 2:128,131-133; 3:67).
We are to live and walk by faith (10:19 - 12:29)	Salvation is by works (*Surah* 2:177; 277).
Christ was resurrected and lives (4:14; 7:24)	Christ was not resurrected (*Surah* 4:157-58).

The Epistle to the Hebrews has a compelling message in the context of Muslim evangelism. It makes a clear connection between conscience and justification (9:9,14; 10:22; 13:18), while at the same time it shows the deficiency of the earthly traditions.

In order to apply God's grace to the functioning of the conscience, we must differentiate between a true and healthy sense of guilt before Almighty God and psychological guilt introduced by 'external regulations' — cultural standards.

Chapter 3 of Genesis demonstrates the dawn of fear and guilt as man experiences them today. When Adam and Eve sinned against God, they hid themselves because they became aware of their nakedness and shame. Their guilt feelings compelled them to hide behind fig leaves — an act that was not necessary before the Fall. But since the moment of the Fall, man has continued to mask his guilt by inventing new brands of fig leaves, including the use of man-made religious rituals as means of seeking to atone for one's own sins. The attempt by the Pharisees of Jesus' day to keep their traditions and perform ceremonial washings to pay for their own sins was nothing more than Adam and Eve's fig leaves — an inadequate attempt to rid them of their sense of shame and guilt.

Thus making the connection between sin, guilt and conscience should be our strategic starting point in Muslim evangelism as we seek to learn from the way their conscience has been formed and attempt to articulate the truth of the gospel convincingly. Such an approach helps Muslims to acknowledge their need for forgiveness and to discover from their own experience, as Paul did, that any attempt to make atonement for one's own sin, on the basis of legalistic observances, meticulous acts of ceremonial cleansing and other rituals, is altogether inadequate to eradicate a sense of guilt or to obtain the forgiveness of sins and thus secure salvation.

Applying certain passages from the Epistle to the Hebrews is helpful in driving these truths home as the missionary relates the gospel to Muslims. The Word of God must be our final authority on this subject. As we have seen, Scripture is not silent on the subject of conscience. Moreover, it does not only describe the function of conscience, but it also prescribes solutions to the problems associated with it. The book of Hebrews is resourceful and constructive in providing us with basic foundations for resolving the conflicts of conscience and is therefore important in our endeavour to evangelize Muslims.

As have seen, the Word of God gives concrete teaching that we can never satisfy the demands of conscience through our own efforts. It only can be accomplished through the efficacy of Christ's sacrifice, which provides the ground for justification. The writer of Hebrews affirms: '... the gifts and sacrifices being offered were not able to clear the conscience of the worshipper. They are only a matter of food and drink and various ceremonial washings — external regulations applying until the time of the new order' (Heb. 9:9-10). There is something about the conscience that could not be fully satisfied by the Old Testament sacrificial system despite its being ordained by God. For the sacrifices were nothing more than a shadow of the perfect sacrifice on the cross. This simply means that all the religious rituals in world religions cannot achieve the desired end of cleansing the conscience from uneasiness, guilt and sin. There is an inherent impotency and barrenness in all man-made systems. They are incapable of reconciling a sinful man with a holy God. For this reason, the writer of Hebrews explains that the blood of Christ is the only means 'to cleanse our consciences from acts that lead to death, so that we may serve the living God' (Heb. 9:14).

Herein lies one of the major weaknesses of Islam. Outward conformity to any legal system can never make the heart clean. Moreover, such conformity brings with it the condemnation of conscience. Accordingly, being legalistic to its very core, Islam can never satisfy the demands of the conscience, and therefore will always keep its followers in a constant state of guilt and discontentment. Thus, unless a person acknowledges his inability to attain forgiveness through his own efforts, there will never be a genuine experience of inner peace and harmony.

Building upon these basic principles must be our starting point in communicating the gospel to Muslims. Perhaps the same Muslim conscience that has been programmed to resist the gospel's message can be our initial contact point in leading to repentance and faith in Jesus Christ.

Learning to care for the conscience of the new Muslim believer in Christ

It cannot be an over-exaggeration to say that the ultimate goal of mission work is to be instrumental in the conversion of sinners. The conversion of sinners was the object of Christ's first command to Paul when he commissioned him on the road to Damascus. Christ appeared to Paul to make him a 'martur' (one who bears witness by testimony, even to the point of death). The charge was loud and clear: 'I am sending you to them to open their eyes and turn them from darkness to light, and from the power of Satan to God, so that they may receive forgiveness of sins and a place among those who are sanctified by faith in me' (Acts 26:17-18).

This passage suggests that conversion is a clear break with the former life of sin and a complete turning to Christ. The *Willowbank Report* of the Lausanne Committee, in its discussion of conversion, reminds us that it often involves a painful sacrifice, even the loss of family and possessions (e.g., Luke 14:25-33).[14] It is of the utmost importance to keep in mind this potential consequence, as we look briefly at the process of conversion in the Muslim context and its relation to conscience. While it is true that conversion is the work of God the Holy Spirit, at the same time, at 'the heart of every culture is a "religion" of some kind, even if it is irreligious religion like Marxism. "Culture is religion made visible" (J. H. Bavinck). And a religion is a whole cluster of basic beliefs and values. True conversion to Christ is bound, therefore, to strike at the heart of our cultural inheritance.'[15]

Perhaps the 'cultural inheritance' is of greater potency in Arab Muslim society, which is extremely closely knit and has religious and moral values ingrained in its very fabric. In interviewing a number of Muslim converts to Christianity about the circumstances surrounding their conversion, one of the questions was: 'Did you know about the possible reaction of your family, friends and community to your conversion?' 'Definitely,' they all replied. But in answer to the question, 'What was your main concern as you were making your decision to follow Christ?', four out of five gave unexpected responses. My assumption had been that the primary concern of the converts from Islam would be the consequences of the law of apostasy, which prescribes harsh penalties, including death. Instead, their main concern was losing their family bonds. One interviewee said something which left an indelible impression on me: 'If I die, I know that I will be in heaven, so I am gaining, not losing, but when I lose my family, I will lose everything, including my identity and my possessions. But even more importantly, I will lose the opportunity to share Christ with them.'

A much-publicized case of conversion from Islam to Christianity, at least in Christian circles, was that of Hussein Ali. He abandoned Islam and converted to Christ in his native country, Kuwait. An Islamic court declared him apostate. He lost his family, being forcibly divorced and losing the right to visit his children. Numerous agencies spoke out for Hussein to help him leave his native country unharmed. However, in its issue dated 21 February 1997, under the title, 'Hussein Reverts to Islam,' the *World Pulse* publication reported: 'Robert Hussein, who drew international attention to his native Kuwait after announcing his conversion to Christ, has returned to Islam. Hussein had been declared an apostate by a Muslim court last May 29. Hussein returned to Kuwait in January.' *Christianity Today*, in its April 1997 issue, made a perceptive comment about Hussein's alleged return to Islam: 'It illustrates the complicated dynamics of motives and pressures on Muslim converts: It is true that Muslim converts, perhaps more than most other converts, often experience directly and personally what it means to take up the cross and follow Jesus in suffering (Matt. 10:38-39).'

But why do so many of them, after professing faith in Christ, revert to Islam? It is certainly a complex issue, but one thing is certain: for most converts the initial sacrifices are just the beginning in a long journey of costly discipleship. The convert moves from external hardships to inner moral and spiritual conflicts, creating a crisis deep in his conscience.

The convert embraces a faith that is in every way distinctive and stands in sharp contrast to his former faith. This often creates an immense crisis in the process of discipleship. For one thing, the Christian concept of discipleship is totally new to the Muslim way of thinking. Christianity depends on how we answer the question: 'Who do you say that I [Christ] am?' (Mark 8:29). When a Muslim convert avows, 'You are the resurrected Son of the living God,' he is precipitating a simultaneous mental, spiritual and moral crisis that finds its roots in the training he has received from early childhood.

A former missionary to Muslims recognizes the conflict: 'Whenever a Muslim, in spite of all the hindrances, begins to come close to Christ, he is confronted with the basic sin in Islam which for him corresponds to the sin against the Holy Spirit [in Christianity]. Whoever places a partner or another god beside God will never receive forgiveness (*Surat Imran* 116), and whoever leaves Islam is condemned and is regarded as eternally lost (*Surat Imran* 90).'

We also should not overlook the power of Satan to incite discouragement and tempt new converts to revert to Islam. Satan seeks to blind people's eyes to the gospel (2 Cor. 4:3-4); to snatch the Word of God from their hearts before it can take root (Matt. 13:19); to incite disobedience against God (Eph. 2:2); and to destroy God's people and God's kingdom (Eph. 6:11-12). Moreover, Satan comes to the new convert knowing his vulnerability, the cracks in his armour, and attempts to allure the convert back to his former life. To be successful in our war against Satan, we cannot afford to minimize his power and the nature of his methods of attack, least of all in the Muslim context. The Word of God calls us to be self-controlled and vigilant (1 Peter 5:8), prepared for the trials (1 Cor. 10:13), and aware of Satan's methods (2 Cor. 2:11).

Moreover, we need to be reminded that Islam is a post-Christian religion that has consciously dealt with Christ and has developed from its very inception into an anti-Christian power. Therefore, people tend gradually to become immune to Christianity. They have been, as it were, vaccinated at an early age against the teaching of the gospel. Another spirit holds them captive, which could be described as their being in the grip of a collective possession. A break from such an ongoing inculcation of inhibitions is a difficult and bitter process in each convert and cannot be forced.

To further complicate the problem, after much inner conflict when a convert leaves his former faith, he turns to the local church for spiritual and moral support. As the convert enters the new fellowship, he experiences a new dilemma. For example, since the onslaught of Islam in the seventh century, the Middle-Eastern Arab church has been suspicious and fearful of Muslims and has therefore had very little success in winning converts and providing them with much-needed support and Christian fellowship. It is not unusual for members of a local church to suspect the new converts as agents for the Muslim government, or what are known as 'rice Christians' (i.e. people who make a profession of Christianity in the hope of receiving some material benefit). But the sad reality is that the converts often find themselves 'rejected by the very people whom they imagined to be saints and children of God according to the Bible; this sobering fact shocks them deeply'.[16]

In sum, many problems of conscience arise when a convert from Islam embraces Christ. When they survive their conversion, not having matured in their faith in Christ, they find themselves in a state of bewilderment concerning Christian liberty. Two reasons might be suggested here.

First, their weak consciences play a role in restricting their Christian liberty. The Bible speaks clearly concerning this problem. In his first letter to the Corinthians, the apostle Paul gives certain principles concerning the weak, scrupulous conscience. He says that 'Some people [this is particularly true of new converts] are still so accustomed to idols that when they eat such food they think of it as having been sacrificed to an idol, and since their conscience is weak, it is defiled' (1 Cor. 8:7).

Commenting on this verse, the *Anchor Bible Dictionary*, says, 'The scrupulous conscience of the "weak" is pained by the apparently idolatrous acts of the strong (vv. 7,12) because it has been informed by previous experiences of idolatry and so bears a witness to non-Christian morality; and when inconsistency to that standard is perceived, pain is produced. Yet the pain produced in the conscience of the "weak" is rarely the result of competing conceptions of *gnosis* which have in turn produced competing consciences between those who live either in accord with Pauline *gnosis* or with pagan *gnosis*. Thus, the conscience of the "weak" is not itself weak or faulty; rather, it distorts the truth, turning an innocent act into an evil one, because of a misguided standard of truth.'[17]

By the same token, though it is true that a Muslim convert accepts the God of the Bible through Jesus Christ, because of past experiences, his concept of God remains distorted. The result is that a weak conscience, lacking proper education, forbids what is permissible. Moreover, when such a conscience applies its faulty principles to other spiritual matters, it can restrict the discipleship process and growth in grace and may even contribute to spiritual lapses and a return to the old ways of life.

The second problem concerning Christian liberty is that it becomes a stumbling block (1 Cor. 8:8-11). Eating food sacrificed to idols has no ethical or spiritual value in itself. Nevertheless, Paul says that when such liberty becomes a stumbling block to another person's weak conscience, it becomes an ethical and spiritual concern (1 Cor. 8:9). The word *xousia* mentioned in this verse is rendered 'liberty', 'freedom' or 'authority', but a Christian is not free to use such liberty or authority if it becomes an obstruction to the weak.

It is fitting to conclude with these words written by the great missionary to Islam W. H. T. Gairdner:

> I want to say what has been borne in upon my soul with increasing force: 'How far the Christian community is a home for those who turn to Christ from Islam?' For the Church or congregation which desires to be, sets out to be, and succeeds in being a home for those converted to Christ from Islam, is in itself a gospel — preaches thereby the best, highest, and most Christ-like gospel of all: the gospel that will be most easily understood and most easily loved by those without, and will most powerfully attract them to come in... If any church

desires to be a spiritual home for those who come to Christ from Islam, a brotherhood, a spiritual garden, then it must have a very definite and well thought-out plan for teaching and training them in the Christian faith; and it must also, having determined its responsibility with regard to their human needs, be ready to shoulder the same. A church that makes this preparation in a spirit of thoughtful love, is already more than halfway to the ideal of being a home.[18]

Notes

Chapter 1 Questions about early Islam

1. Hastings, *Encyclopaedia of Religion and Ethics* (Edinburgh, T. & T. Clark, 1911), see under the heading 'Arabs'.
2. Thomas Hughes, *Dictionary of Islam* (London: Allen & Co., 1895), p.285.
3. George Sale, *The Koran: Translated into English from the Original Arabic* (Frederick Warne and Co., 1734), p. 36.
4. F. F. Bruce, *The Epistle to the Hebrews* (Grand Rapids, Michigan: Eerdmans, 1966), p.54.
5. Raphael Patai, *The Jewish Mind* (New York: Charles Scribner's Sons, 1977), p.18.
6. Muhammad Ali, *A Manual of Hadith* (NY: Olive branch Press, 1977), pp.261-2.
7. *Ibid.,* p.265.
8. Cf. Bat Ye'or, *The Dhimmi: Jews and Christians under Islam* (London: Associated University Presses, 1985), DS 36.9 / D 47.

Chapter 2 — Questions about West-East encounters

1. *Associated Press Network,* 10 March 2003.
2. *U.S. Department of State Annual Report on International Religious Freedom for 1999* (published 2000).
3. Donald McKim, ed., *Encyclopaedia of the Reformed Faith* (Edinburgh: St Andrew Press, 1992), pp.85-6.

Chapter 3 — Questions about faith and practice

1. Ismail Faruqi and Lamya Faruqi, *Cultural Atlas of Islam* (New York: MacMillan Publishing, 1986), p.105.
2. Joseph Schacht, *An Introduction to Islamic Law* (Oxford: Oxford University Press, 1993), p.9.
3. Ali, *Manual of Hadith,* p.396.
4. Sale, *The Koran,* p.36.

Chapter 4 — Questions about cultural themes

1. Lausanne Committee for World Evangelization, *The Willowbank Report no. 2, Gospel and Culture* (Wheaton, Illinois: Lausanne Committee, 1978), p.7.
2. Cf. Mazhar U. Kazi, *A Treasury of Hadith and Sunnah* (Markazi Maktabat Publications, 1992), pp.123-36.
3. B. Lemu and F. Heeren, *Women in Islam* (London: International Islamic Conference, 1976), pp.34-5.
4. Halim Barakat, *The Arab World* (Berkeley: University of California Press, 1993), p.23.
5. John Esposito, ed., *The Oxford Encyclopaedia of the Modern Islamic World* (Oxford: Oxford University Press, 1995), vol. 4, p.323.
6. Kazi, *A treasury of Hadith and Sunnah,* p.117.
7. Margaret Nydell, *Understanding Arabs: A guide for Westerners* (Yarmouth, Maine: Intercultural Press Inc., 1987), p.82.
8. Philip Greven, *The Protestant Temperament* (Chicago: University of Chicago Press, 1988).
9. Robert H. Springer, *Conscience and the Behavioural Sciences* (Washington & Cleveland: Corpus Books, 1969), p.2.
10. Lemu and Heeren, *Women in Islam,* pp.36-7.
11. Hughes, *Dictionary of Islam,* p.51.
12. Bilquis Sheikh, *I Dared to Call Him Father* (Bromley, England: STL Books, 1979), pp.25-6.
13. R. Abdur, *Shariah: The Islamic Law* (Ibabam: Iskan Publishing, 1990), p.5.
14. Ignaz Goldziher, *Introduction to Islamic Theology and Law* (Princeton, New Jersey: Princeton University Press, 1981), p.59.
15. *Ibid.,* pp.66-7.
16. See Raphael Patai, *The Arab Mind* (New York: Macmillan Publishing Company, 1983).
17. See Nydell, *Understanding Arabs.*
18. Cf. Ali, *A Manual of Hadith.*
19. Bruce Thomas, 'The gospel for shame cultures: How we failed to reach Muslims at their point of deepest insecurity', *Evangelical Missions Quarterly,* 30 (1994), pp.285-90.
20. *Ibid.,* p.286.
21. Patai, *The Arab Mind,* pp.90-91
22. Ali, *A Manual of Hadith,* p.71.
23. Ellis C. Nelson, *Don't let Your Conscience be Your Guide* (New York: Paulist Press, 1978).
24. J. H. Bavinck, *An Introduction to the Science of Missions* (Philadelphia, PA: Presbyterian and Reformed Publishing Co., 1960), p.260.
25. *Ibid.,* pp.263-4.
26. Daniel Pipes, *In the Path of God: Islam and political power* (New York: Basic Books, 1983), p.38.
27. Charles Malik, *God and Man in Contemporary Islamic Thought* (Beirut: Centennial Publications, 1972), p.53.

28. Anwar Chejne, *The Arabic Language: Its role in history* (Minneapolis: University of Minnesota Press, 1969), p.21.
29. Stephen Neill, *Christian Faith and Other Faiths* (Oxford: Oxford University Press, 1961), p.45
30. Cf. Patai, *The Arab Mind*, pp.42-43.
31. *Ibid.*, p.44.
32. Quoted by Barakat, *The Arab World*, p.126.
33. Quoted by Chejne, *The Arabic Mind*, p.9.

Chapter 5 —Questions about sharing the faith
1. Christy Wilson, *The Christian Message to Islam* (New York: Fleming H. Revell Co., 1950), p.33.
2. B. B. Warfield, *Biblical Doctrine*, vol. II, pp, 139, 167.
3. Quoted in *The Fathers of the Church*, vol. 37 pp.162-3.
4. Kenneth Cragg, *The Call of the Minaret* (New York: Oxford University Press, 1956), pp.261-2.

Chapter 6 — Conscience — A forgotten factor in Muslim evangelism?
1. Abraham Kuyper, *Godgeleerdheid*, vol. III, pp.449ff.
2. Robert Priest's 'Missionary Elenctics: Conscience and culture,' *Missiology: An International Review*, 22, no. 3 (July 1994), pp.291-315. is perhaps the best available article on this subject.
3. Steven Masood, *Into the Light* (Carlisle: OM Publishing, 1994), pp.16, 17, 129.
4. Claude A. Pierce, *Conscience in the New Testament: a study of* syneidesis *in the New Testament* (London: SCM Press, 1955), p.108.
5. United Nations General Assembly 1984, Thirty-ninth Session, Third Committee, Sixty-fifth Meeting. Quoted in Ann Elizabeth Mayer, *Islam and Human Rights* (Boulder and San Francisco: Westview Press, 1995).
6. Cf. Priest, 'Missionary Elenctics'.
7. Reza Safa, *Blood of the Sword, Blood of the Cross* (Carlisle: STL Books, 1993), p.11.
8. Cornelius Van Til, *The Defense of Faith* (Philadelphia, PA: Presbyterian and Reformed Publishing Co., 1972), pp.152-3.
9. Joseph Schacht, *An Introduction to Islamic Law* (Oxford: Oxford University Press), p.1.
10. Kenneth Barker, ed., *The NIV Study Bible* (Grand Rapids, Michigan: Zondervan Bible Publishers, 1985), p.166.
11. Samuel Zwemer, *Islam a Challenge to Faith* (New York: Student Volunteer Movement), p.120.
12. James Childress and John Macquarrie, eds, *The Westminster Dictionary of Christian Ethics* (Philadelphia: Westminster Press, 1986), entry for 'Guilt'.
13. Donald Guthrie, *The Letter to the Hebrews: An Introduction and Commentary* (Grand Rapids, Michigan: Eerdmans, 1983), p.32.
14. *Willowbank Report*, no. 2, see under 'Conversion'.
15. *Ibid.*, p.19.

16. Abd-Al-Masih, *Why is it Difficult for a Muslim to Become a Christian?* (Schorndorf, Germany: EV. Karmelmission, 1987), p.26.
17. David Freedman ed., *The Anchor Bible Dictionary* (NY: Doubleday, 1992), article on 'Conscience'.
18. W. H. Gairdner, 'The Christian Church as a Home for Christ's Converts from Islam,' *The Muslim World,* vol. 14 (July 1924), pp.236, 241.

Select bibliography

Abdur, R. *Shariah: The Islamic law* (Ibabam: Iskan Publishing,1990)

Adeney, Bernard. *Strange Virtues: Ethics in a multi-cultural world* (Downers Grove, Illinois: Inter-Varsity Press, 1995)

Al-Faruqi, Ismail and Lois A-Faruqi. *The Cultural Atlas of Islam* (New York: Collier Macmillan Publishers, 1986)

Ali, Muhammad. *A Manual of Hadith* (NY: Olive Branch Press, 1977)

Arkoun, Mohammed. *Rethinking Islam* (San Francisco: Westview Press, 1994)

Atiyah, Edward. *The Arabs* (Edinburgh: Penguin Books, 1955)

Azmi, Omar. *In Quest for Islamic Ideals of Education* (Temple University, 1993)

Barakat, Halim. 1993. *The Arab world* (Berkeley: University of California Press)

Bavinck, J. H. *An Introduction to the Science of Missions* (Philadelphia, Pennsylvania: Presbyterian and Reformed Publishing Co., 1960)

   The Church Between the Temple and Mosque (Grand Rapids, Michigan: Eerdmans,1966)

Boulton, Wayne. *Is Legalism a Heresy?* (NY: Paulist Press,1982)

Bruce, F. F. *The Epistle to the Hebrews* (Grand Rapids, Michigan: Eerdmans Publishing Co., 1964)

Chejne, Anwar. *The Arabic Language: Its role in history* (Minneapolis: University of Minnesota Press,1969)

Childress, James and John Macquarrie, eds. *The Westminster Dictionary of Christian Ethics* (Philadelphia: Westminster Press, 1986)

Conley, William. *The Kalimantan Kenyah: A study of tribal conversion in terms of dynamic cultural themes* (Philadelphia, Pennsylvania. Presbyterian and Reformed Publishing Company, 1976)

Constantelos, Demetrios J. 'The "neo-martyrs": As evidence for methods and motives leading to conversion and martyrdom in the Ottoman Empire', *Greek Orthodox Theological Review*, 23: 216-34 (1978)

Coon, Carlton S. *Caravan: The story of the Middle East* (New York: Henry Holt & Co., 1951)

Muhammad and the Christian: A question of response (Maryknoll: Orbis Books, 1984)

The Christ and the Faiths (Philadelphia: Westminster Press, 1986)

Cragg, Kenneth. *The Call of the Minaret* (New York: Oxford University Press, 1956)

De Boer, T. J. *The History of Philosophy in Islam* (New York: Dover Publications, 1967)

Doi, Abdur Rahman. *Shari'ah the Islamic Law* (London: Ta-Ha Publishers, 1990)

Donaldson, Dwight M. *Studies in Muslim Ethics* (London: William Clowes and Sons, 1953)

Ellul, Jacques. *The Theological Foundation of Law* (New York: Seabury Press, 1960)

Esposito, John. ed. *The Oxford Encyclopaedia of the Modern Islamic World* (Oxford: Oxford University Press, 1995)

Faruqi, Ismail and Lamya Faruqi. *Cultural Atlas of Islam* (NY: MacMillan Publishing, 1986)

Fehderau, Harold W. 'Keys to Cultural Insights' *Practical Anthropology* 10 (Sept.-Oct. 1963): 193-8.

Freedman, David, ed. *The Anchor Bible Dictionary* (NY: Doubleday, 1992)

Freeman, James C. *Ten Great Religions* (Boston: Houghton Publishing Co., 1892)

Forde, Daryll. *African Worlds: Studies in the Cosmological Ideas and Social Values of African Peoples* (London: Oxford University Press, 1954)

Fort, Timothy L. *Law and Religion* (Jefferson, North Carolina: McFarland & Company, 1987)

Foxgrover, David L. *John Calvin's Understanding of Conscience* (Ann Arbor: University Microfilms, 1982)

Fry, George C. and James R. King. *Islam: A Survey of the Muslim Faith* (Grand Rapids, Michigan: Baker Book House, 1982)

Gairdner, W. H. 'The Christian church as a home for Christ's converts from Islam' *The Muslim World*, vol. 14 (July 1924), pp.236-41.
The Vital Forces of Christianity and Islam (London: Oxford University Press, 1915)

Galwash, Ahmad. *The Religion of Islam* (Cambridge, Massachusetts: Murray Printing Co., n. d.)

Garnett, Campbell A. *Religion and the Moral Life* (New York: Ronald Press Company, 1955)

Gaudefroy-Demombynes, Maurice. *Muslim Institutions* (London: George Allen & Unwin Ltd, 1968)

Gervers, Michael and Bikhazi Jibran. *Conversion and Continuity: Indigenous Christian communities in Islamic lands, eighth to eighteenth centuries* (Toronto: University of Toronto Press, 1986)

Gibb, Hamilton A. R. *Studies on the Civilization of Islam* (London: Routledge and Kegan Paul, 1962)
Christ in Islam and Christianity (Villach, Austria, Light of Life, 1984)
The Textual History of the Qur'an and the Bible (Villach, Austria: Light of Life, 1988)

Glaser, John. 'Conscience and superego: A key distinction', *Theological Studies* (March 1971) 32: 30-47

Glassman, Eugene H. 'Theological stumbling-blocks in Christian / Muslim communication and their implications for Bible translators', *Bulletin of Christian Institute of Islamic Studies* 4 (1981): 167-207.

Godit, F. *Commentary on the First Epistle of St Paul to the Corinthians* (Grand Rapids, Michigan: Zondervan Publishing Company, 1957)

Goldsack, William. *Selections from Muhammadan Traditions* (Madras, India: Christian Literature Society for India, 1923)

Goldsmith, Martin. 'Community and controversy: Key causes of Muslim resistance', *Missiology* 4 (1976): 317-21

Goldziher, Ignaz. *Introduction to Islamic Theology and Law* (Princeton, New Jersey: Princeton University Press, 1981)

Griffiths, Paul J. *Christianity through Non-Christian Eyes* (Maryknoll, New York: Orbis Books, 1992)

Hadrill, Wallace. *Christian Antioch: A study in the early Christian thought in the East* (London: Cambridge University Press, 1982)

Haines, Byron L. and Frank L. Cooley. *Christians and Muslims Together: An exploration* (Philadelphia, Pennsylvania: The Geneva Press, 1987)

Hallesby, O. *Conscience* (Minneapolis: Augsburg Publishing House, 1933)

Hassan, Riffat. 'Messianism and Islam', *Journal of Ecumenical Studies* 22 (1985): 261-91.

Hastings, J., ed. *Encyclopaedia of Religion and Ethics* (Edinburgh: T & T Clark, 1911)

Henry, Carl. 1977. *Christian Personal Ethics* (Grand Rapids, Michigan: Baker Book House)

Hexham, Irving R. *Calvinism & Culture: A historical perspective* (Otchefstroom, Instituut Vir Reformatoriese Studie, 1979)

Hitti, Philip K. *Islam: A way of life* (Chicago, IL: Henry Regenery Company, 1970)

Horani, Albert. *A History of the Arab People* (Cambridge, Massachusetts: Harvard University Press, 1991)

Hudson, Lofton. *The Religion of a Mature Person* (Nashville, Tennessee: Broadman Press, 1952)

Hughes, Thomas. *Dictionary of Islam* (London: Allen and Company, 1895)

Joseph, John. *Muslim-Christian Relations and Inter-Christian Rivalries in the Middle East: The case of the Jacobites in an age of transition* (Albany, N.Y: State University of New York Press, 1983)

Kateregga, B and D. Shenk. *Islam and Christianity* (Grand Rapids, Michigan: William B. Eerdmans Publishing Company, 1980)

Kazi, Mazhar U. *A Treasury of Hadith and Sunnah* (Markazi Maktabat Publications, 1992)

Kedar, Benjamin Z. *Crusade and Mission: European approaches toward the Muslims* (Princeton, New Jersey: Princeton University Press, 1984)

Kifaystullah, Allama M. *Taleem al-Islam* (Lahore: Ahraf Publishers, 1991)

Kirk, Kenneth E. *The Threshold of Ethics* (London: Skeffington, 1933)

Kraemer, H. *The Christian Message in a Non-Christian World* (Grand Rapids, Michigan: Kregel Publications, 1969)

Kroeber, A. L. and Clyde Kluckhohn. *Culture: A critical review of concepts and definitions* (New York: Vintage Books, 1963)

Kung, H. *Christianity and World Religions* (NY: Orbis Books, 1996)

Kung, H. and J. Moltmann. *Islam: A challenge for Christianity* (London: SCM Press, 1994)

Lausanne Committee for World Evangelization. *The Willowbank Report. No. 2. Gospel and Culture* (Wheaton, Illinois: Lausanne Committee, 1978)

Law, Howard W. *Winning a Hearing: An introduction to missionary anthropology and linguistics* (Grand Rapids: W. B. Eerdmans Pub. Co., 1968)

Lee, Francis N. *The Central Significance of Culture* (Philadelphia: The Presbyterian & Reformed Publishing Co., 1976)

Lemu, B. and F. Heeren. *Women in Islam* (London: International Islamic Conference, 1978)

Lewis, Bernard. *The Arabs in History* (New York: Harper & Row Publishers, 1966)
Islam in History: Ideas, people, and events in the Middle East (Chicago, Illinois: Open Court, 1993)
Islam and the West (New York: Oxford University Press, 1993)

Malik, Charles. *God and Man in Contemporary Islamic Thought* (Beirut: Centennial Publications, 1972)

Masood, Steven. *Into the Light* (Carlisle, England: OM Publishing, 1994)

Mayer, Ann Elizabeth. *Islam and Human Rights* (Boulder and San Francisco: Westview Press, 1995)

Mayers, Marvin K. *Christianity Confronts Culture* (Grand Rapids, Michigan: Zondervan Publishing House, 1987)

Mazrui, Ali A. 'Religion and political culture in Africa', *Journal of the American Academy of Religion* 53, no. 4, pp.817-39 (1985)

McKim, Donald, ed. *Encyclopaedia of the Reformed Faith* (Edinburgh: Saint Andrew Press, 1992)

Michel, Thomas F. *A Muslim Theologian's Response to Christianity* (Delmar, N.Y.: Caravan Books, 1984)

Miller, Roland E. *Muslim Friends: Their faith and feeling* (Saint Louis: Concordia Publishing House, 1995)

Molla, Claude F. 'Can the clock go back?: Islamic fundamentalism', *One World*, no. 121 (1986): 7-9.

Nadwi, Syed H. *Islam in a Changing World* (Lucknow, India: Islamic Research & Publications, n. d.)

Naipaul, V. S. *Among the Believers: An Islamic journey* (New York: Vintage Books, 1981)

Narramore, Bruce S. *No Condemnation* (Grand Rapids, Michigan: Academic Books. 1984)

Nasr, Seyyed Hossein. *Islamic Life and Thought* (Albany: State University of New York Press, 1981)

Naydel, Margaret. *Understanding Arabs* (Yarmouth, Maine: International Press Inc., 1987)

Neill, Stephen. *Christian Faith and Other Faiths* (Oxford: Oxford University Press, 1961)

Nelson, Ellis C. *Don't let your Conscience be your Guide* (NY: Paulist Press, 1978)

Nydell, Margaret. *Understanding Arabs: A guide for Westerners* (Yarmouth, Maine: Intercultural Press Inc., 1987)

Omar, Azmi Bin. *In Quest of an Islamic Ideal of Education* (Ann Arbor, MI: UMI, 1993)

Parshall, Phil. *New Paths in Muslim Evangelism: Evangelical approaches to contextualization* (Grand Rapids, Michigan: Baker Book House, 1980)
    Inside the Community: Understanding Muslims through their traditions (Grand Rapids, Michigan: Baker Book House, 1994)

Patai, Raphael. *The Jewish Mind* (New York: Charles Scribner's Sons, 1977)
    The Arab Mind (New York: Macmillan Publishing Company, 1983)

Pickthall, Muhammad Marmaduke. *The Glorious Qur'an* (New York: The Muslim World League, 1977)

Pierce, Claude A. *Conscience in the New Testament: A study of syneidesis in the New Testament* (London: SCM Press, 1955)

Pipes, Daniel. *In the Path of God: Islam and political power* (New York: Basic Books, 1983).

Pittman, Samuel. *The Liberty of the Gospel versus Legalism in Islam* (Portland: Theological Research Network, 1989)

Priest, Robert. 'Missionary elenctics: Conscience and culture' *Missiology: An international review* 22, no. 3 (July 1994): 291-315.

Rappin, A. and J. Knappert, eds. *Textual Sources for the Study of Islam* (Manchester: Manchester University Press, 1986)

Rauf, Muhammad A. *Islam Creed and Worship* (Washington, D.C.: Islamic Center, 1974)

Richardson, Don. *Eternity in their Hearts* (Ventura, California: Regal Books, 1981)

Robertson, Palmer O. *The Israel of God: Yesterday today and tomorrow* (New Jersey: P & R Publishing, 2000)

Roheim, Geza. *Psychoanalysis and Anthropology: Culture, personality and the unconscious* (New York: International Universities Press, 1950)

Roxborough, John. 'From guilt to awareness: Gospel and culture, conscience and mission', *Evangelical Review of Theology* 18, no. 4 (1994): 196-203.

Safa, Reza. *Blood of the Sword, Blood of the Cross* (Carlisle, England: STL Books, 1993)

Sale, George. *The Koran: Translated into English from the Original Arabic* (Frederick Warne and Co., 1734)

Samirs, S. K. and J. S. Nielsen, eds. *Christian Arabic Apologetics during the Abbasid Period (750-1258)* (New York: E. J. Brill,1994)

Schacht, Joseph. *An Introduction to Islamic Law* (Oxford: Oxford University Press,1993)

Schlossberg, Herbert. *A Fragrance of Oppression: The church and its persecutors* (Wheaton, Illinois: Crossway Books, 1991)

Sheikh, Bilquis. *I Dared to Call him Father* (Bromley, England: STL Books, 1979)

Siddiqui, Abdul-aleem. *Elementary Teaching of Islam* (Takoma Park, Maryland: Crescent Publications, 1978)

Siddiqui, Abdul Hamid. *Translation of Sahih Muslim*: http://www.usc.edu/dept/muslimfundamantals/hadithsunnah/muslims

Siraju'd, Din. *The Vital Forces of Christianity and Islam* (London: Oxford University Press, 1915)

Smalley, William A., ed. *Readings in Missionary Anthropology* (Pasadena, California: William Carey Library, 1978)

Smith, Wilfred C. *On Understanding Islam: Selected studies* (Netherlands: Mouton Publishers, 1981)

Smyth, Newman. *Christian Ethics* (New York: Charles Scribner's Sons, 1922)

Spier, J. M. *An Introduction to Christian Philosophy* (Philadelphia, Pennsylvania: Presbyterian and Reformed Publishing Co., 1954)

Syrjanen, Seppo. *In search of Meaning and Identity* (Vammala, Helsinki: Vammalan Kirjapaino, 1984)

Thomas, Bruce. 'The gospel for shame cultures: How we failed to reach Muslims at their point of deepest insecurity', *Evangelical Missions Quarterly* 30 (1994): 285-90.

Tillich, Paul. *Theology of Culture* (New York: Oxford University Press, 1959)

Tisdall, W. *The Original Sources of the Quran* (London: SPCK,1905)

United Nations General Assembly. Thirty-Ninth Session, Third Committee, Sixty-Fifth Meeting (1984). Quoted in Ann Elizabeth Mayer, *Islam and Human Rights* (Boulder and San Francisco: Westview Press, 1995)

Van Til, Cornelius. *The Defense of Faith* (Philadelphia, Pennsylvania: Presbyterian and Reformed Publishing Company, 1972)
Common Grace and the Gospel (Philadelphia: Presbyterian and Reformed Publishing Company, 1973)

Van Til, Henry R. *The Calvinistic Concept of Culture* (Philadelphia, Pennsylvania: Presbyterian and Reformed Pub. Co., 1972)

Van Til, John. 'The Appeal of Conscience', *Christianity Today,* May 1969, pp.6-8.

Von Grunebaum, G. E. *Modern Islam: A search for cultural identity* (New York: Random House, 1963)

Williamson, G. I. *Westminster Confession of Faith* (Philadelphia, PA: Presbyterian and Reformed Publishing Co., 1964)

Wilson, Christy. *The Christian Message to Islam* (New York: Fleming H. Revell Co., 1950)

Woodberry, Dudley, Charles Van Engen and Edgar Elliston, eds. *Missiological Education for the 21st Century* (New York: Orbis Books, 1996)

Ye'or, Bat. *The Dhimmi: Jews and Christians under Islam* (London: Associated University Presses, 1985)

Yusuf, Ali. *The Holy Quran* (United States: McGregor & Werner, 1946)

Zwemer, Samuel. *Across the World of Islam* (New York: Fleming H. Revell Company, n. d.)

The Moslem Doctrine of God (New York: Young People's Missionary Movement, n. d.)

Islam a Challenge to Faith (NY: Student Volunteer Movement, 1909)

Index

For information about the ministry of Children of Abraham, or to arrange speaking engagements involving the author visit the web site:

http://www.coabraham.org

or contact the address below:

P. O. Box 508
Clinton, MS 39056
USA

Tel. 601-923-1612

A wide range of excellent books on spiritual subjects is available from EP. If you would like a free catalogue please write to us or contact us by e-mail. Alternatively, you can view the whole catalogue online at our website: http://www.epbooks.org

EP BOOKS
Faverdale North, Darlington, DL3 0PH, England
e-mail: sales@evangelicalpress.org

EP BOOKS INC.
P. O. Box 825, Webster, New York 14580, USA
e-mail: usa.sales@evangelicalpress.org